AF846879

ECONOMIC THEORY AND THE ROMAN MONETARY ECONOMY

Modern economics tantalizes historians, promising them a set of simple verbal and mathematical formulas to explain and even retrospectively predict historical actions and choices. Colin P. Elliott challenges economic historians to rethink the way they use economic theory. Building upon the approaches of Max Weber, R. G. Collingwood, Ludwig von Mises and others, Elliott reconceptualizes economic theories such as the quantity theory of money and Gresham's law as heuristic and counterfactual constructs – constructs which help historians identify and understand the unique modes of thought and embedding contexts which characterized economic action in the Roman Empire. The book offers novel analyses of key events in Roman monetary history, from Augustus' triumph over Mark Antony and Cleopatra, to third-century AD coinage debasements. Roman history has long been a battleground for polarizing methodological debates, but this book's accessible style and conciliatory tone invites historians, economists, sociologists and other scholars to use economic theory for understanding.

COLIN P. ELLIOTT is an Assistant Professor in the Department of History at Indiana University. He has published interdisciplinary research on the economic, social and environmental history of the Roman Empire, and his next project explores intersections between its economy and the environment.

ECONOMIC THEORY AND THE ROMAN MONETARY ECONOMY

COLIN P. ELLIOTT
Indiana University, Bloomington

CAMBRIDGE
UNIVERSITY PRESS

CAMBRIDGE
UNIVERSITY PRESS

University Printing House, Cambridge CB2 8BS, United Kingdom

One Liberty Plaza, 20th Floor, New York, NY 10006, USA

477 Williamstown Road, Port Melbourne, VIC 3207, Australia

314–321, 3rd Floor, Plot 3, Splendor Forum, Jasola District Centre, New Delhi – 110025, India

79 Anson Road, #06–04/06, Singapore 079906

Cambridge University Press is part of the University of Cambridge.

It furthers the University's mission by disseminating knowledge in the pursuit of education, learning, and research at the highest international levels of excellence.

www.cambridge.org
Information on this title: www.cambridge.org/9781108418607
DOI: 10.1017/9781108290531

© Colin P. Elliott 2020

This publication is in copyright. Subject to statutory exception and to the provisions of relevant collective licensing agreements, no reproduction of any part may take place without the written permission of Cambridge University Press.

First published 2020

A catalogue record for this publication is available from the British Library.

Library of Congress Cataloging-in-Publication Data
NAMES: Elliott, Colin P., 1982– author.
TITLE: Economic theory and the Roman monetary economy / Colin P. Elliott, Indiana University, Bloomington.
DESCRIPTION: Cambridge ; New York, NY : Cambridge University Press, 2020. | Includes bibliographical references and index.
IDENTIFIERS: LCCN 2019038678 (print) | LCCN 2019038679 (ebook) | ISBN 9781108418607 (hardback) | ISBN 9781108407595 (paperback) | ISBN 9781108407595 (epub)
SUBJECTS: LCSH: Money–Rome–History. | Coinage–Rome–History. | Monetary policy–Rome–History.
CLASSIFICATION: LCC HG237 .E55 2020 (print) | LCC HG237 (ebook) | DDC 332.4/937–dc23
LC record available at https://lccn.loc.gov/2019038678
LC ebook record available at https://lccn.loc.gov/2019038679

ISBN 978-1-108-41860-7 Hardback

Cambridge University Press has no responsibility for the persistence or accuracy of URLs for external or third-party internet websites referred to in this publication and does not guarantee that any content on such websites is, or will remain, accurate or appropriate.

For Aunt Donna

Contents

List of Figures

Preface

Near the end of his life, Moses Finley opined that "very few ancient historians are introspective: one must infer their most fundamental presuppositions from their substantive accounts, since they refuse to discuss methodological questions."[1] In the more than thirty years since Finley wrote this statement, economic theory has come to enjoy an established presence in the sub-field of Roman economic history. Many factors are behind this significant methodological shift. It is true that simple inertia may be partly responsible – as economics has crept into the vacuum left by the waning influence of Finley's own ideas. At the same time, some Roman economic historians have introspectively and reflectively chosen to incorporate formal economic analysis into their investigations and arguments because many of the theories of modern economics appear to offer straightforward and testable explanations for historical economic phenomena. Economic models seem to help fill in the gaps where evidence is inadequate or even absent. At the same time, critics of the recent turn toward economic formalism in Roman economic history suggest that serious ideological and teleological problems have accompanied this development. Is it responsible, or even possible for that matter, to reduce the complexity present in any given historical society into simple verbal or mathematical formulae? Is economization a universal component of or even a synonym for human rationality? Does the analytical power of economic theory come with costly side-effects: the privileging of capitalism and capitalism-centered value-judgments?

My own struggle with such challenging questions has, at the time of writing this book, left me in the uncomfortable position of accepting many of the critiques against formalist economic history while, at the same time, still remaining convinced that economic theory is useful for understanding Roman economic and monetary history. The universalizing claim of one

[1] Finley (1985a), 105.

prominent Roman economic historian – that "ancient economies clearly differed from modern ones, but the principles of economics still hold true" – strikes me as both persuasive and at the same time troubling.[2] Some economic theories indeed seem to contain a universal and undeniable logic – a logic which provides a sense of objectivity against many of the seemingly indefinite or 'soft' models in the other social sciences. At the same time, economic theory's appearance of objectivity is often rhetorical and superficial; historical narratives constructed upon economic theory are often ideal-typical at best and, more often, they are woefully mistaken, anachronistic and in some cases may, to paraphrase Chris Wickham, do violence to historical understanding.[3] Economic historians must continue to wrestle with a fundamental question: if economic theories rest upon supposedly *a priori* epistemological foundations, why do applications of economic theory to history – especially to pre-modern history – so often generate anachronisms and misappropriations? The answer I offer in this book – an answer which has certainly occurred to others before, to be sure – is that economic history tends to go wrong when it forsakes what should be the main aim of history-writing: understanding. The problem is that the discipline of economics left questions of understanding behind about a century ago. As a consequence, economic history, especially under the aegis of neoclassical economics and cliometrics, tends to avoid questions of understanding; instead, history serves as the laboratory in which the deductive hypotheses of modern economics are 'tested'. While many polemical books have been written which critique cliometric methods and similar 'positivist' applications of economics to history, I wanted to write a book which not only scrutinizes formalist economic history methodologies but also takes the risk of putting forward new if not experimental solutions. It is especially important to me, moreover, to present these solutions in a tone which avoids hostility and instead invites economic historians of all ideological and methodological persuasions to patiently consider my arguments. These arguments are not revolutionary; in the end, the book outlines, illustrates and defends an approach to economic history which embraces economic theory as a useful if not necessary tool for understanding historical societies.

Investigating broad methodological issues required an immersion into the intellectual history of economics, especially the pivotal scholarship which followed the *Methodenstreit* – the late nineteenth-century 'war of methods' among German-speaking economists. It is difficult to

[2] Temin (2012a), 45. [3] Wickham (2005), 823.

over-emphasize the powerful and lasting changes the *Methodenstreit* brought to the social sciences. The *Methodenstreit* either birthed or re-birthed the modern disciplines of economics, history, sociology and economic history.[4] As in most wars, the composition, aims and unity of the various 'sides' involved in the *Methodenstreit* were often in flux, but intellectual historians tend to identify one prominent group as the German historicists, epitomized for better or worse by Gustav von Schmoller. The historicists made much of the importance of embeddedness: of the individual actor within the *Volkswirtschaft* ('national economy'), of the *Volkswirtschaft* within broader social and cultural frameworks and even of economic theory as embedded in modernity.[5] In the historicists' inductivist framework, economic 'laws' were constructed from descriptions of comparable empirical phenomena – descriptions which were themselves derived from observations of evidence.[6] On the other side was Carl Menger and the so-called 'Austrians' – a term coined by Schmoller himself which plays upon prejudicial stereotypes of Habsburg Austria as intellectually backward compared to Schmoller's native Prussia. Menger, and many who sympathized with his views, advanced an economics founded upon a belief in *a priori* economic laws – an epistemological position which necessitated that economic theory be deduced, formulated and applied *before* empirical observation. Menger had harsh words for his historicist adversaries:

> Testing the exact theory of economy by the full empirical method is simply a methodological absurdity, a failure to recognize the bases and presuppositions of exact research. At the same time it is a failure to recognize the particular aims which the exact sciences serve. To want to test the pure theory of economy by experience in its full reality is a process analogous to that of the mathematician who wants to correct the principles of geometry by measuring real objects.[7]

To many historians of the *Methodenstreit*, the subsequent emergence and eventual dominance of neoclassical economics suggests that Menger and his 'Austrian' allies won the war of methods.[8] Their victory was secured through the discovery of the principle of marginalism – the idea that the value of goods and services is determined by the subjective importance of the wants they satisfy. In Menger's words:

4 Boldizzoni (2011), 151. 5 See, for example, Schmoller (1896), 3–4.
6 Camic, Gorski and Trubek (2005), 11. 7 Menger (1985), 69–70. 8 Häuser (1988).

> Value is thus nothing inherent in goods, no property of them, nor an independent thing existing by itself. It is a judgment economizing men make about the importance of the goods at their disposal for the maintenance of their lives and well-being. Hence value does not exist outside the consciousness of men.[9]

The neoclassical revolution which followed the *Methodenstreit* adopted marginalism in concept, but Alfred Marshall and later several other (mostly British) economists turned economics toward mathematical and so-called 'scientific' approaches, not only to marginal utility, but to economic analysis as a whole. Menger's version of marginalism was soon abandoned for the mathematical versions elucidated by British economist William Stanley Jevons and French economist Léon Walras. The emergent neoclassicals also adopted a modeled man: *homo economicus*, whose crude unwavering economizing rationality, ironically, made him just as passive and reactive as the embedded individual theorized by the historicists. The 'Austrian' victory was, therefore, short-lived – and within decades Menger's methodology lost influence in post-*Methodenstreit* economics.

The Austrian economist Ludwig von Mises, initially an aspiring historian, became enamored of Menger's approach to economics while studying at the University of Vienna.[10] Mises, however, found few friends among the ascendant neoclassicals, as he maintained that humans' autonomy and purposefulness made their actions immune to mathematical prediction. Mises also rejected modeled men like *homo economicus*. The principles of economics, Mises claimed, must instead be deduced from unmodeled choice. Furthermore, Mises – influenced by his friend German sociologist Max Weber – acknowledged that the historicists were right about the indispensability of understanding for studying human choice in past societies:

> The specific task of history for which it uses a specific method is the study of these value judgments and of the effects of the actions as far as they cannot be analyzed by the teachings of all other branches of knowledge. The historian's genuine problem is always to interpret things as they happened. But he cannot solve this problem on the ground of the theorems provided by all other sciences alone. There always remains at the bottom of each of his problems something which resists analysis at the hand of these teachings of other sciences. It is these individual and unique characteristics of each event which are studied by the *understanding*.[11]

9 Menger (2007), 121. 10 Mises (2009), 25. 11 Mises (1949), 49.

Sociologists and historians embrace and even revere Weber's work; many economists, however, both past and present, treat Mises' insights with skepticism and even hostility.[12] Mises and his Austrian-School followers reject far too much of the neoclassical orthodoxy. As a consequence, few historians are aware of Mises' work, and especially of the methodological dialogue between Mises and Weber. Although Mises and Weber sharply disagreed on many points, there are understudied overlaps in their methodologies which are of great value to economic historians.

Mises and Weber concomitantly held to what has since been called 'methodological dualism' – the idea that the social sciences should be studied with different methodologies than the natural sciences. Both scholars also based their work on a particular form of 'methodological individualism' – the idea that the study of human societies must begin with the study of individual human beings. These concepts have since enthralled a few historians, such as British historian and philosopher Robin George Collingwood – but many Roman economic historians have made little conscientious use of either concept. One of the aims of this book is to expand upon the value of these concepts as a basis for understanding the economic history of the Roman Empire. Both concepts help redirect formal economic analysis away from sterile, positivistic or otherwise 'de-contextualized' treatments of the *products* of the Roman economy (prices, wages, growth) and toward understanding the meanings, mentalities, choices and motivated actions of Roman money-users. After Collingwood, I argue that Roman economic historians ultimately study not merely the historical products of Roman minds but Roman minds themselves.[13] Studying the choices made by actors in the Roman economy and the consequences of these choices is a fruitful way for Roman historians to understand the Roman monetary system itself.

The arguments in this book appeal to scholars whatever their views on economic theory, as well as to the uninitiated who wish to engage economic theory with introspection and reflection. It is my desire that formalist readers will be convinced of the importance of understanding over prediction and explanation – and that they will consider how the models and approaches they currently use might be redeployed toward this end. For substantivist readers and those who tend to be critical of economic formalism – most of whom already view understanding as a core tenet of historical study – I hope to persuade them that economic theories can be a helpful component in the construction of meta-theoretical

[12] Gane (2014), 1104; Gane (2013), 6.

[13] Collingwood (1999), 45–6.

frameworks. I want skeptics to see that economic theories can be used in ways which avoid anachronisms and in fact highlight social and cultural difference in historical societies. On these matters, however, this book is a beginning not an end; although it provides a general framework as well as some practical illustrations, it is an experimental effort to introduce and engage questions which move the discussion in new directions. *Histoire totale* cannot be achieved by scholars working alone. Including time spent on my PhD dissertation – a portion of which was used to create this book – a full ten years' worth of work has been invested in this project in one form or another. Despite the inadequacies and limitations which remain, I now wish to invite others to help move the discussion forward.

Acknowledgments

This book has benefitted from many scholars' advice, comments, access to unpublished work, helpful conversation and/or support of some kind that it is simply not possible for me to recollect and, therefore, properly acknowledge their generosity. Some names come to mind now, but I am sure that many more should be listed: Katherine Blouin, Kevin Butcher, Carmen Dorobăţ, Kyle Harper, Chris Howgego, Max Koedijk, Myles Lavan, Robert Murphy, Roderick Long, Chris Pelling, Matthew Ponting, Charlotte Potts, George Selgin, Tony Woodman. I should also thank the referees commissioned by Cambridge University Press for their thoughtful suggestions during this book's long journey to publication. Their advice has helped me avoid many errors and omissions, and they have helped me keep the book focused on methodological issues. Michael Sharp facilitated a productive dialogue with the referees, and he guided everyone involved in this book's production toward a positive conclusion.

Although this book is very different from my PhD thesis, many of the ideas for this book were generated during my four years at the University of Bristol. I am especially thankful for the patience and grace shown by Ellen O'Gorman, Genevieve Liveley and Gillian Clark as I fumbled through postgraduate study, teaching and adapting to life in the British academy. Fellow postgraduates Greta Hawes, Loriel Anderson, Shushma Malik, Heather Hunter-Crawley, Rob Crowe and Alex Wardop were kind and gracious. My PhD examiners, Peter Bang and Dominic Rathbone, generously offered observations, questions and guidance which helped me think clearly and carefully about the integrity of my methodological approach and my selection and use of evidence. Neville Morley was and is a true *Doktorvater* and an ongoing exemplar of academic excellence and personal integrity. This book may bear little similarity to my original dissertation; nevertheless, I hope that it retains an imprint of Neville's invaluable influence and mentorship.

I am grateful to colleagues at Washington and Lee University and Indiana University. As caretakers of Washington and Lee's traditional language-focused Classics program, Kevin Crotty, Rebecca Benefiel, Michael Laughy and Miriam Carlisle took a risk in inviting a social-science-oriented historian to join their department. Their wisdom, advice and encouragement, as well as the collegiality shown to me by colleagues Isabel Köster and Caleb Dance, nurtured me as I made some of the most drastic and difficult changes to the manuscript. Furthermore, it was a special privilege to engage Washington and Lee's bright, inquisitive and enthusiastic students. Colleagues in History and Classics at Indiana have been similarly supportive in guiding this book to completion. There are too many names to list here, but I should at the very least mention a few of the colleagues who provided especially helpful mentorship, comments or professional advice over the past four years: Eric Robinson, Deborah Deliyannis, Cynthia Bannon, Jonathan Ready, Matt Christ and Jeremy Schott.

I thank my parents and brother. I thank my children: Eva, Lillian and Reuben. Most importantly, I thank Sadie, my wife. Words are insufficient, both in quality and quantity, to recount her practical, emotional and spiritual support. Her fellowship and faithfulness undergirds each and every word in this book.

CHAPTER 1

On Writing Roman Economic History

... it is our critical intelligence which is prior to the sources.

Keith Hopkins[1]

History-writing is a *subjective* art. The historian is an agent – an individual who selects, arranges, interprets and emplots a series of 'facts' within a narrative determined, whether consciously or subconsciously, by ideology.[2] There is a fundamental difference between the past – events which empirically occurred in physical, temporal reality – and what historical theorist Hayden White calls "the historical past" – "a construction and only a highly selective version of the past."[3] Even the historical 'facts' themselves – the building blocks of historiography – are inescapably subjective, even intangible. Neville Morley pithily observes "a fact is a verbal statement, an idea, with no empirical existence outside people's minds."[4] Although not all historians are willing to embrace such a deconstructionist or otherwise broadly postmodern dissonance between 'history' and 'the past', there is broad agreement in the mainstream of the discipline that history-writing is a process of argumentation, interpretation and weighing plausibilities. History-writing, therefore, cannot be called 'objective'.

Not so with many of the theories of modern economics – a result of many developments, but especially the early twentieth century's distinction between 'value-free' (*wertfrei*) and 'normative' economics as well as the widespread adoption of Chicago School economist Milton Friedman's concept of "positive economics" in the 1950s.[5] Now central within the overarching methodology of modern economics is the idea that economic propositions are 'testable' in the same way as scientific statements about the natural world. Economic propositions – accompanied scientific-sounding terminology – hold the status of *hypotheses* which can and must

[1] Hopkins (2002), 196. [2] White (2000). [3] White (2014), xiii. [4] Morley (1999), 57.
[5] Friedman (1953), 3–43; Weber (1949).

be either 'confirmed' or 'falsified' against observations.[6] Friedman won a Nobel Prize, in part because his use of mathematical models, combined with simplifying assumptions about the efficiency of markets and the economizing and utility-maximizing rationality of all human beings, reified economics' abstract logic into measurable and objective 'science'. Prior to these developments, economics in fact had much more in common with sociology; hence, economic models were often employed with the purpose of understanding and explaining human behavior, whether in the present or the past. Now, however, economics is a collection of scientific 'laws' which have been verified by repeated testing – laws which offer the tantalizing promise of predicting human behavior, whether in the future, present or past.[7]

How should this 'objective' economics accommodate the 'subjective' art of history-writing? Perhaps anticipating this conundrum, Friedman himself offered a solution which is still widely practiced: economic historians are to be *predictors of the past*:

> the 'predictions' by which the validity of a hypothesis is tested need not be about phenomena that have not yet occurred, that is, need not be forecasts of future events; they may be about phenomena that have occurred but observations on which have not yet been made or are not known to the person making the prediction. For example, a hypothesis may imply that such and such must have happened in 1906, given some other known circumstances. If a search of the records reveals that such and such did happen, the prediction is confirmed; if it reveals that such and such did not happen, the prediction is contradicted.[8]

Something like the approach Friedman advocates is at the core of what many call 'new economic history'; sometimes it is called 'cliometrics', most often by those who oppose it.[9] Roman historians became late adopters of the new economic history, but it is now safe to say that many who study the Roman economy do so after the fashion of Friedman's 'predicting the past' approach – testing models against evidence in one form or another, whether or not formal economic theory is explicitly involved. There are a few nuances to such an approach. The historian, for example, must assume that the model deployed is both internally consistent and historically applicable. Also, sufficient evidence must be available for testing the model. If the model is 'confirmed' by the evidence, however, then the

[6] Keynes (1936), 378. [7] Davidson (2012). [8] Friedman (1953), 9.
[9] E.g. Boldizzoni (2011).

historian can more plausibly state what 'actually happened' without necessarily having empirical evidence for what 'actually happened' – a prospect as intriguing as it is unsettling.

Divisions and Debates

The use of the new economic history by Roman historians has not met with universal approval. Current disagreements over methodology, however, are merely the latest skirmishes in one of the most enduring and inimical disputes in all of scholastic history. As what would become neoclassical economics was emerging in the late nineteenth century, a clear division formed in the writings of several prominent German intellectuals. The economist Karl Bücher, building upon the foundations of nineteenth-century economist Johann Karl Rodbertus, argued that ancient economies were culturally and conceptually bound by the *oikos* – the autarkic household – and, therefore, were qualitatively different than the modern, exchange-dominated economy of the nation-state (*Volkswirtschaft*).[10] It was the ancient historian Edward Meyer – an ardent believer in the comparability of classical antiquity and modernity – who first labeled Bücher and others "primitivists."[11] Meyer's views were bolstered with the publication of Michael Rostovtzeff's *Social and Economic History of the Roman Empire* (1926) – a work many now see as the height of what would become primitivism's antonym: "modernism."[12] For Rostovtzeff, like Meyer before him, the differences between ancient and modern economies were merely quantitative.[13] "Ancient capitalism," as Rostovtzeff named it, was different from modern capitalism only in terms of scale, techniques and technologies such as "factory mass production with the use of complicated machinery."[14] Rostovtzeff's work roundly discredited primitivism. The modernist perspective, in turn, dominated the next several decades of scholarship on the ancient economy.

It was not until the 1950s and 60s that the primitivist remnant found an unlikely ally in anthropologist Karl Polanyi, whose work emerged in ideological, theoretical and analytical opposition to the modernizing tendencies in his own field.[15] In *The Great Transformation*, Polanyi argued that economic activity prior to the Industrial Revolution was "embedded"

[10] Bücher (1917). A long list of Rodbertus' relevant works is found in Schiavone (2000), 227 n. 2.
[11] Meyer (1924). Commentary in Cohen (2002), 1; Bang (1998).
[12] Southern (2001), 38; Bang (2007), 5; North (2009), 93; Saller (2002).
[13] Rostovtzeff (1933). Commentary in Morley (2006a), 43; Meikle (2002), 239.
[14] Rostovtzeff (1936), 250, 252.
[15] Granovetter (2007), 85–7.

in society – that is, that the economizing action of individuals was itself submerged within the political, religious and cultural aspects of society. The "great transformation" which took over the agendas of many industrialized societies in the nineteenth century, however, was a complete subversion of the historical position of the economy. The autonomous, self-governing market that efficiently regulates all human activity was not merely a theoretical abstraction, but a utopia to be adopted. Attempts to bring about such a system made society "an adjunct to the market" – a result which Polanyi saw as not only undesirable but unsustainable.[16]

Polanyi's skepticism of capitalism's excesses was not mere polemic. A central and lasting tenet of his interpretive framework was the observation that human societies have provided for their material well-being in three primary modes of economic interaction, two of which were non-capitalistic: redistribution (typically by political structures), reciprocity (in tribal, familial or gift-giving relationships) and exchange (by market institutions).[17] According to his analysis, the first two modes were dominant in the ancient Mediterranean world.[18] Despite the grand scale of economic activity in the Roman world, "it formed no exception to the rule that up to the end of the Middle Ages, markets played no important part in the economic system."[19] The only responsible means of studying pre-industrial societies, therefore, was through "substantive" approaches which accounted for the material realities of embeddedness.

By the middle of the 1960s, Polanyi's main theses were applied to the Roman economy by Arnold Hugh Martin Jones and then in the 1970s with Michael Crawford's *Money and Exchange in the Roman World*. Jones' and Crawford's work in turn prepared the scholarly landscape for the emergence of Moses Finley's foundational monograph *The Ancient Economy*, a book based upon his Sather Lectures given a few years prior at the University of California, Berkeley. Finley produced an account which crafted, mostly through cleverly selected anecdotes, an image of antiquity in which market exchange was important but ultimately constrained by overriding cultural and social frameworks.[20] *Homo economicus* – the idealized actor of neoclassical economics, 'perfectly rational' and self-interested in his pursuit of maximum profit, whether psychic or material – was not to be found anywhere in the classical world.[21] The actors in the ancient

16 Polanyi (1944), 60. 17 Ibid., 47–61, 71–2; Polanyi (1957), 256. 18 Polanyi (1957).
19 Polanyi (1944), 57.
20 Bang (2007), 7. Another thoughtful revision of Finley's primitivism is in Hitchner (2007).
21 Mises (1949), 286–91.

economy, according to Finley, played by their own unique and embedded set of rules, constrained by the pursuit of status and other non-economic goals and incentives.[22] Elements superficially shared by both antiquity and modernity – trade networks, monetization, prices and markets – did not self-evidently imply the historical ubiquity of a *market system*.[23] "Trade," for example, Finley revised as "redistribution" or "administered trade."[24] Finley's rich conceptual framework – illustrated through carefully selected references from primary sources – showed the folly of the previous generations of modernizers who had uncritically classified and described the economic structures of antiquity within modern capitalistic concepts and constructs.

The embedded economy framework inspired a new generation of ancient economic historians. Almost concurrent with economists' embrace of Friedman's positive economics – a methodology which saw history as the testing ground for deductive economic hypotheses – a group of ancient historians, led by Finley, was showing that the inhabitants of the ancient world could not easily be forced into the mentality of modern capitalism. Division and conflict among ancient historians inevitably followed.[25] Keith Hopkins described Finley's framework as something like an inoculation which protected the classical world from analysis by modern economic models:

> [Finley and his followers] believe that it is impossible or at least unprofitable to use modern economic concepts in order to analyse a pre-industrial embedded economy. For them, the ancient economy was a cultural system, which was dominated by nonrational considerations of status and ritual and so was immune to cold rational analysis or reconstruction.[26]

Finley immunized Greece and Rome using a distinct strain of Polanyi's substantivism. As a side effect, scholarly positions took on distinctly ideological meanings. Many ancient historians found themselves on either side of a divide between substantivism and "formalism" – the use of formal theories and models in the study of ancient economies.[27]

In this environment, Finley's version of primitivism served as the rally flag for adherents or, conversely, as the main target of critics. Finley, however, was not nearly as ideological as Polanyi, but it is true that Finley's politics were shaped during his time in New York by members of the exiled Frankfurt School of neo-Marxists.[28] Indeed, the idea of antiquity's

[22] Von Reden and Scheidel (2002), 2; Morley (2004), 40–1. [23] Dale (2010), 141.
[24] Garnsey and Saller (1987), 48. [25] Andreau (2002), 33. [26] Hopkins (2009), 200–1.
[27] Cartledge (1998), 114–5. [28] Tompkins (2013), 18–9.

"fundamental break" with modernity was crucial to Karl Marx's materialist historiography.[29] Finley drew upon this aspect of Marxism (through the lens of Weber's revisions) to address a question of transcendent ideological significance: is capitalism inevitably conjoined with human society? The primitivism of *The Ancient Economy*, more than any other previous iteration of the idea, painted a vivid picture of a thriving society in the midst of a world which operated under different rules than the modern capitalistic order.[30] The implications were almost eschatological in scope: "we might now look to Rome to see how else things might have been – for example, it offers a reminder that capitalism is not the only way of organising a society – and perhaps also *how else things might be*."[31]

Finley's ideas were compelling, convincing and powerful. Although primitivists – whether or not they self-identified as such – never fully dominated the field, their contributions to the discipline easily overcame their smaller numbers.[32] The counter-reformation was led by Hopkins. In the *Journal of Roman Studies*, Hopkins constructed a 'taxes and trade' model of the Roman economy, which showed how taxation stimulated and directed trade in the Roman world. The model was what Hopkins called a "wigwam argument" – an amalgamative approach which collected scattered pieces of empirical evidence, weak generalizations and theoretical models into an argument greater than the sum of its parts; each element was like the poles of a wigwam – structurally sound and circumscribing of the truth.[33] Some of Hopkins' formulas were patently neoclassical, such as the one he employed to calculate the gross domestic product (GDP) – an estimate of the monetary value of all final-order or "consumer" goods – in a model year – within the territory of the Roman Empire. The same is true of Hopkins' use of the equation of exchange (sometimes called the 'Fisher equation'), which assumes an unbreakable mathematical connection between money supply, the speed at which money circulates, the total quantity of goods in the economy and the prices at which those goods are successfully exchanged.[34] The mathematics of the equation of exchange are predicated upon a certain verbal logic – that if the economic output of the economy stays the same while the amount of money increases, then prices must proportionally rise. Hopkins used hypothetical numbers in his equation to illustrate relationships rather than make predictions, yet he still

[29] Marx (1847), 120–1; Morley (2006a), 42; Morley (2010), 39.
[30] Cohen (2002), 5; Morris (2002), 27.
[31] Morley (2000)(b), 207. Emphasis added. See also Morley (2004), 39.
[32] Morris (2002), 27; Morley (2006a), 46. [33] Hopkins (1978), 19–20. [34] See 108ff.

felt the need to assure his assumedly skeptical readers of the purely speculative nature of the exercise. While Hopkins used neoclassical methods, his approach was not quite the same as the pure positive economics of Friedman (and some of the ancient economic historians who have since followed Hopkins) in which models are tested by data and either confirmed or falsified. Hopkins' model needed merely to be plausible enough to compare with the fragmentary data; his was ultimately a qualitative if not ideal-typical enterprise. By deploying theory heuristically, Hopkins avoided the circularity of positivist economic analysis, where it is often unclear whether theory is testing history or if history is testing theory. Instead, 'taxes and trade' provided what might be thought of as 'bounding' knowledge about the structure and scale of economic activity in the Roman world.

Both Hopkins' model and his imaginative but controversial methodology provoked the ire of primitivists. He was criticized most famously and enduringly in the work of Richard Duncan-Jones throughout the 1980s and 90s.[35] Duncan-Jones overwhelmed his readers with tables of coin finds and carefully dissected hoard analyses – a strategy which directly attacked the empirical pole of the 'taxes and trade' wigwam. Hopkins, however, like Finley, had his own methodological inoculation: deductivism.

> The logical connections [of Hopkin's argument] cannot be proved or disproved by examples, or by counter-examples. The only proper disproof, I claim, is by counter-argument ... some critics, true to the positivistic traditions of history, have simply taken for granted that showing errors of fact would be sufficient disproof of my propositions. I do not think that disproof is so simple.[36]

Hopkin's saw Duncan-Jones' coin hoards as counter-examples, not counter-arguments; they did not damage the logical core of Hopkins' deductive model and, hence, were ultimately impotent in fully discrediting it according to Hopkins.[37] Over the years, Hopkins became worn down by the constant need to defend both his 'taxes and trade' model, as well as the deductive approach behind it, from mischaracterizations and misunderstandings. Near the end of his life, Hopkins lamented that induction was "the dominant orthodoxy" while his approach was a "heresy."[38] Hopkins was a rhetorical savant, and the "protestant atheist's" use of religious

[35] Duncan-Jones (1990), 30–47; Morley (2014). See also Garnsey and Saller (1987), 49–53; Goldsmith (1984), 273. On rhetorical style, see Morley (2006a), 33–5.

[36] Hopkins (2002), 210–11. See also Hopkins (1980), 103.

[37] Morley (2004), 24–6; Manning and Morris (2007), 38.

[38] Hopkins (2002), 192.

language may reveal his evaluation of the nature of many of the arguments made against him.[39] Alternatively, Hopkins may have simply been expressing humility, or perhaps reflection, or even hyperbole.[40]

Nevertheless, Hopkins' claims about the epistemological structure of his model demands a level of methodological reflection and debate with which few ancient historians have engaged. Instead, there persists a certain amount of methodological schizophrenia in the field of Roman economic history: things have changed, but they have also stayed the same. Confusion persists, for example, over the differing epistemological statuses of theories, hypotheses and models as well as the role of empirical evidence within these categories of argumentation. The main historiographical dichotomies of ancient economic history – primitivism/modernism and substantivism/formalism – are muddled almost beyond usefulness. Primitivism and substantivism, for instance, are often used interchangeably.[41] Furthermore, ancient historians practice the age-old scholarly pastime of distinguishing 'new' work by segregating the 'old' work into extreme characterizations and subsequently arguing against these stereotypes.[42] Approaches which were once nuanced and complex are now straw men which show the 'extremism' which new research will supposedly avoid through a 'third way', compromise or moderation.[43] The primitivist/modernist and substantivist/formalist binaries have been unfortunately reduced into caricatures, as over time short-term efforts to create 'third ways' have cumulated in diluting these otherwise helpful historiographic categories.

In addition to the need for clarity in the field of Roman economic history is a need for reflection. Social-scientific theories, models and organizing concepts should be evaluated for "their usefulness, the extent to which they can offer a persuasive view of the evidence, rather than being automatically ruled invalid and unacceptable."[44] Theoretical constructs should channel historians' inquiries toward questions the empirical evidence does not ask of itself.[45] Pure induction is a myth, not a method. Generalization may be problematic, yet it is impossible to write history without it. One of the more eloquent commentaries upon methodology and the ancient economy is found in the editors' introduction to *Ancient Economies, Modern Methodologies*:

39 See his obituary in The Telegraph (2004).
40 Manning and Morris (2007), 15. Contra Schiavone (2000), 176.
41 As observed by Saller (2002), 252–5; Morley (2004), 44.
42 Katsari (2011), 4.
43 Bang (1998); Saller (2002), 155–6.
44 Morley (2004), 44–5.
45 Harris (1993), 15.

> the historian cannot simply withdraw from the realm of ideas to find safe and firm ground in the world of sources. We perceive the world through ideas and concepts. They determine what questions we ask of ancient material and how we organize the answers.[46]

Inductivism may offer the promise of substance, even objectivity, but there is no *self-evident* framework for organizing or examining the facts.[47] Historians can and must debate the degree to which generalizations are useful; yet they cannot pretend to be pure inductivists, as it is impossible to write history without prior assumptions.[48] Hopkins rightly notes that our critical intelligence is prior to the sources.[49] It seems imprudent, therefore, to dismiss economic theory on ideological or political grounds alone.[50]

How then should Roman economic historians account for the *otherness* of the various cultural contexts for economic activity in the Roman world? One approach is to subvert it to supposedly universalizing concepts. *The Roman Market Economy*, the title of a recent book by one of the most influential economic historians of the late twentieth century, for example, seems to beg the question.[51] The book's provocative title is no doubt meant to summarize the author's characterization of production and distribution in the Roman economy as driven by market forces in both qualitative and quantitative terms.[52] The Roman 'market' would therefore tend toward equilibrium and prices would reflect supply and demand.[53] Characterizations such as these, in which the economic forces of markets, integration and money are dominant, justify the use of neoclassical and new institutional economics: "ancient economies clearly differed from modern ones, but the principles of economics still hold true, and economics can bring clarity to the analysis of how resources were allocated in the ancient world."[54] Such characterizations, however, are odious to scholars sympathetic to substantivist approaches derived from economic anthropology, cultural history, classical philology and economic sociology.[55]

Roman economic historians are rapidly becoming more literate in social-scientific approaches – a change which brings new opportunities but also some challenges. Paleoclimatology and other 'hard' science is also becoming increasingly relevant if not essential for understanding the

46 Bang, Ikeguchi and Ziche (2006), 7. 47 Mises (1933), 107–8.
48 Bang (2008), 3; Morley (2006b), 320–1. 49 Hopkins (2002), 196.
50 Bang (1998); Katsari (2011), 34. 51 Temin (2013).
52 Some, however, maintain that Temin's work has "made the issue effectively closed" and "puts to rest Finley's claim"; see Grantham (2015), 59.
53 Temin (2013), 6; Temin (2001), 170. Contra Bang (2007), 25 n. 59; Haley (2003), 11–2.
54 Temin (2012a), 45. 55 Viglietti (2018).

Roman world.[56] New methodologies now confront Roman historians on a regular basis – an exciting but also potentially overwhelming situation.[57] Navigating the nuances of, for example, post-Keynesianism or economic anthropology is a burdensome dilemma for Roman historians who have already acquired background philological and historical knowledge and, in many cases, theory common to history-writing. In the case of economics, some practical helps have appeared such as Donald Jones' *Economic Theory and the Ancient Mediterranean* or Morris' now aged but still apropos "Hard Surfaces" chapter in the edited volume *Money, Labour and Land*.[58] Morris' chapter, which contrasts the approaches to model-building in neoclassical economics versus those of economic sociology, performs an invaluable service to the field by unpacking concepts otherwise foreign to many ancient historians. The expanding methodological menu has also brought new and more sophisticated challenges to the formalist enterprise broadly. Naïve substantivism (why study theory which is inapplicable if not alien to antiquity?) has been replaced by theoretically literate critiques of formalism and the use of economic theory broadly. Recent debates have taken place upon a fitting battleground: new institutional economics. The ideas of new institutionalist and Nobel laureate Douglass North –both a critic and a proponent of neoclassical economics – wield tremendous influence over the use of economic theory in the field of Roman economic history. Assessing the presence of new institutionalism in Roman history is not only valuable for understanding the present state of the field, but it is also possible to signal trajectories for future debates on the place for economic theory in the study of the Roman economy.

New Institutional Economics and Beyond

New institutional economics enjoys something like 'third way' status in the field of ancient economic history because the new institutional framework seems to enable (primitive) pre-industrial economies to be studied using (formal) economic theory. Roman economic historians friendly to new institutional economics tend to use the version articulated by North in which economic analysis accounts for 'institutional frameworks' – the rules, laws, political bodies and social norms which play a key role in controlling, guiding or influencing the actions and interactions of

[56] Harper (2017a); Harper (2016b); McConnell et al. (2018); McCormick (2013); McCormick et al. (2012); Elliott (2016); Elliott (forthcoming).

[57] Morris (2002), 24.

[58] Jones (2014); Morris (2002). See also Manning and Morris (2007).

individual actors.[59] 'Institutions' are typically defined as the practical mechanisms by which economic exchanges take place in societies – e.g. legal systems, property rights and money are all 'institutions'. Dennis Kehoe argues that thinking in terms of institutional frameworks helps historians categorize and subsequently analyze a broad range of activities, laws and customs in the Roman world, both 'formal' and 'informal'. Kehoe provides a succinct of explanation of the difference between formal and informal institutions in his book *Law and the Rural Economy in the Roman Empire*:

> The formal institutions include the rules that the Roman state established to define property rights, legal rules relating to farm tenancy and other aspects of land tenure, as well as the courts and other institutions through which individuals could defend their rights. The formal institutions also include policies of the Roman government, such as how it defined and defended property rights, how it mediated between competing claims by various classes of landowners and tenants, and, ultimately, whose property rights it tended to foster. But institutional environment also embraces the informal institutions that helped determine how formal institutions worked, that is, the social values and practices that helped establish the 'rules of the game' for the rural economy in the Roman Empire.[60]

Kehoe is one of many Roman economic historians who have found in North's new institutionalism a body of both abstract concepts and practical models seemingly tailor-made to overcome the unique methodological problems that have hitherto plagued the historiography of the Roman economy.[61] Perhaps more than any other school of economics, new institutionalism appears best equipped to handle the persistent problem of limited empirical evidence; at the same time, the approach seems to reveal new (although often hypothetical) 'evidence' about the costs and incentives created by 'institutions' and the response these elicited in economic actors.

The practical power of new institutionalism is in its use of 'transaction costs' to analyze and explain economic activity, whether such activity occurs in individual transactions or in a wider social context. Transaction costs are the costs associated with making an exchange – costs, for example, of defining and protecting property, negotiating contracts and completing transactions – all of which are often unexamined in the 'clean' models of

[59] North (1981); North (1990). [60] Kehoe (2007), 29–30.
[61] See, for example, the authors in recent volumes: McGinn (2012); Kehoe, Ratzan and Yiftach (2015b).

neoclassical economics.[62] The 'frictionless' world of neoclassical models, North thoughtfully observes, "appears to beg all of the interesting questions."[63] Neoclassical models, for example, assume perfect information – that prices, quality and value (utility) are thoroughly known by individuals. By contrast, new institutional economics factors (or attempts to factor) the cost of searching for goods, price comparisons, gathering information and information asymmetry. Markets in neoclassical models are usually perfectly or 'purely' competitive, in that no individual or firm is powerful enough to affect the equilibrium price – the price at which supply and demand are in balance. New institutional economics, however, acknowledges that there are costs involved when parties agree to exchange, such as the need to draw up contracts. States or other enforcement agencies are also important for policing contracts and perhaps providing legal systems; the costs of these must be factored into the 'institutional environment'. Finally, neoclassical models usually assume rule-enforcement – that property rights, contracts and the rule of law will be upheld and respected without deviation – as a given. A framework of transaction costs, however, allows the models of new institutional economics comparative flexibility against those of neoclassical economics. Identifying and quantifying transaction costs in the Roman economy, however, is difficult. Only occasionally do ancient sources seem to mention transaction costs, such as when Tacitus claims that slave traders raised their prices after Nero required traders to pay the tax on slave purchases.[64] Furthermore, to what extent is it even possible to assign cardinal values to these costs? One might, for example, look at taxes paid as a way to calculate the costs of the judicial system, but not all taxes go exclusively to the provision of justice and rarely (if ever) has any justice system given equal treatment to all taxpayers.

New institutional economics also offers a different approach to rationality. Neoclassical economics tends to model rationality after *homo economicus*' instinctive disposition toward profit-maximization and omniscience.[65] The use of this 'perfect' rationality for analyzing non-capitalist societies outraged Polanyi as well as Finley and his followers, and for good reason, as "neither the drives and psychological profile attributed to *homo economicus*, nor the assumption of the effective operation of price mechanisms, can be applied across the spectrum of ancient societies without creating a gross travesty of reality."[66] New institutional

[62] Nee (1994), 50; Lo Cascio (2006), 218–9. [63] North (1981), 5.
[64] Tac. *Ann.* 13.31. Koops (2016), 612. [65] Madra (2017), 116.
[66] Davies (2007), 130. See also Bresson (2015), 13.

economics' understanding of transaction costs problematizes the rationality of *homo economicus*, as the presence of these costs in exchanges – costs which are often implied or even hidden during the decision-making process – leaves little room for a purely 'rational' actor to exist. Instead, new institutional economics uses the more nuanced 'bounded rationality' to theorize and analyze human decision-making under conditions of limited information, limited ability to assess value and the limited amount of time individuals have to make decisions. North posits that

> institutions are a creation of human beings. They evolve and are altered by human beings; hence our theory must begin with the individual. At the same time, the constraints that institutions impose on individual choices are pervasive.[67]

North's bounded rationality seems to find itself somewhere between 'methodological individualism' – the idea that the study of society must begin with the study of individuals – and neoclassical 'ontological individualism' – the idea that only individuals *exist*. North here draws upon the idea advanced by fellow Nobel laureate Herbert Simon that human knowledge is "local" rather than "global."[68] In practice, individuals rarely make "optimal" decisions; most often, they make "satisfactory" decisions instead.[69] Compared to perfect rationality, bounded rationality offers historians a better way to think about microeconomic factors and how economic activity might work within an embedded economy.[70]

Is the wholesale adoption of new institutional economics *the* answer to the substantivist/formalist debate?[71] Evaluations are mixed. Historian of capitalism Francesco Boldizzoni argues that new institutionalism's accommodation of embeddedness is a deception, and that new institutional economics is a mere rebranding of neoclassical economics, only with a more refined set of categories and a consistent although sometimes vague lexicon of jargon: "what [North] did was to extend the neoclassical explanatory model to the realm of social relations."[72] North himself called his efforts a "modification" of neoclassical theory, as his approach retains most of neoclassical microeconomics as well as many basic neoclassical assumptions about scarcity and competitive markets.[73]

Some historians believe that the Roman Empire is "a test case for Douglass North's claim about the importance of institutions," but how should economic historians perform such tests and would these tests differ

[67] North (1990), 5. See also 86ff. [68] Simon (1957); Simon (1955); Metcalfe (2010), 61–3.
[69] Simon (1983). [70] See for example Kehoe (2007), 38–9; Bannon (2009), 30–6.
[71] Scheidel (2005), 35. [72] Boldizzoni (2011), 18. [73] North (1996), 344.

substantially from the kind of testing performed in neoclassical analyses?[74] How meaningful is a term like 'institution', for example, which encompasses many facets of the process of exchange and even the wider political, legal, social and cultural context in which exchange takes place? Economist and economic historian Peter Temin's use of new institutional concepts in his scholarship on the Roman world has led him to conclude that market systems were dominant in classical antiquity.[75] Bruce Frier and Kehoe, by contrast, use new institutional concepts in ways which are surprisingly compatible with and even at times reinforce a primitivist and substantivist view of the ancient economy: "ancient evidence can seldom if ever be used to test the hypotheses that are characteristic on the current research agenda in new institutional economics."[76] Even Bang's primitivistic "Roman bazaar" economy is rooted in a comparative analysis of institutions, albeit an analysis which emphasizes the dominance of predation and prevailing cultural norms. Therefore, while Boldizzoni's critiques no doubt apply to many applications of new institutionalism, there are also noteworthy exceptions.

Roman economic historians' use of new institutionalist concepts has now spanned multiple decades – enough time to afford some hindsight on the results. Despite its clear improvements over neoclassical analysis, some Roman historians remain unconvinced that new institutional economics offers a credible way forward. Is it a form of cliometric abuse, for example, to mine ancient sources for 'statistics' (and in the process discard cultural and social contexts) in order to quantify transaction costs and the wider 'institutional environment'? Are analyses driven by new institutional concepts more likely to ignore historical problems which are not answered by appeals to quantitative data or statistics – especially questions of *meaning*? Roman historians have long understood, for example, the social and cultural stigmas held (at least superficially) by Roman elites against certain forms of trade and entrepreneurship.[77] Making money as an end in itself implied a lack of self-control – the willful indulgence in a never-ending cycle of insatiable greed, as the accumulation of money merely precipitated the need to exchange it to gain more.[78] In a recent book, Neil Coffee provides economic historians with a thorough survey of Roman writers' frequent condemnation of 'money-making' for its own sake, especially

[74] Saller (2002), 266. [75] Temin (2013).
[76] Frier and Kehoe (2007), 142. See also Kehoe (2012). [77] Morley (2007), 83–5.
[78] Schaps (2003), 179–93.

through money-lending.[79] As Kehoe, Bang and others have shown, new institutionalism offers Roman historians some tools for productively exploring such issues, but new institutionalism's vestigial neoclassicism limits the historical applicability of many of its concepts.

As is the case with the agenda of neoclassical economics, new institutionalism prioritizes questions of causality over questions of meaning. Tacitus, for example, claims that Tiberius injected 100 million sesterces into the Roman economy via "banks" (*mensae*) in AD 33.[80] Recently, scholars seem much more interested in theorizing about how this injection may have influenced GDP than understanding the social and cultural meanings of, let alone the motivations behind, Tiberius' intervention.[81] Collingwood summarized the insufficiency of mere causal analysis in matters of economic history:

> No historian can claim to have shown that a certain sequence of events must have fallen out thus and not otherwise. The fall of a man's income may lead him to retrenchment or to bankruptcy: which it does, depends certainly on what kind of man he is, but what kind of man he is can never be finally determined: he determines it himself in his own action as he goes on. He goes on to bankruptcy and we say he was an extravagant and thriftless man, but this does not explain *why* he chose that alternative, it is only a way of saying that he *did* choose it.[82]

New institutional economics may have better concepts and more accommodating jargon than its neoclassical parent, but new institutionalism offers historians few if any tools for evaluating the meanings of historical actors' choices, economic or otherwise. The potential for reorienting new institutional approaches toward identifying and understanding the sorts of *ex ante* attitudes, mentalities and ideologies which were ultimately articulated in 'costs' – economic costs to be sure, but also social and cultural costs – seems limited.

Another consequence of new institutionalism's presence in the field of Roman economic history is a gradual but unmistakable modernist resurgence. Many Roman historians would now agree that the 'institutions' of the Roman Empire promoted, either by accident or design, markets and economic growth. Finley's lingering influence has likely prevented excesses here; at least Roman historians have selected North's new institutionalism (which focuses upon the state as the entity which sets the "rules of the game"),

[79] Coffee (2017). [80] Tac. *Ann.* 6.17. [81] See 89ff. [82] Collingwood (1999), 142.

and not a more ideologically capitalist flavor.[83] Yet while Finley and his followers focused upon the state's redistributive and predatory role, many new institutional studies reorient the state's role toward raising or (more often) lowering transaction costs and thus facilitating market exchange and economic rationality. The triumph of this flavor of new institutionalist historiography is surely *The Cambridge Economic History of the Greco-Roman World*:

> the creation of more peaceful and safer conditions translated to a marked decrease in transaction costs. The suppression of piracy in the final decades of the Republic, the diffusion of a 'technology of measurement' and of common metrological systems, and above all the creation of a unitary monetary zone and of common legal rules, especially in the field of commercial law, were all quite remarkable contributing factors in this reduction of transaction costs, in so far as they reduced uncertainty and improved access to information. The imperial state could define and enforce the fundamental 'rules of the game,' in particular exclusive property rights, not only in the Italian core but also in the provinces. The spread of the Roman notion (and practice) of private property was fostered by the increase in the number of urban communities of Roman or Latin status.[84]

The most recent new institutional analyses give the Roman state an even more powerful and conscientious role as market facilitator:

> both economic growth and intensification of trade . . . was not merely the unintended and unexpected result of the unification of the Mediterranean under Roman rule, but also the product of the role that the political organization of Rome purposely undertook in regulating market transactions . . . [this regulation] aimed at guaranteeing that the price in the *forum rerum venalium* would always be the market price, formed through the encounter between supply and demand: a market price conceived as a 'fair price'.[85]

In other words, the Roman state did not merely passively benefit markets; rather, the state *designed* the institutional environment *for the purpose* of growing markets. Such claims seem to vindicate those who fear that new institutionalism is merely a thinly veiled modernism. These skeptics believe that "cultural biases" are embedded in new institutional models

[83] As opposed to that of, say, Oliver Williamson, who assumes the primacy of the market: "in the beginning there were markets," Williamson (1975), 20. Rather than the state, Williamson focused upon "firms" which correct information asymmetries and promote the smoother operation of markets. See Williamson (1985); Williamson (1981).

[84] Lo Cascio (2007), 626. See also Katsari (2011), 1; Bowman and Wilson (2009), 56; Morley (2010), 83–5.

[85] Lo Cascio (2018), 120.

and concepts, and these biases make it difficult for new institutionalists to distinguish the cultural elements which constrain *their own thinking* with what might be called "constants of nature."[86] Both Boldizzoni and Jérôme Maucourant observe, for example, that despite North's effort to incorporate non-market "substitutes" (not "alternatives"), North still premises these "substitutes" on capitalist concepts: contracts, property rights, economic efficiency and a pre-existent market mentality.[87] The rules adopted by institutions, North argues, "are derived from self-interest ... with compliance costs in mind."[88] If North's new institutionalism assumes that "institutions," even non-market ones, are magnetically drawn to market-like characteristics, then is it surprising that the adoption of new institutionalism by Roman historians has coincided with a distinctly modernist turn or, even more problematically, a teleology which idealizes (American) capitalism?[89]

New institutionalist studies (again, with some exceptions), tend to underappreciate the pervasive problems of violence and predation in the Roman world.[90] Scheidel rightly characterizes the Roman imperial economy as "a product of organized violence and coercive integration."[91] Some applications of new institutionalism retroject the modern notion of property rights, with its clear division between public and private, onto Roman ideas and practices of property ownership. In fact, property ownership in the Roman world often came with public obligations. Moreover, coercion and violence were common mechanisms by which the elite shareholders in the empire's social hierarchy grew their share of resources at the expense of others' (including fellow elites') so-called 'property rights':

> Monopolies *normally* abuse their power to charge a monopoly rent. Interpretations, therefore, that emphasize the benign institutional conditions produced for economic life by the Roman state, need to develop an explanation why the imperial government did not abuse its monopolistic position.[92]

Behind senators' terror of the rise of soldier emperors of the third century AD, for example, was concern that the coercive power apparatus, which had hitherto benefited the landholding elite, would be turned upon them.

86 Boldizzoni (2011), 23.
87 Maucourant (2012), 196–201; Boldizzoni (2011), 21–3. The specific object of their critique is North (1977).
88 North (1990), 48.
89 Maucourant (2012), 197.
90 Bang (2012).
91 Scheidel (2012), 108.
92 Bang (2009), 205. See also von Reden (2010), 13–5; Bang (2008), 97–103; Weber (1968), 164.

In fact, the subsequent course of events justified these fears. Many Roman historians, including myself, are the passive beneficiaries of exploitative systems – an embedding context which easily blinds us to fully appreciating the violence and coercion undergirding the societies we study.

Sociologist Mark Granovetter forcefully argues that research on markets must study "the actual patterns of personal relations by which economic transactions are carried out."[93] In the case of the Roman economy, the role of coercion, predation and violence must be accounted for. Unfortunately, the networks of interpersonal connections, whether violent or voluntary, of pre-modern economies are impossible to quantify and exploit via formal economic modeling; even new institutional economics, despite being an improved version of neoclassical economics, offers limited avenues for circumventing the problems raised by embeddedness (of both observers and subjects). Cultural historians and economic anthropologists, most of them skeptical of economic theory, are unlikely to find the approaches offered by new institutional economics more useful than the tools they already know and use. Still, new institutionalism provides Roman economic historians with novel concepts, even if new institutionalism as a whole clearly cannot pull the field out of well-worn dichotomies. Despite its promise, the agenda of new institutionalism has thus far not materialized as a true 'third way' between either primitivism and modernism or substantivism and formalism. I do not believe that new institutionalism should be discarded entirely, but historians would be wise to use care and caution.

Conclusions

All historical applications of formal economic models require justification – not merely within their own closed system of logic, but in a wider historiographical context which includes serious and thoughtful substantivist critiques of the formalist enterprise more generally and especially of applied economic theory. New institutional economics may not be the final solution, but are there other ways Roman economic historians might use economic theories to better understand economic choices as well as the embedding contexts which channeled such choices? Although I share many of the substantivists' concerns about new institutional economics, I wonder: can some new institutional concepts (e.g. transaction costs and

[93] Granovetter (1985), 504.

bounded rationality) be redeemed in order to help historians understand the Roman monetary system? History and economics, despite fundamental differences embedded in each discipline, can meaningfully and symbiotically intersect. While I hesitate to suggest that the two disciplines are entirely reconcilable, economics offers Roman historians valuable and helpful organizing concepts, so long as these concepts are used *within* an agenda of historical understanding.

CHAPTER 2

Embedding Contexts of Roman Money

> In Western societies money was fetishized by scholars nearly as much as by stock brokers. If we aim to free ourselves from this tradition we have to accept that money can change its character and function according to the context in which it is used.
>
> Sitta von Reden[1]

What exactly was the Roman monetary system? It is often too easy to conceive of Roman money as a collection of sterile, disembedded objects and instruments – coins, commodities and credit arrangements. Similarly, the 'system' into which these items were integrated can be easily reduced to the economic relationships between such items. Roman money, however, emerged from and continually operated within a variety of contexts. Anthropological studies of money emphasize social and cultural contexts. Ecology also seems to have influenced monetization, and ever accumulating environmental and climate evidence presents historians with new questions about money production in ancient societies.[2] There was also the looming presence of the Roman state. Political power invariably framed money use and value, but historians vigorously debate both the structure and scale of state influence.

In this chapter, I define the Roman monetary system of the Principate as a complex, dynamic and ultimately embedded network of values in which various moneys – coins, credit instruments, commodities and a variety of special-purpose monies – obtained value and acceptability from a dynamic matrix of embedding political, social, economic and cultural contexts (what I summarize in this book 'embedding contexts'). These embedding contexts were not mutually exclusive, but their influence on money use and value could change depending upon local conditions. A wide range of laws, cultural rituals, informal social rules and practical

[1] Von Reden (1995), 172. [2] E.g. Elliott (forthcoming).

economic factors (scarcity, demand, convenience, use-value) could exert influence on the subjectively determined value that money-users gave to whatever monies they held. The use of coins and other media of exchange in the Roman world is incomprehensible without at least some study of embedding contexts.

The complexity and dynamicity of embeddedness is not too difficult to grasp. Roman coinage's *raison d'être*, for example, was as a means of state payment as well as a mechanism for redistribution, taxation and tribute collection. The coinage created by the state nevertheless had an enduring afterlife in social customs, cultural rituals and market exchange – an afterlife which influenced the use and value coinage differently from place to place and context to context.[3] Different notions of value sometimes complimented each other; for example, state guarantees of nominal value made coinage more acceptable in most economic transactions, even those in which the state was not involved. Roman historians are also aware of periods of monetary tension which created dissonance in the system (e.g. when state guarantees failed, or when debasements made it more difficult for coin-users to accurately or conveniently value coins). During these periods, coin-users may have found that the power of the Roman state to dictate or guarantee the exchange-value of money was less influential than economic factors, especially use-value (in the broadest sense possible – not merely 'economic' use-value).

In summary: the Roman monetary system was historically unique. Its complexity arose out of several intersecting and sometimes contradictory embedding contexts. This chapter identifies several important (but by no means all) embedding contexts and provides a broad and loosely diachronic outline of their influence in the development of Roman money. Some of Rome's Republican-era experiments with coinage, for example, were inescapably influenced by Greek practices and concepts; monetary developments in the Greek world, therefore, must be touched upon. It is also true, however, that Roman territorial expansion seems to have been correlated with the rise of impersonal exchange in Rome, Italy and beyond – presenting unique cultural challenges for Roman elites in the Republican period.[4] Notions of monetary value in the Principate remained tethered to historical monetary contexts – but shifts in value and in the prominence of certain contexts over others could and did happen. Oscillations in the

[3] Rowan (2014), 78.

[4] Problems which are now generating renewed scholarly interested; see Bernard (2018); Coffee (2017); Viglietti (2014).

intensity and breadth of state power, for example – perhaps the most significant embedding context during the Principate – influenced money use, value and the scope for market exchange. It is impossible to import modern economic theory into Roman monetary history without first accounting for some of the key embedding contexts which shaped monetary practices, processes and concepts in the Roman world.

Embeddedness

When Finley updated *The Ancient Economy* in 1985, he emphatically stated that ancient "money was essentially coined metal and nothing else."[5] Here as elsewhere in *The Ancient Economy*, Finley's prose is dour – emphasizing absence, lacking, deficiencies. Finley believed that materiality placed hard limits on monetary developments in ancient Greece and Rome. There could be no such thing as ancient 'fiduciary money' – a term Finley used but did not define. Usually, fiduciary money is money that is valued by trust or confidence (*fiducia*), presumably in the issuing authority. Fiduciary money is different from 'token money', which Finley defined in the same place as "base metal circulating at conventional values." Finley's short (two and a half page) discourse on ancient money frames interpretations of the Roman monetary system in at least two important ways. First, if Roman monetary instruments were inseparable from their material substance, then the amount of physical coin produced intrinsically limited the supply of money in the Roman world. Inflexibility, sluggish circulation and chronic currency shortages would therefore have characterized the system. A second implication is methodological: modern economic theory, apart from the most commonsensical notions, gives few insights into a money system primarily composed of physical money – a system radically different from those found in modern capitalist economies. Ancient economic historians who hold Finley's view will likely view non-theoretical (i.e. rhetorical, metaphorical) comparisons with modern monetary institutions with suspicion.

Historiographical treatments of the Roman monetary system typically start where Finley did: with the materiality of money – namely, coins: their nominal values, metal composition, and such. In a book about *money*, however – not *coinage* – it seems necessary to start with conceptual and organization frameworks – e.g. state power, market exchange, informal rules, social and cultural customs, and other contexts – which dictated the

[5] Finley (1985b), 196.

values and acceptability of currency instruments, including coinage. Coins are themselves merely *a posteriori* physical articulations of money, which is ultimately a preexistent abstraction: indirect exchange. Now, if Finley was right that materiality limited money, then the distinction between money and coinage at least for antiquity is merely semantic. To talk about the 'Roman monetary system' would be to talk about Roman coins, their metal content, their circulation (presumably at low velocity, mostly via state redistribution) and perhaps their users (those few urban and elite inhabitants who dwelled outside the ever-dominant subsistence economy). Roman economic historians, however, especially over the past two decades, have questioned or outright rejected Finley's money–coinage equivalence. Instead, historians tend to describe the Roman economy as highly integrated and healthily monetized – an economy thoroughly permeated by both coinage and credit instruments.[6] Roman money in its various forms, especially during the Principate, is now seen as composing a true *system*: an interconnected, even purposefully designed arrangement of legally fixed coin denominations, credit instruments, commodity monies, monetary regulations – including legal tender laws – and institutional mechanisms, both formal and informal, for enforcing these regulations.[7] It goes without saying that such a dynamic system, in stark contrast to Finley's view, allows and even seems to encourage theoretical analysis of prices, money supply and, ultimately, economic growth across the vast monetary zone administered by Roman authorities.

Scholars who retain a primitivistic disposition, whether inspired by Finley, Crawford, Duncan-Jones or other scholars, tend to see ancient monetary systems as part of the embedded economy. Primitivists typically seem to think of 'system' differently than their more modernist counterparts – as analogous to 'contexts' or even 'determinants': the social and cultural channels which limited monetary exchange and dictated the meanings of money.[8] It necessarily follows that if *any* theories are used to study such systems, they should be informed by 'emic' approaches which prioritize cultural-social context as determining the meaning of currencies in societies. The conventional economic theories deployed to study monetary systems are, by contrast, 'etic' in nature; they rest upon generalizations which universalize the meanings of money in ways roughly analogous to those meanings found in the modern experience of money.

[6] Harris (2008b); Temin (2014); Temin and Kessler (2008).
[7] Lo Cascio (2000), 79. Similar thoughts in Katsari (2011), 84; Lo Cascio (2008), 160.
[8] I use 'meanings' here after Geertz (1973).

Such meanings, in the words of anthropologists Maurice Bloch and Johnny Parry, give money "an intrinsically revolutionary power which inexorably subverts the moral economy of 'traditional' societies."[9] In other words, money exogenously and autonomously *reshapes* and *reorients* societies and their cultures toward a modernistic (if not capitalistic) horizon. This anachronistic assumption, which sometimes goes unacknowledged or unappraised by scholars of the Roman economy, has the effect of conflating monetization with marketization. It is difficult for some to imagine that the Roman Empire could have featured high levels of monetization for several centuries without also developing many of the elements we associate with highly monetized post-industrial economies.

A recent influential book by Philip Kay, for example, observes that proceeds of imperialism ("war booty, indemnities, and silver from the Spanish mines" among other gains) brought Rome a sustained flow of bullion in the second and first centuries BC – bullion which was converted into an unprecedented amount of coinage.[10] The resulting monetization of the Roman Mediterranean, the author argues, "marketized" a variety of economic institutions (agriculture, trade, manufacturing, physical infrastructure and financial intermediation). This economic revolution created an agricultural economy shaped by enterprising landowners who maximized the production of their lands by means of "radical technological advances" including the use of water power and water lifting, crop rotation regimes, food processing technology and machinery such as the olive press.[11] Geographically broad, interconnected and "monetized urban and international trade networks" offered opportunities for export for these specialized, capital-generating "investment farms."[12] Markets were also nurtured by a "pervasive and institutionalized" credit system – a "liquid and sophisticated market for lending and borrowing money on a very significant scale."[13] This perspective challenges Finley's ancient Mediterranean, which was dominated by subsistence farming and elite estates managed "by tradition, habit and rule-of-thumb."[14]

The interpretive framework also departs from Finley. A robust engagement with economic theory and a comprehensive, detailed analysis of empirical evidence supports Kay's imaginative argument. Even more impressive, Kay's optimism bears little resemblance whatsoever to the naïve modernism of Rostovtzeff. His book, along with Temin's *The*

[9] Parry and Bloch (1989), 12; Maucourant (1991), 155; Coffee (2017), 13–4.
[10] Kay (2014), 105.
[11] Finley (1985b), 117. Kay (2014), 155–60; Wilson (2002).
[12] Kay (2014), 317, 2.
[13] Harris (2006), 13; Kay (2014), 194.
[14] Finley (1985), 110.

Roman Market Economy, is in the vanguard of a revised modernism – a synthesis of cliometrics, new institutionalist frameworks and an optimistic view of the structure and scale of market exchange in the Roman world. These 'new' modernist arguments often rest upon unstated but foundational theoretical assumptions. Why, for example, would a dramatic burst in the supply of money necessarily lead to expansive monetization? When second-century BC Italians encountered (*a posteriori*) coined money, especially for the first time, did they also simultaneously adopt the (*a priori*) mental and ultimately culturally learned habit of impersonal exchange and market calculation? Historians must be cautious about correlating the presence of monetary objects with the processes and habits of monetization, as Koenraad Verboven rightly notes:

> No pre-industrial economy ever came near to being fully monetized. Gift exchange, command economics and redistribution remained important structuring principles that governed the flow of resources in ancient and other pre-industrial societies. Money may be drawn into gift-exchange practices (as gifts and free loans) and command and redistribution systems, but the presence of money as such does not imply that transactions were monetized.[15]

Anthropological and archaeological studies of coinage in Celtic Gaul and Britain support Verboven's claim. Despite a healthy presence of foreign and later domestic gold and silver coinage in pre-Roman Gaul and Britain, these societies incorporated coinage into pre-existing ritual exchange and ostentation practices.[16] Contemporary Roman writers, such as Tacitus, noted these practices – which included "the exchange of commodities" – probably to reinforce notions of Roman cultural superiority:

> The population nearest to us, however, value gold and silver for their use in commerce, and are familiar and prefer some of our coins. The tribes of the interior use the simpler and more ancient practice of the exchange of commodities. They like the old-fashioned money – coins with milled edges or which show the two-horse chariot. They also prefer silver to gold, not from any special preference, but because a large number of silver pieces is more convenient for buying cheap and common goods.[17]

For elite Roman writers, the use of coined money *as money* was one of many culturally defined markers of civilization. Is it also possible that modern historians, whether consciously or not, use norms and assumptions embedded

[15] Verboven (2009), 105.
[16] Roymans and Aarts (2009); Hunter (2007); Jersey and Haselgrove (2006).
[17] Tac. *Germ.* 5.

in our own monetary culture to evaluate ancient societies? At least in this case, it seems prudent to question whether an expanded money supply was itself sufficient to spark a cultural transformation and hence "encourage an increase in effective demand" in Roman Italy.[18] Modern historians cannot always expect that those who encountered Roman money were predisposed to demanding markets and monetization – that such people simply lacked the physical objects and subsequent credit instruments to put the pre-existing principles of their dormant pre-capitalist thinking into practice.

Very recently, some scholars have begun investigating Roman monetary developments in the Republic through an anthropological lens. Economic anthropologists typically frame money as a cultural *product*: money does not change society, rather it emerges and evolves *from* society. The meanings a society attaches to exchange and the instruments of exchange are entrenched within the wider constraints of culture.[19] Some economists, by contrast, are disposed toward viewing monetization as a self-contained, non-contextualized *process* across time and space; in effect, monetization is *autonomous* rather than embedded.[20] Historical accounts (whether of Rome, ancient China or other geographies and temporalities) influenced by such thinking tend to exhibit narratives in which money use evolves from barter to money to credit. Anthropologist David Graeber argues (as have others before) that this economic-historical formula lacks historical merit.[21] Study after study in Bloch and Parry's collection shows the importance of embedding contexts in shaping both exchange practices as well as monetary objects themselves.[22] In their introduction, Bloch and Parry argue that the meanings of money in the diachronic story of 'Western civilization' derive directly from our own culture and perceptions of its historical development; in other words, these meanings are historically specific, not universal.[23] The ideological problem that economic historians must grapple with is that our predilection to universalize the modern experience of money necessarily and problematically subverts and distorts non-conforming historical meanings.

Because of the role context plays in their methodology, economic anthropologists and economic historians using anthropological approaches tend to ask questions about phenomena which the models and teleologies of modern economics often assume or ignore. Studies of the origin of coinage in the Greek world by Sitta von Reden (1995), Leslie Kurke

[18] Kay (2014), 107–8. [19] Aarts (2005), 13. [20] Maucourant (1991), 155.
[21] Graeber (2011), 21–41; Hart (2012). [22] Parry and Bloch (1989). [23] Ibid., 1.

(1999) and Richard Seaford (2004), for example, have much to offer historians of Roman money by showing how the anthropological lens clarifies histories of monetization in ancient societies. For von Reden, for example, money was one facet within a larger system of exchange, not an autonomous, exogenous, culture-transforming 'force'. If anything, money was quickly appropriated – first by social elites and then by the *polis* broadly – into existing systems of value and exchange – a struggle seen, in part, in the diverse styles of the late sixth century BC *Wappenmünzen* coins minted at Athens. Kurke also sees Greek monetization as synchronous with the development of the democratic *polis*, but in her view money antagonized the distinctions between elites and non-elites – the *kakoi* and *deiloi* who "do not understand or respect the proper workings of gift exchange."[24] Coins were part of a new regime of value which competed with (and ultimately superseded) aristocratic value systems, into which gift-exchange was embedded. Seaford's study emphasizes the money-shaping role of Greek animal sacrifice which transferred its characteristics of reciprocity and redistribution to coinage. A sacrifice creates a reasonable expectation that the deity will give something in return, but the ceremony itself is redistributive, as all share equally in eating the meat offered. According to Seaford, "it was this traditional, sanctified equality that we saw as a factor in that communal confidence in multiple symbols of identical value that is a *prerequisite* for the communal adoption of coinage."[25]

Economic factors, too, explain the gradual use of metal coins in ancient Greek societies. It is true, for example, that gold and silver likely offered Greek elites and those who took coins in payments a durable, homogenous and divisible medium of exchange which was likely more attractive than other commodities. Coined precious metals, however, retained attributes of precious metal broadly – attributes which carried cultural weight in the Hellenic societies that first minted them into coinage. Greek culture imbued gold, for example, with moral, social and religious meaning. Gold was tested and purified, justly sovereign, even immortal – a metal of gods, kings and men of virtue.[26] In archaic Greek communities, precious metals were pragmatic, but also given sacrality. Exchanging precious metals connected human beings with the deities and heroes they worshiped in a tangible, embodied way.

[24] Kurke (1999), 103. [25] Seaford (2004), 294. Emphasis added.
[26] Kurke (1999), 41–64, 91; Kurke (1995).

The Greek cultural context for coin development – again, expounded upon especially by von Reden, Kurke and Seaford – is important for understanding the meanings of Roman coinage, as Rome likely encountered coins through contact with Greek city states in the south of Italy. These communities had been minting precious-metal coins from the second half of the sixth century BC. Elites in the city of Rome, however, despite regular interactions with Greek monetary practices, seem to have avoided minting Greek-style coins for several centuries. Did cultural and social contexts shape Romans' avoidance of coined money? It is true that reliable gold and silver sources are rare in Italy, but this fact only tells historians about the availability of material for certain kinds of monetary objects; it tells historians nothing about whether and why Roman monetary ideas and mentalities diverged from those of their southern neighbors in Magna Graecia.[27] In her study of archaic Greek exchange, von Reden observes that "money can change its character and function according to the context in which it is used" – a principle which applies to both ancient and modern societies.[28] Roman historians need to ask: what were the embedding contexts for monetary developments in the early-to-mid Roman Republic?

Parallels between Roman and Etruscan cultures suggest a close connection between monetary developments in both societies. One obvious link is between Etruscan *ramo secco* and Roman *aes signatum* bronze bars. The Etruscan bars, produced sometime within the sixth through third centuries BC, may have served a monetary function, but no one can say for certain.[29] *Ramo secco* bars, named after the branch-like emblem that appears on their surface, lack any kind of discernable weight or metallurgical standard. The *aes signatum* bars used in and around Rome, however, are of standardized weight and the bronze of which they are composed is of a consistent alloy – the same alloy used for Greek bronze coins in the south of Italy.[30] Does the absence of standards in Etruscan bars suggests that they were initially non-monetary objects that derived their value from ritual uses? Many *ramo secco* bars have been found in votive and religious contexts, but why?[31] A forthcoming study by Charlotte Potts proposes that the design on *ramo secco* bars represents growing wheat.[32] Potts argues that this symbol could have both economic and religious meanings. Growing wheat may represent wealth and prosperity – a way to associate the bars with a valuable

[27] Forsythe (2006), 336. [28] Von Reden (1995), 172. [29] Crawford (1985), 3–6.
[30] Burnett (2012), 302; Von Reden (2010), 50. [31] Potts (forthcoming). [32] Ibid.

commodity and perhaps promote exchange. It is also true, however, that ancient Italians perceived minerals and ores as akin to living organisms.[33] Potts speculates, reasonably in my view, that the wheat symbols on *ramo secco* bars draws upon the association between metals and plants and, therefore, may explain why so many *ramo secco* bars were offered to the gods. Perhaps, like Celtic 'coins', these bars obtained their value primarily from their ceremonial and ritual uses.[34]

The autarkic agricultural economy and militaristic culture of archaic Rome also may have minimized the usefulness of precious-metal coins. From the Twelve Tables and limited archaeological evidence, it appears that monetary transactions in archaic Rome were processed chiefly through the media of livestock, weighed bronze ingots of various shapes and other commodities.[35] The functions of early Roman money appear to have been limited to justice and restitution within the community of the city. Monetary developments in this period are largely a matter of speculation, but by the mid-fourth century BC – well before the city first minted coins – it appears that Roman soldiers received payments in commodities, probably in weighed bronze. Some scholars believe that war booty was distributed in "weighed heaps" of bronze, but the low numbers of cast bronze bars (*asses signata)* and discs (*asses gravia*) makes it unclear how often physical bronze was used for purposes of military pay.[36] Landed wealth, essential for establishing position in the *comitia centuriata*, was measured in weights of bronze from around the sixth century BC.[37] Bronze, whether by account or in tangible form, was seemingly the money of landed citizen-soldiers. Coins of precious metal, however, were foreign to the status-producing rule of early Republican culture. In fact, the first 'Roman' coins, which were minted in the late fourth century BC, were produced to Greek standards, likely for making short-term payments to Greek cities or mercenaries.[38] Coinage, even if Romans perceived it as 'foreign', was unquestionably a more economically efficient form of money compared to their own incoherent 'system' of weighed bronze objects and commodities; yet it took until the third century BC – when foreign conquest and political reconfiguration enabled elites to begin to draw significant wealth from outside the Roman social order – for the Roman monetary system to move toward the regular use of standardized coinage.[39]

[33] Fiorini and Torelli (2007). [34] Roymans and Aarts (2009); Jersey and Haselgrove (2006).
[35] Crawford (1985), 17–24. [36] Kroll (2008), 13; Burnett (1987), 14. [37] Burnett (1987), 15.
[38] Crawford (1985), 29. [39] Bernard (2018).

Whatever the exact reason, Rome's systematic refusal to adopt coinage in the early-to-mid republic shows how powerful and unique embedding contexts could supersede economic convenience.

Unfortunately, limited surviving evidence makes it difficult for historians to identify the specific cultural practices and values which shaped Roman monetary developments; yet the looming presence of embeddedness is impossible to ignore. As a consequence, arguments for Rome's embedded monetary economy are prone to circularity; in many cases, the monetary objects are themselves the same sources for the economic, social and cultural contexts into which they were incorporated.[40] Scholars generally agree that even by the third century BC, Roman monetary instruments were a diverse mixture of weights of metal, Greek-style coins, bronze bars and disks. This idiosyncratic situation implies that the Roman monetary system of the early-to-mid republic blended many 'special-purpose' monies – monetary objects which have an exchange-value that is limited only to certain goods, categories of transaction or social contexts.[41] In fact, calling it a monetary 'system' may be generous.[42]

Only out of the necessities brought on by the Second Punic War was Rome forced to adopt a more coherent (and Hellenized) monetary system.[43] The *denarius* system which emerged at the end of the third century BC – for a 'system' it quickly became – offered in its coin denominations a 'general-purpose money' – a money with which *anything* could be bought or sold by *anyone.* More importantly, however, the coherence and prevalence of the denarius system "reinforced not only social relations but also an intuitive awareness of the cohesion of the community, symbolized by the political authority that minted money."[44] Thus, by the second century BC, Roman money was dualistic, having both 'top-down' political functions and 'bottom-up' social and economic ones – what Weber called 'formal validity' and 'substantive validity'.[45] These differing and sometimes antagonistic embedding contexts, as well as the diverse practical functions Roman money performed in the late Republic and onward, necessarily complicates the use of generalizing paradigms – including and especially economic theory – that modern scholars use to theorize about monetary use and value.

40 Haselgrove and Krmnicek (2012), 236. 41 Polanyi (1968); Maucourant (1995), 10.
42 Burnett (2012), 310. 43 Crawford (1964), 29; Harl (1996), 30–2; Woytek (2012), 315–6.
44 Andreau (1999), 2. 45 Weber (1968), 178–80; Hart (1986).

Value Paradigms

In addition to the complexities introduced by notions of embeddedness and the limits of the empirical evidence, those who study pre-modern monetary systems must wrestle with questions of value. How did embedding contexts influence notions of value and money use in the Roman world? Did Roman coins have value, for instance, simply because they bore markers of state authority (i.e. Weber's 'formal validity')? Alternatively, did such markers merely verify or communicate values already determined by society outside of state power (i.e. 'substantive validity')?[46] Scholars tend to organize the study of such questions within a formal dichotomy: the chartalist/metallist division. These two overarching paradigms help historians identify, organize and generalize about the different mechanisms for creating money value in complex monetary systems. Indeed, several recent studies of Roman money have productively used these paradigms to advance scholarly understanding of monetary value in Roman monetary history.[47]

A chartalist monetary system operates primarily due to two forces: *power* and *obligation*. The state creates money, sustains its use and dictates its value through the state's practical power to demand tax payments in money. Obligation's role, although central, is less immediately obvious. Sociologist Geoffrey Ingham speaks of a "primordial debt" owed "by the living to the continuity and durability of the society that secures their individual existence."[48] Money is, therefore, a direct output of social relationships.[49] The state quantifies this "primordial" obligation through monetization and collects it via taxation.[50] Power and obligation thus combine to create monetary value and acceptability.[51] Some chartalists, therefore, after the once-neglected work of British economist Alfred Mitchell Innes, make no absolute distinction between money and credit.[52] As a further consequence of its value-creating mechanisms, chartalism accounts little influence to the quality or physical properties of whatever monetary instrument(s) the state authorizes and requires in payments.

'Metallism' is the primary alternative to chartalism. As with the 'primitivist' moniker, the term 'metallism' was originally pejorative. Economist

[46] De Cecco (1985), 818.
[47] Haklai-Rotenberg (2011); Bransbourg (2011) and (2013); Scheidel (2010b).
[48] Ingham (2004a), 90. Extended commentary on the idea of primordial debt in Graeber (2011), 55–71.
[49] Ingham (1996). [50] Graeber (2011), 43–72; Goodhart (1998). [51] Ingham (2012).
[52] Innes (1913); Innes (1914); Ingham (2012), 121.

and father of chartalism Georg Friedrich Knapp called his opponents 'metallists' in order to differentiate their 'metal fetishism' from his chartalism.[53] As a result, superficial definitions of metallism – whether these take the form of straw men set up by critics, or naïve metallists' own oversimplifications – focus exclusively on precious metals in currency. Metallism, however, describes a *process* of valuation, not the *product* of the process (i.e. precious-metal coins). In that sense, like Ingham's chartalistic 'credit theory of money', social relationships also uphold value under metallism. A socially formulated metallism is in fact present even in Menger's *Methodenstreit*-era writings. In *Principles of Economics* (*Grundsätze der Volkswirtschaftslehre*), coinage arose in the social setting as part of an organic, evolutionary progression due to "economic relationships" rather than "a legislative act":

> The origin of money (as distinct from coin, which is only one variety of money) is, as we have seen, entirely natural and thus displays legislative influence only in the rarest instances. Money is not an invention of the state. It is not the product of a legislative act. Even the sanction of political authority is not necessary for its existence. Certain commodities came to be money quite naturally, as the result of economic relationships that were independent of the power of the state.[54]

Money was not merely an inert technology or gimmick, according to Menger, but the physical articulation of a complex principle of social interaction: indirect exchange, which is not something "invented" *ex nihilo* by a monetary authority.[55] Instead, over time, societies began to produce surplus goods for their value in exchange rather than their end use – that is, for exchange for other goods rather than for direct consumption.[56]

As neoclassical economics emerged after the *Methodenstreit*, economists gradually abandoned the distinction between use-value and exchange-value.[57] Only economists in a few heterodox traditions – especially Marxist and Austrian economists – preserved the use-value/exchange-value distinction.[58] Marx and Menger themselves, however, held little in common when it came to the basis of value which underpinned currency. Marx, consistent with many Classical economists, believed that the value of money was objective – directly determined by the amount of labor required to produce it. Menger, however, saw money's value as subjective – that is, monetary value was determined in the mind of each individual based upon the extent to which a good or service is perceived to meet

[53] Knapp (1924). [54] Menger (2007), 261–2. [55] Von Reden (2010), 3.
[56] Howgego (1995), 12–4. [57] Meikle (2002), 250. [58] Hong (2000).

desired ends. Still, both Marx's labor theory of value and Menger's subjective value theory are broadly and theoretically metallist. Marx, for example, called gold a monetary commodity par excellence because "all commodities, as values, are realised human labour . . . money as a measure of value, is the phenomenal form that must of necessity be assumed by that measure of value which is immanent in commodities, labour-time."[59] Gold money has value, according to Marx, because of the labor (mining, refining and minting) involved in its production. Marx here is unquestionably speaking about a process of valuation in which objects are given value by the labor required to make them and thus Joseph Schumpeter was right to identify him as a "theoretical metallist."[60]

Metallism, therefore, is ultimately a metatheory of value – one far more flexible and encompassing than its critics often suggest. A gold coin can have value because of the labor involved in mining, refining and striking the metal or, conversely, because gold is seen as desirable and useful by a great many people for achieving a great many ends, whether these ends are practical (tools, weapons), ritualistic (sacrifice, offerings) or status-driven (display, euergetism). It is true that metallists tend to focus upon the use and endurance of precious-metal money; such an outcome, however, is by no means *required* for a system to be metallist. Precious metals seem to have been the commodities used as money in many societies throughout history – but, of course, it did not *have* to be that way. Although von Reden seems more sympathetic to chartalism than metallism, metallists can nevertheless agree with her when she observes that "precious metal coinage . . . is not a natural consequence of monetary evolution, but a specific historical development."[61] Metallism, in theory, allows for the preference of any scarce thing (or even non-things, e.g. cryptocurrencies) by individuals involved in indirect exchange – precious metal, livestock, tobacco or labor-time. Transactions in barley and silver in third millennium BC Babylon are just as metallist as uncoined silver exchanges in Hellenistic societies, cigarette exchange in mid-twentieth-century prisoner of war camps (or modern prisons) and receipts for labor-hours in modern-day Ithaca, New York.[62]

Metallism emphasizes a specific set of properties which create exchange-value: durability, divisibility, scarcity, homogeneity, ease of transport and other properties. The development of coinage, therefore, was an

59 Marx (1887), 66; Schumpeter (1954), 289–90.
60 Schumpeter (1954), 288; Vasudevan (2017).
61 Von Reden (2010), 5.
62 Widell (2005); Panagopoulou (2007); Radford (1945); Lankenau (2001); Jacob et al. (2004).

evolutionary, accidental process. It is unlikely that a single ruler, or body of officials, immersed in a world of reciprocity and/or barter exchange could spontaneously conceive of and successfully impose money upon an uncomprehending population by law. At the same time, as many economic anthropologists have observed, there is admittedly little empirical evidence which supports the Mengerian metallist story either. It is true that some of the earliest hoards of Lydian coins contain small globules of electrum at mostly uniform weights, but only some of these pieces bear stamps and are therefore categorized as 'coins' – the rest are seen as 'bullion'.[63] The fineness of electrum was especially difficult to verify and so a mark was a sensible addition to the metal. The fact that the 'coins' were mixed with 'bullion' in a single hoard, however, may suggest that both types of objects were viewed as having the same value basis, at least for purposes of storing wealth.[64] Marks of value, in the metallist framework, do not represent an imbuing of value from an external authority, whether civic or religious, but rather they are a declaration and guarantee of either the internal characteristics of monetary object itself or the value that society has placed collectively upon the metal through some process, whether formal or informal.

Stamping metal into coins of standardized weights or fineness made metals much easier to use as objects of indirect exchange. Aristotle wrote, for example, that early coinage "had a certain stamp, to save the trouble of weighing, and to express its value."[65] In Aristotle's statement, it seems that value *precedes* the expression of value, not the other way around. Metallists interpret such marks as *communicating* value. Chartalists see such marks are *creating* value by imbuing coins with a new kind of value (fiduciary) derived from trust in the power and practices of the state.[66] Metallism too makes a place for fiduciarity, but as a consequence of the lower transaction costs of coins (which can be counted) as opposed to uncoined bullion (which must be weighed). A coin's stamp *communicates* that it conforms to a homogenous standard of weight (and perhaps fineness). Chris Howgego, for example, gives a delicate explanation of the way in which the "officialization" of coinage by the Roman state interacted with pre-existing and socially determined exchange-value:

> it is important to ask why a single means of exchange came to be used in all these spheres. The use of coin by the state to make payments is presumably part of the answer, but to be effective payments must be useful to the

[63] Karwiese (1991), 9–10; von Reden (1997), 157. [64] Kroll (2008). [65] Arist. *Pol.* 1.4.1257a.
[66] Harris (2006), 20. Similar thoughts in Strobel (2002), 97; Katsari (2011), 247.

> recipient. Some recipients will have been able to return the coins to the state to settle obligations such as enforced contributions, taxes, or fines, but it is tempting to see the usefulness of coin for market exchange as underpinning the whole system.[67]

States may create and legitimize monetary objects, but the process of indirect exchange itself precedes the definition of such objects as exchange media. Hence, outside of the context of the state, the subjective preferences of coin-users themselves ultimately dictate the value and acceptability of media of exchange. Monetary systems which integrate, whether purposefully or accidentally, their subjectively chosen monetary objects within existing value-making embedding contexts – contexts which include political power as well as cultural customs and social rules – seem to be more sustainable than systems which minimize either the economics or embeddedness of money.[68]

Was the Roman monetary system chartalist, metallist or something else? The Roman state seems to have commanded the kind of hegemonic power which would have allowed for the creation of a monetary monopoly – a crucial component of a chartalist system.[69] Several historians argue that the Roman state appears to have made a fiduciary coinage "as good as gold" by guaranteeing it as an acceptable form of payment for taxes, debts and private transactions.[70] At the same time, such fiduciary power is itself a kind of "practical metallism" due to its core operating principles.[71] Because metallism merely requires a commodity-money – said commodities need not be metal or even physical – even a currency which 'commodifies' debased coins or paper banknotes can still operate under metallist principles. Even immaterial cryptocurrencies operate under the principle of "digital metallism": "the supposed grounding of value, inspired by gold standard economics, through algorithmic control of the money supply."[72] The success or failure of commodity-like currencies, according to metallism, rests upon how well they behave *as* commodities, even if they are not commodities themselves. Verboven explains that "the social nature of money" or the "self-evident assumption that it will be generally accepted as a means of payment and a discharge of obligations," even if supported by measures such as legal tender laws and other formal institutional arrangements, "does not derive from government intervention."[73]

67 Howgego (1995), 15. 68 Kurke (1999), 46; von Reden (1995), 184–7.
69 Weber (1968), 178; Swedberg (2005), 133–4.
70 Rathbone (1996a), 325; Katsari (2011), 101; Wassink (1991), 469; Hasler (1980), 26–7.
71 On "practical metallism" see Ingham (2004b); Schumpeter (1954), 274–6.
72 Swartz (2017); Maurer, Nelms and Swartz (2013), 262. 73 Verboven (2009), 92.

Therefore, although chartalism and metallism are diametrically opposed concepts in the abstract, historical monetary systems often share features of both paradigms. Two crucial periods in Roman monetary history show the influence of both metallism and chartalism. The first period is roughly between the Second Punic War and the Social War, when Roman bronze coinage was reduced in weight and silver *denarii* were given marks of nominal value. The second period is in the first half of the AD 270s when the silver fineness of billon *antoniniani* improved and the coin was stamped with a mark of value. In both cases, the state as minting authority attempted to declare by fiat the value of coins while, at the same time, manipulating precious-metal content, presumably because fiat alone was not enough to make the coin acceptable to coin-users. Scholars who have recently analyzed both periods conclude that the Roman monetary system featured elements of both chartalism and metallism.[74]

Characterizing such complexity and even contradiction is challenging for Roman historians. One scholar invented the term 'fiscal metallism'; fiscal metallism assumes a Roman state, conscious of the economics of money production and supply, that cooperated with "free-market" monetary forces to ensure "the long term survival of the Augustan economy and the prosperity of the empire."[75] The idea relies upon Karl Strobel's critique of the predominant view of a third-century crisis caused, in part, by currency debasement.[76] For Strobel, part of the reason that the third-century monetary system was stable, even if it went through "structural change" (*Strukturwandel*), was because Roman money had effectively come to operate under chartalistic principles; how else, for example, could the mid-third-century AD *antoninianus* – a coin which contained almost no silver whatsoever – continue to circulate? 'Fiscal metallism' answers that "the markets" had developed "an uncontested habit" of money use and, therefore, "the debasement of silver currency into billon coins brought the demise of the entire monetary system."[77]

Some of the methodological premises of 'fiscal metallism' open the concept to criticism. In fiscal metallism, metallism is equated with modernism and chartalism with primitivism – equivalences which make it seem as though fiscal metallism successfully balances between the extremes of "un-Roman modernism" (*unrömischer Modernismus*) and the "traditionalism

[74] Rowan (2014); Haklai-Rotenberg (2011); Bransbourg (2011); Bransbourg (2013).
[75] Katsari (2011), 253. [76] Strobel (2002); Strobel (1993).
[77] Katsari (2011), 250–1. An idea also seen in Strobel (2002), 136: "Die allgemeine Verwendung des umlaufenden Münzgeldes war eine Selbstverständlichkeit des Alltags geworden."

of primitivism" (*das traditionelle Bild des Neoprimitivismus*).[78] Fiscal metallism follows Strobel by fusing a modernistic outlook on the Roman economy (total monetization, economically aware officials, integrated markets, coordinated monetary policies aimed at promoting economic growth) with chartalism. This fusion has an existing scholarly literature and even a term: 'modern monetary theory' – the chartalism of Knapp's *State Theory of Money* (*Staatliche Theorie des Geldes*) adapted to the institutional reality of the modern economy which is thoroughly permeated by independent central banks and exclusively fiduciary money.[79] Modern monetary theory, which assumes central banking and pro-growth monetary policies, is in some respects antagonistic to primitivism. Equally, the connection between metallism and market economics is a mischaracterization which arose when proto-metallist economists elucidated their theories in terms of markets to make their arguments accessible to their late nineteenth-century readers. Currency value and acceptability – elements which dictate the success or failure of currencies in the metallist framework – need not come exclusively from either markets or states. In many historical cases, and in the Roman case specifically, layered interactions among and between social, cultural, political and economic embedding contexts created and sustained value and acceptability.

Certainly for the Roman world, if not for modernity, a hard dichotomy between states and society is problematic. The two realms necessarily overlapped; it is, however, useful to separate them for heuristic purposes – to think about notions of value in the Roman monetary system. Since there is evidence for both chartalism and metallism in the Roman monetary system, it seems sensible to embrace the complexity and explore Roman money as a product of several processes and sustaining contexts; contexts which include embedding cultural and social frameworks, markets as well as the state.

States, Markets and Models

The Roman monetary system emerged and operated within a complex and interdependent web of embedding contexts, perhaps the most important of which was the state. Some scholars, such as Alan Bowman and Andrew Wilson, emphasize the role of the Roman state as a provider of impressive economic infrastructure which included:

[78] Strobel (2002), 149. Translation mine. [79] Baronian (2013), 58.

> the military peacekeeping presence ... the monetary and commercial instruments, the legal framework that government modes of economic ... and the physical structures – ports, harbours, and other commercial/industrial establishments ... and transportation networks.[80]

Lists of Roman achievements similar to the one above are now standard fare in works on the Roman economy, but they often beg methodological and ideological questions. Assuming such descriptions are accurate, does the existence of such infrastructure act as its own evidence of the quality, effectiveness or the frequency with which the infrastructure was used? Similarly, does the existence of such infrastructure prove that certain mentalities, motives and policies were behind its creation and maintenance? It is true that the Roman state had at its disposal many of the same institutional ingredients which fostered markets in other (usually more recent) times and places, but how far should historians draw comparisons?

Primitivists understand the Roman state differently. They typically argue that (1) state officials' thought about and carried out their duties more like household managers than modern civil servants, and (2) the Roman state's physical and ideological scale was vast, even 'total', allowing it to dominate the paradigm of the ancient economy. Finley certainly saw the state's presence as totalizing:

> The authority of the state was total, of the city-states as of the autocracies, and it extended to everyone with the territorial borders ... Classical Greeks and Republican Romans ... lacked, and would have been appalled by, inalienable rights. There were no theoretical limits to the power of the state, no activity, no sphere of human behaviour, in which the state could not legitimately intervene ... Only the methods varied.[81]

Through its regular but sometimes capricious interventions and assumed prerogative to do so, the actions of state officials invariably framed the use, ownership and exchange of property – including the validity of contracts and the formal value of any currencies – even if the methods and mechanisms were inconsistent, irregular or unpredictable. Bang echoes and amplifies Finley's 'total state' by showing some of the ways in which 'inalienable rights' or even 'property rights' were disregarded or, in fact, never conceived of (at least in the post-Enlightenment sense) in the first place.

> Whenever it suited its purposes, [the Roman state] never hesitated to bypass the market: for example, by using tax grain for the corn-dole in Rome, or by

[80] Bowman and Wilson (2018), 8. [81] Finley (1985b), 154–5.

> imposing forced requisitions in order to obtain supplies for the army. Furthermore, inability to control society was not simply a matter of leaving the economy to the market. It also entailed very patchy enforcement of law and order, and very uneven regulation and administration of society.[82]

What are the repercussions of state dominance for money, especially as a facilitator of markets? If the theoretical authority of the state was total, but its practical authority was "patchy" and "uneven," then was there room in the space in-between for markets to form and perhaps even thrive?[83] To what extent was market activity dependent upon state power?

One ideal-typical model for characterizing the type of activity between and within theoretical and practical state power is Bang's "bazaar economy" model. For Bang, the Roman economy was neither "a 'failed' version of modernity" nor "an agrarian economy approaching modernization"; it was, instead, characterized by slow and disconnected transport (whether by sea or land), out-of-date price information (on unequilibrated markets), unstandardized goods, small-scale and mobile merchants and, finally, risk-minimizing trade via social networks.[84] Rome's 'bazaar economy' was paradoxical: the inherent fragility of the system placed practical limits upon structure and scale while, at the same time, offering impressive flexibility and resilience to arbitrary state power and enforcement. The *otherness* of the 'bazaar economy' model challenges modern scholars to envision the Roman economy on its own unique terms instead of as an antecedent of modernity. In fact, the comparison with the Mughal bazaar challenges Rome's assumed position within the narrative of European economic development culminating in neoliberal (American) capitalism. More broadly, it subverts Rome's exclusive position within the construct of Western Civilization.

The bazaar economy contains elements of what Weber called "politically- oriented capitalism" (*politisch orientierter Kapitalismus*) – a mode in which profit derives "from political organizations or persons connected with politics . . . by virtue of domination by force."[85] Weber concluded that politically – oriented capitalism dominated the ancient world – a perspective reinforced by Bang's study as well as several others.[86] This predatory form of economic organization is at odds with 'market' or 'rational' capitalism because political capitalism "has a powerful retarding effect on the potential development of market capitalism."[87] A large

[82] Bang (2007), 12. [83] See also Finley (1985b), 155.
[84] Bang (2008), 292, 137, 225, 286–7, 296. [85] Weber (1968), 164–6.
[86] Ibid., 201, 710; North, Wallis and Weingast (2009), 44–9. [87] Love (1991), 51.

predatory state influenced the mixture of exchange modes in the Roman economy – creating more scope for redistribution and reciprocity. Market exchange was hardly ubiquitous in the Roman world. State administration and state economies of scale influenced many of the prices scholars typically think of as 'market prices' – prices which reflect an equilibrium between unregulated supply and demand. Scott Meikle argues that "the institutions and relations of exchange-value were peripheral to ancient society, not central and dominating as they have become in modernity" – a statement which, if true, suggests that 'free-market' prices would have been rare in classical antiquity.[88] How, therefore, would 'economically rational' state officials, whether at the imperial or municipal level, be able to regulate economic activity without true market-generated statistics and, it follows, an apparatus for collecting such information?[89] Moreover, how would 'monetary policy' function under such conditions? Some argue that the Roman state manipulated coin quality to preserve exchange rates between denominations.[90] In order to engage in such a policy, however, the state required, at minimum, (1) a monetary monopoly, (2) quantified information about the number of coins circulating of each denomination, (3) the precious-metal content and weight in each issue and (4) the current market prices of precious metals.[91] Even modern states have trouble quantifying and tracking their money supplies and the levels of commodity prices.

Weber argued that a kind of duality existed in the Roman world:

> the eminent families of the Roman nobility consumed the services of a great number of slaves who . . . produced a considerable part of the household needs in the manner of the *oikos* economy and yet food and clothing for the slaves, however, were to the largest part obtained in the money economy.[92]

How can Roman historians reconcile the presence of both a 'money economy' and the dominance of the '*oikos* economy' paradigm in the Roman world? The answer requires historians to acknowledge that *oikos*-oriented systems have plenty of capacity for economic complexity.[93] In many historical societies, families, tribes even entire villages survived and even prospered without economic calculation. Even today, economic

88 Meikle (2002), 247.
89 Cohen (1992), 27. This situation changes by the middle of the fourth century AD, as several Oxyrhynchus papyri show efforts to collect prices, see *P. Oxy.* 3773 and the early fifth-century reports, *P. Oxy.* 3628–3636. Commentary in Bang (2008), 156–73.
90 Lo Cascio (1981). 91 Lo Cascio (2000), 79; Katsari (2011), 84. 92 Weber (1968), 1342.
93 Mises (1920).

calculation hardly factors in family life across a range of ethnic, national, social and cultural contexts. Modern states and even modern firms operating in capitalistic economies manage and administer many of their operations by principles other than those of the market.[94] Intra-family labor and exchange is not wage or price-based; similarly, the state's figures, budgets and costs – whether the state is ancient or modern – are also part of a 'closed' economy, with market information only coming from outside, from markets themselves.[95]

Must a society adopt capitalism and the mentality of free markets in order to experience economic expansion and complexity? The Roman state itself developed in an almost ad hoc fashion in order to solve practical political-military problems; this is also true of the major constitutional and structural changes of the late republic and Principate.[96] The Roman Empire was managed by a household economic model – albeit it was one of the largest household economies in human history.[97] The various relationships between those who moved goods and services around the Roman Mediterranean, whether we call them 'entrepreneurs' or 'firms' were ultimately rooted in 'household' principles: "webs of favours" and "effective ties of obedience."[98] The point is this: the quantitative size of the Roman economy and much of the movements of people and goods across large distances could be (and was, in my view) achieved within the *oikos* mode of economic management.

Still, markets must have played their role, but creating sufficiently dynamic and complex models of the Roman economy has thus far been difficult. Some admirable efforts have been put forward. Davies sketched several visual representations for how 'flows' (movement or exchange of goods and services) might operate in societies which were complex but also not dominated by market exchange. His rough models account for the fact that, for example, 'social returns', in the form of ostentation, euergetism and other forms of status-building, were often part of an exchange and thus needed representation. Such sketches, even if they are rough, hint at the complexity of ancient economies as well as possible non-economic connections within them. Davies' *Kleinstaat* model, for example, emphasizes the complex relationship between the state and other institutions and activities: the temple economy, autarkic households, family farms, physical marketplaces, renters and others. Even in the *Kleinstaat*, the state is

[94] Temin (2012a), 48. [95] Lazear (1991), 11–16. [96] Drinkwater (2007).
[97] Davies (2007), 129; Davies (1998), 238–42. See also Davies (2006).
[98] MacMullen (1988), 121, x.

dominant but not 'total'. Both inside and outside the boundary of the regional polity, there are flows (loans, transactions, wages, reciprocal exchanges, offerings and obligations) which avoid direct contact with the state.

The imperial Roman government could hardly be called a *Kleinstaat*; indeed, any model of the Roman imperial economy would necessarily be so complex that it is doubtful that it could be summarized or sketched easily. Economies of various scales (municipal, provincial, regional and long-distance, to use three blunt categories) crisscrossed the Roman Mediterranean. Each economy, furthermore, operated within a wide variety of cultural and geographic contexts. Davies' models and charts are not definitive maps which sort out this complexity (and were never intended to be such), but they are heuristic devices – mostly useful for thinking about how economic flows (exchanges, redistributions, gifts etc.) work in non-capitalist systems. Davies' flow charts, nevertheless, show the capacity for Weber's duality: the presence of market-oriented activity within and subsumed by an overarching household economy. State power in the Roman Empire may have been theoretically absolute, but its practical interventions were limited. Theoretical models must account for this duality. The state was dominant, but not total; markets were peripheral, but not absent. Plenty of historians have observed this duality. Paul Erdkamp's model of a state-directed Roman grain 'market', for example, envisions markets operating "in the margins of a system that was characterized by public supply channels."[99] Bang's 'bazaar economy' too provides space for markets.

There is also the issue of rationality and even *mentalité*. Does the presence of market activity also leave room for market mentalities: economization, profit maximization and other economically rational modes of thought? Some scholars might see such a question as irrelevant if they presume that utility maximization is hardwired into all human beings, whether they lived in antiquity or modernity. While there is a good case to be made that the practical limits of state power left room for market activity, proving the universal presence of *homo economicus* is another matter altogether.[100] Already, it should be clear that the social and cultural contexts of the Roman world bounded and even at times directed economization along particular routes, some of which differed markedly from economic developments in modernity.

[99] Erdkamp (2005), 257. [100] Manning and Morris (2007), 31.

What about money specifically? Did space exist for money to take on functions beyond those dictated by the embedding constraints of culture and state power? Did ancient people use money, for example, to 'make money' (Marx's M–C–M)? Were the Greek writers who condemned 'money-making' (*chrēmatistikē*) responding to behaviors which were prevalent in their societies or were they merely engaging in a slippery slope fallacy – arguing merely against what *might* go wrong?[101] The answer is probably more elusive than either economics-minded or anthropology-minded scholars might prefer. The dominant medium of exchange in the ancient world (i.e. coinage) was state-created and the state's power to tax unquestionably reinforced its value. At the same time, the process of indirect exchange itself in all societies is not so mechanical. Indirect exchange also requires money-users to act upon their means–ends economization – in other words, their capacity to choose or to rationalize. Ancient monetary systems therefore simultaneously embodied both political and economic meanings – meanings which could and did diverge in known historical cases – and therefore carried endemic tensions.

It is easier to see the dualistic nature of ancient money on the small-scale economies of the *Kleinstaat* in *poleis* such as Syracuse and Athens. A Pseudo-Aristotelian author recounts how the fourth-century BC tyrant Dionysius of Syracuse used bait-and-switch schemes for his own enrichment.[102] Dionysius would establish trust with the Syracusan people by making and keeping simple promises. He would then trade on this trust by making more grand promises with the intention of breaking them for personal gain. The Pseudo-Aristotelian author discusses coinage debasement within this context. Dionysius persuaded the Syracusan assembly to accept a tin coinage at the value of the normal silver coinage. He also paid back money he borrowed from citizens with *didrachmae* which contained only one *drachm* of silver. Whether or not the stories are true, they play upon the audience's familiarity with the duality of monetary value and the tension between state power and their own willingness to accept and use the coinage. Was Dionysius' token coinage immoral because of the debasement itself or because he debased his coinage while also showing a pattern of faithlessness in other political matters? Athens also, for example, issued an emergency bronze coinage near the end of the Peloponnesian

101 Gallagher (2018), 9.

102 Ps.-Arist. *Oec.* 2.1349a, 1349b. Commentary in von Reden (1997), 175.

War, presumably to be redeemed back later for silver.[103] Unlike Dionysius, however, the Athenian government kept the promise to honor the value of the token coinage. In the meantime, however, what kept the emergency money circulating? Did token money circulate because the citizens trusted that their intrinsically valuable silver would be returned to them or because they simply trusted the state's markings on whatever coins they used? Did Athens, in fact, need to redeem the debased coins? There are different forms of public trust here: one trusts in the state itself while the other trusts the value of the metal the state promises to return in the future.

The Roman monetary system featured this same duality, but with far greater complexity owing to the system's multi-metallic coinage and multicultural context. Both aspects of the system were in flux from the mid-Republic onward. By the end of the Second Punic War, the Roman monetary system rested upon a *denarius* of pure silver.[104] The new silver coin was linked to tokenized bronze coins, first at an exchange rate of 1:10, and later at 1:16 from around 141 BC.[105] Augustus regularized the gold *aureus* and minted copper-alloyed coins of bronze and brass. The introduction of brass was a novelty to the Roman system – a numismatic practice which was borrowed (as so many other Augustan-era innovations) from the Hellenistic world.[106] Monetary value in the system was precariously balanced between the state's power to dictate coin value and the use-value of the metals and alloys of which imperial coins were made. The gold *aureus*, for example, nominally exchanged for twenty-five silver *denarii*. A *denarius*, in turn, could be obtained in exchange for either four brass *sestertii* or sixteen copper *asses*. These nominal exchange rates probably held as long as the prices of the various metals remained stable and also as long as coins themselves maintained standardized weights and fineness. As I discuss in Chapter 6 of this book, even this well-defined and generally well-understood layer of the Roman monetary system had its intrinsic tensions.

The multicultural composition of the Roman Empire and Roman officials' willingness to allow the persistence of local currencies increased the complexity of the system. In fact, archaeological finds from southern Italy show that as late as the early Principate, old local coinages decades and even centuries out of production continued to function as money based on the use-value of their metal.[107] Under the Principate, several

103 Giovannini (1975); van Alfen (2012), 94–5. 104 Crawford (1974), 28–35.
105 Woytek (2012), 320. 106 Wallace-Hadrill (1986), 81; Zanker (1990), 51, 297.
107 Visonà and Frey-Kupper (1998).

societies within the empire continued to mint their own coinages at unique weight and fineness standards. Scattered hints in the source material suggest that formal exchange rates existed between imperial and provincial coinages. An early third-century AD letter from a soldier to his sister, for example, mentions that thirty *denarii* are worth 120 *drachms.*[108] Most scholars believe exchange rates like these were legally enforced, regardless of whether the rates were the invention of the state or widely shared social conventions. Some areas, the most notable of which was Egypt, preserved their closed currency zones and required that foreign coins (the coins of imperial Rome were considered foreign) be exchanged for the local currency. Silver *cistophori* were minted in Ephesus and Pergamum through the mid-second century AD.[109] While some polities retained rights to mint silver or billon (alloys with a minority silver component) coins, many local coinages produced under the Principate were copper or copper alloys. The explanation for the ongoing presence of these coins in the Roman monetary system could be economic – i.e. they acted as small change for the supply of local markets. It is interesting, however, that it was not until the third century AD that a Roman writer (Cassius Dio) proposes a transaction cost-reducing change which would have made the system more economically efficient: "none of the cities should be allowed to have its own separate coinage or system of weights and measures; they should all be required to use ours."[110] The persistence of local coinages is about much more than economic convenience. The right to mint coinage had long been a sign of authority and autonomy in Eastern Mediterranean societies. It makes sense that local elites continued to mint local coin denominations as a means of signaling their position in the social and political hierarchy. Their position could be politically anxious; local elites needed to show deference to their imperial betters while also asserting their superior status to their local inferiors. By emblazoning local coinage with iconography glorifying Rome and her emperors, local elites clarified their dependence upon and loyalty to Rome's *imperium*. Clare Rowan's study of the coinage of southern Italy shows a similar phenomenon during the Second Punic War.[111] Despite the inconvenience caused by having such disparate monetary standards across the empire, emperors may have permitted or even appreciated the voluntary gestures of supplication and submission.

The use and value of both imperial and local coinages was also influenced by the persistence of reciprocity and in-kind transactions in the largely subsistence economy of the Roman countryside. The autarkic

[108] *P. Meyer* 20. [109] Metcalf (1980). [110] Dio Cass. 52.30.9. [111] Rowan (2014), 78–9.

peasants who made up the bulk of the population of the Roman Empire rarely required coined money. Comparative advantage among subsistence-oriented peasants was imperceptible, negating any need to use money to carry out market-based exchanges with family members and neighbors.[112] In practice, Romans thought of 'money' as coinage, but legal writings from the Principate suggest additional money-commodities, indicating "an economy in which monetary functions are still dispersed among a variety of objects rather than unified in a single form of currency."[113] Jean-Jacques Aubert goes so far as to suggest that barter and commodity-money were "common" in the Roman economy:

> Some people and some areas remained however non-monetized or partially monetized, while being nonetheless involved in intense commercial activities whereby goods and services were exchanged for non-monetized counterparts in the form of all kinds of commodities. Even in places where money was available, payments in kind, both private and public (taxes, liturgies), were common, because at times commodities such as grain are viewed as more desirable than coinage.[114]

Even though the Roman state minted an unprecedented amount of coinage, monetized market exchange was not ubiquitous, as the archaeological record of Northwestern Europe seems to suggest.[115] Coins were available, but they were not always used as money. Inhabitants of Egypt too, even under the Principate, show similar adherence to non-coinage monies. Papyri show that numerous commodities served the functions of money (e.g. stores of value, means of payments, units of account and instruments of obligation).[116] The most prominent of these was grain. Grain in Egypt, like gold in Greece, performed both economic functions as well as religious and cultural functions – especially in the life–death–rebirth mythology of Osiris.[117] Exchange and accounting via uncoined precious metals and wine appears in private contracts from both the Ptolemaic and Roman periods. Moreover, as Andrea Jördens' thorough survey of Roman Egypt's fiscal administration shows, both local and imperial officials recognized and sustained the use of commodity monies by preserving the collection of at least some taxes in these goods.[118] The symbolic power of the Roman state's monetary monopoly may have been vast, but its functional extent was clearly limited.

112 Jongman (2003), 185. 113 Hollander (2007), 7. 114 Aubert (2014), 110–1.
115 Roymans and Aarts (2009), 40. 116 Bagnall (1993), 330–2. 117 Rowlandson (2001).
118 Jördens (2009), 211–23.

Finally, there is the matter of credit money. Despite Finley's argument that "there was not . . . any machinery for the creation of credit," credit money clearly existed in the Roman world. Several of Cicero's letters give the impression that elites could move large amounts of money over vast distances by means of paper transfers.[119] The Sulpicii of Puteoli moved mostly large sums of money for elites and members of their households, although usually commodities were used as security.[120] Non-elites also made credit arrangements with both cash and commodities.[121] Retailers, traders and artisans could extend credit to customers if cash was unavailable and, in turn, their suppliers extended goods to them on credit.[122] Dominic Rathbone's study of the Appianus estate also shows uses of credit or "account money" which "extended the monetization of the rural economy beyond the limit of the quantity of coin in circulation."[123] The practical workings of this credit-kind system, however, are nuanced. Laborers exchanged their services for the produce of the estate, but the transactions were accounted in monetary units. Only seasonal or other temporary workers were paid in physical cash.[124] Similar practices are attested well beyond the confines of the Appianus estate. A declaration of AD 246 made by Calpurnia Herakleia, a wealthy Oxyrhynchite estate owner, notes that she paid her "managers, bailiffs, farmers, servants and monthly [salaried, permanent] workers" in grain.[125] Similar arrangements are present in the late first- and early second-century AD papyrus archive of the Sarapion estate.[126] As for the city of Rome, and perhaps Italy broadly, studies by Verboven and now Coffee show that Roman credit was intrinsically intertwined with systems of patronage and friendship customs.[127] The credit systems of the Roman world, therefore, were diverse and in many respects historically unique, tied as they were to social, cultural and even geographic frameworks.

The summarizing implications of all of these social, cultural and economic factors is best characterized by von Reden: "there was no continuous expansion toward a single monetary zone" in the whole of classical antiquity.[128] Instead, changes in "monetary networks" – a term which

[119] Cic. *Fam.* 2.17.4, *II Verr.* 1.102, *Att.* 7.18.4. See comments in Harris (2006), 11–2.
[120] Bransbourg (2014); Temin (2006), 145; Andreau (1999), 71–9.
[121] Bowman and Thomas (1983), 118–20; Meyer (2004).
[122] Hawkins (2017).
[123] Rathbone (1991), 327. Contra Harris (2006), 14.
[124] Rathbone (1991), 160–1.
[125] *P. Oxy.* 42.3048. Commentary in Rowlandson (1998), 237. Discussion of permanent, salaried employees and the terms for these in papyri is in Rathbone (1991), 91–2.
[126] Erdkamp (2005), 117.
[127] Verboven (2002); Coffee (2017). See also Saller (1982), 120.
[128] Von Reden (2010), 16.

seems to encompass the standards (weight, fineness and iconographic) which were sustained by "a complex interplay of political, ideological and economic factors" – were intimately connected with changes in the political landscape.[129] Von Reden's studies of exchange in Greece, Ptolemaic Egypt and the Roman world show the overriding importance of non-market factors, but her interpretations often helpfully avoid dogmatic thinking about the total absence of markets. Clearly, markets were extended by monetization. Ultimately, however, market activity was bounded by the political frameworks and ideologies of ancient states and societies. Markets were themselves *embedded.* Those who disagree with von Reden might point to the impressive levels of monetization in the Roman world during the second and third centuries AD – a period in which it is tempting to connect high levels of monetization with marketization and real, per capita economic growth.[130] Economic complexity, however, was not only a possible outcome in an otherwise 'primitive' world, but a plausible outcome; 'complex' and 'primitive' are not mutually exclusive.

The complexity of the Roman monetary system – complexity derived from the simultaneous presence of multiple embedding contexts – is difficult to model, but it is possible to witness the influence of some embedding contexts change over time or in response to certain events in Roman monetary history. From the reign of Augustus until midway through the reign of Caracalla (AD 214), Roman coinage retained consistent nominal values, but the metal content of several denominations shifted over this period. The gold *aureus* changed only a little, maintaining its purity and only diminishing in weight by about one-tenth.[131] The *denarius*, however, lost about a seventh of its weight and, most significantly, about half of its silver content.[132] The brass coins (the *sestertius* and *dupondius*) were purged of zinc and hence were effectively transformed into bronze coins.[133] The copper *as* appears to have lost a fraction of its weight (around one- or two-tenths) but coin wear makes it impossible for numismatists to establish weight standards with any kind of exactitude.[134] The mint ceased production of the smallest denominations below the *as* – the *semis* (1/2 *as*) and *quadrans* (1/4 *as*).[135] There is no obvious explanation for the stoppage. Prices may have risen by the mid-second century – invalidating the necessity of such small denominations, or perhaps these small coins were never much in demand in the first place due to low levels

[129] Ibid., 66. [130] Harper (2017b), 11. [131] Duncan-Jones (1994), 216.
[132] Elliott (2014). [133] Duncan-Jones (1994), 236. [134] Butcher and Ponting (2015a), 37, 91.
[135] Corbier (2005), 332.

of monetization. Whether the sum of all these changes can be aggregated into a monetary crisis, especially during the third-century AD, is a question almost exclusively rooted in theoretical debates concerning the source of monetary value. The current drift in the scholarship is toward the idea that the nominal consistency of the Roman monetary system, including the obvious fact that coin denominations and exchange rates stay the same, was the chief source of monetary stability in the first two centuries of the Principate. Exceptions to this stability, however, tend to surface in studies of the third century AD, where debasement of the silver currency and an inconsistent gold coinage are widely believed to have been key ingredients in a third-century crisis.

The state dominated the monetary system of the Roman Empire, but its dominance was limited in practice. State intervention may have been unpredictable, even whimsical under certain emperors and officials, but there was ample space for market activity and economizing action, framed as it was by embedding cultural and social contexts. The duality of the monetary system – a system upheld by both political and economic value – produced both complexity and contradictions. The imperial coinage acted in many places as the sole unit of account and means of payment for taxes. Nominally fixed denominational relationships underpinned both the political system and market exchange. At the same time, participation in the system was limited. Municipal and regional monetary systems, whether based upon local coinages or surplus commodities or credit arrangements, offered one alternative to imperial coinage. The persistent presence of special-purpose moneys, barter transactions and reciprocity, however, also factored into the wider paradigm of exchange and value in the Roman monetary system.

Conclusions

The Roman monetary system was complex, historically unique and differed in many respects to the monetary systems of post-industrial Europe and America. Monetary instruments in the Roman world obtained value through both economic process and embedding contexts. The influence of these processes and contexts on monetary value and use was neither static nor monolithic, but could change over time, from place to place or in response to cultural, social or political factors. The Roman monetary system's complexity and uniqueness of its contexts makes the system difficult to model or otherwise constrain into generalized paradigms or theories. How might formal economic theory apply to a system subsumed within such unique embedding contexts? Do existing economic theories – especially those of neoclassical and new institutional economics – sufficiently accommodate the complexity and embeddedness of the Roman monetary system?[136] In answer to this question, the next chapter offers a reflective evaluation of the analytical potential of formal economic theory as well several drawbacks, especially when compared to the main alternative of traditional inductive empiricism. Are there alternative ways to use economic theory to study and understand both Roman monetary history and its embedding contexts?

[136] Scheidel (2005), 35.

CHAPTER 3

Evidence and Theory

We explain nature, but understand mental life.

Wilhelm Dilthey[1]

Roman historians are often trained under the aegis of Classics or Classical Studies; hence, they find comfort in the world of sources – a preference manifest in a broadly empiricist outlook and an affinity for inductive approaches. There are, as this chapter argues, good reasons to question the reliability of traditional empirical approaches to historical questions. Are deductive approaches, especially those which draw upon formal economic theory, necessarily any more reliable? Emergent neoclassical and new institutional studies have produced new questions and new insights, but some uses of economic theory promulgate new anachronisms and perhaps even contribute to 'economics imperialism'. Accusations that economics is slowly colonizing the humanities broadly and Roman history specifically seem to have some merit – although such criticisms are sometimes hyperbolic. How much longer will Roman economic history be caught in methodological tug-of-wars over the use of economic theory? After first discussing these questions and others, this chapter suggests that the sociological tradition of methodological dualism – a framework which unequivocally draws upon economic theory as a tool of 'understanding' rather than of testing or predicting – may offer a way forward for using economic theory to understand Roman monetary history.

Inductive Empiricism

Above, I claim that many Roman historians are disposed toward "traditional empirical approaches." What do I mean by this phrase? Empiricism, broadly conceived, is an epistemological disposition to view knowledge as

[1] Dilthey (1976a), 89.

originating *a posteriori* through the experience of the senses.[2] In other words, knowledge comes through observation. Empiricist historians, whether or not they self-categorize as such, tend to infer generalities from specific observable facts – an approach usually referred to as 'induction'. Induction is often simply *done* by its adherents with little methodological scaffolding; after all, why should historians declare their inductivism if the primacy of the sources is undeniable? Boldizzoni states that "the work of the historian is inductive *by definition*."[3] Few Roman historians self-identify as inductivists or more broadly as empiricists (whether in the classical sense or otherwise). Instead, they follow the empiricist habits in which they were likely trained. In historical writing, for example, the archive is often central to historical claims. Similarly, many historians hold the premise that it is impossible to write history without prior appeals to the primary sources. Collingwood, however, criticized historians who ascertain facts "by sensuous perception" and frame laws "through generalizing from these facts by induction."[4] In the wake of the postmodern turn in history-writing, which emphasizes a fundamental gap between the past and representations of the past, some empiricist-oriented historians defend their inductivism as a distinct methodology rather than assuming it as a self-evident or 'commonsense' approach to organizing and interpreting unambiguous facts.[5]

Among Roman historians generally, empiricist impulses reveal themselves in a variety of ways – through inductivism to be sure, but even the use of formal theory can be empiricist, as I discuss in the next section. Many historians who are skeptical of formal theory typically induce only the most limited conclusions 'allowed' by the sources or, if they wish to take greater risks, they may use the sources to abduce and refine a generalized model. In either case, Roman historians are prone to 'stick to the sources' in some fashion because of the entrenched empiricist notion that the sources intrinsically limit historical questions.[6] On the controversy of the third century crisis, for example, one historians argues that

> we cannot usually press [questions about the causes of changes and crises in the third century AD] beyond a certain point. The half century after the Severi unfortunately remains "a period of rapid transition virtually unilluminated by historical sources" . . . without good historical sources,

[2] Hollis and Nell (1975), 140. [3] Boldizzoni (2011), 151. Emphasis added.

[4] Collingwood (1994), 126–7.

[5] While the work of many historians contributed to the postmodern turn, it is best embodied in the work of Frank Ankersmit. See especially Ankersmit (2001); Ankersmit (2005).

[6] Bang (2008), 3.

> *no complete explanation can be constructed*, and the spectacular military history of the period ... remains largely *inaccessible*.
>
> However, important economic changes can be uncovered in what survives through archaeology. The evidence available here is actually growing. The revolution of systematic survey archaeology, and the increasingly large dossiers of coins, papyri, and inscriptions are capable of opening new perspectives.[7]

In one sense, the point here is hardly controversial: historical sources must form the basis of history-writing, and the sources are prior to interpretation. It follows, therefore, that "growing" (i.e. new) evidence subsequently leads to "new perspectives." New sources for the Roman economy, however, are rarely discovered. In order to cope with this unfortunate reality, inductivist historians collect, categorize and compare previously known sources in a variety of different arrangements in order to refine their historical narratives. Such empirical approaches have been useful in many cases. Due to his careful organization of the sources, for example, Duncan-Jones' catalogue of research on the Roman economy and monetary system will serve Roman historians for decades to come.[8] His 1996 *Journal of Roman Archaeology* article on the economic impact of the Antonine plague, for instance, fundamentally reshaped the discussion of the economy of the High Empire, let alone scholarly debate on the Antonine plague and its impact.[9]

Both Duncan-Jones' methodological approach and his rhetorical preference for statistics and matter-of-fact style continue to elicit imitation, even among economic historians who incorporate economic theory into their arguments. Constantina Katsari's *The Roman Monetary System*, for example, carefully and regularly references numismatic evidence arranged in different ways in order to "reveal interesting patterns."[10] Her book dissects coin hoards by pulling out information (ruler, mint location etc.), quantifying it and then presenting it in varied configurations. Much the same as Duncan-Jones' graphs add a scientific flavor to his arguments, Katsari's approach dazzles readers with waves of graphs as part of a larger argument based on "the structure of coin finds" and "common patterns."[11] Katsari's argument for a generally integrated Roman economy, for example, rests upon inferences about "circulation pools" derived from coin hoards, especially the origins of coins: "it has become evident that the

[7] Duncan-Jones (2006), 22–3. Emphasis added. The quotation within Duncan-Jones' comments is from Reece (1981), 36.

[8] Duncan-Jones (1982); Duncan-Jones (1990); Duncan-Jones (1994).

[9] Duncan-Jones (1996).

[10] Katsari (2011), 12.

[11] Ibid., 45, 117.

eastern Roman empire should be divided into numerous numismatic circulation pools . . . *as the structure of coin finds indicates*."[12] Both Katsari and Duncan-Jones derive their interpretations *from* coin hoards arranged in different ways: "it was argued *from correlations by reign with civilian handouts in Rome* that most coin-hoards in this period originated from the parallel handouts to the provincial armies."[13]

The approaches taken by my two exemplars here – Katsari and Duncan-Jones – differ in scale, but not in kind. Both scholars use empiricist approaches. Katsari abduces broad modernistic conclusions about the Roman monetary system from her sources as well as some economic theories: emperors were aware of liquidity problems and the economic consequences of such problems, and they even constructed policies with the aim of correcting market failures; emperors "supervised closely the minting of precious metals" and commanded monetary policy to the extent that "it was essential for the healthy development of the monetary economy and the continuous operation of the markets"; the emperor's "monetary policies aimed at solving his financial problems and regulating the markets in an effective manner"; even municipal mints had monetary policies aimed at minting coins to meet the economic demands of markets and promote "the efficient operation of markets"; there was co-ordination between different levels of government in making monetary policy and "the different parts of the monetary economy functioned perfectly together"; finally, the "free-market" and the state created a complementary relationship and thus helped the economy survive and prosper.[14] Katsari's modernistic interpretations and willingness to generalize from her evidence offers a different perspective than Duncan-Jones' primitivism and particularism. Both authors, however, despite their different viewpoints, place the evidence before their interpretations, as is consistent with an empiricist epistemology.

One would think that empiricism – an approach which places evidence prior to interpretation – would produce consensus. In reality, the opposite is true – and even fundamental issues divide Roman economic historians. Crawford, and later Duncan-Jones, both concluded "by the finds" that "most coin-types had no regional significance, and no propaganda meaning."[15] In contrast, Erika Manders' inductive survey of Roman coins of the third century AD offers an opposing interpretation: "imperial coinage

[12] Ibid., 199, 192–7. Emphasis added. [13] Duncan-Jones (1994), 86.

[14] Quotations drawn from, respectively, Katsari (2011), 53, 71, 143–4, 154.

[15] Crawford (1983b); Duncan-Jones (1994), 177–8. Quotations from the latter work.

proves to be valuable for interpreting the image of imperial power ... it can be seen as a message medium ... the outcome of a well-oiled propaganda machine."[16] Why do empirical studies, even those which look at very similar bodies of evidence, produce opposing conclusions? An empiricist might claim that different interpretations are the result of one scholar insufficiently allowing the evidence to 'speak'. This argument, however, sidesteps the question of who has a monopoly on accurately 'hearing' what the evidence 'says'. The postmodern turn emphasized that evidence lacks agency; only interpreters have agency. The problem with empiricism is its *a posteriori* epistemology. Without any, dare it be said, *a priori* interpretive framework, there is no definitive way to say that one induced conclusion is better than another. Even if conclusions are inductively 'dictated by the evidence', the evidence was itself selected, arranged and interpreted. Even interpretations which rest upon mountains of ancient coins, papyri, inscriptions or other sources are to some extent, owing to their *a posteriori* nature, arbitrary.

Postmodernists, however, argue that 'sources' and 'facts' are themselves constructs of prior cognitive process. Naming something as 'evidence' requires both justification and, hence, arbitration by an external interpretive and organizational framework. Historians need to (and often do) ask: what counts as evidence and how should it be organized? For examinations of the Roman monetary system, for example, it would seem that coins and coin hoards should be thought of as 'sources', yet numismatic evidence may be organized in many different ways.[17] Three examples dealing with the popular subject of Roman coin debasement in the second and third centuries AD, for example, all published within a two-year period (1994–96), illustrate how data are included and arranged selectively to support different sorts of narratives.

In *Coinage in the Roman Economy*, Kenneth Harl selects *denarius* debasement numbers from the years AD 148–241 and groups averages within imperial reigns (Antoninus Pius to Gordian III). A few emperors receive more than one entry wherever Harl believes a change in weight and/or fineness standards merits noting.[18] Harl's accompanying narrative makes much of different emperors' fiscal policies (e.g. Caracalla's "wars and grandiose buildings") and temperaments (e.g. Commodus'

[16] Wallace-Hadrill (1986). The quotation is Manders (2007), 283. Manders' work came to fruition in Manders (2012).

[17] Helpful thoughts on the categorization of numismatic evidence are found in Christiansen (2004), 13–32.

[18] Harl (1996), 127.

"profligacy"). Numismatic data help Harl tell the story of how emperors, in some ways, *personally* drove Rome's fiscal and perhaps moral collapse.[19]

Duncan-Jones, in *Money and Government in the Roman Empire*, uses categories similar to Harl, but there are key differences.[20] While Duncan-Jones also uses imperial reigns to group and process numismatic data, he details short-term variations in coinage standards and often divides reigns into distinct phases accordingly. Duncan-Jones' narrative context for these data mostly avoids ascribing debasements to the personal choices of emperors, although he mentions some broad governmental factors (military and fiscal) elsewhere in the book.[21] Instead, Duncan-Jones uses emperors organizationally – as markers for key changes. The rhetoric is subtle, but significant: changes in coin standards happen 'under' emperors, not necessarily *because* of them.

Finally, Howgego, in *Ancient History from Coins*, uses a chart which mentions no rulers whatsoever, opting instead to note changes in silver weight rather than fineness within a period of round-numbered years: AD 20 to 260.[22] Unsurprisingly, Howgego's narrative mostly avoids discussing emperors and instead assesses different frameworks for interpreting the numismatic data, including the extent to which changes in standards represent (impersonal, perhaps even bureaucratic) 'policy'.

Why discuss these three different approaches? Remarkably, all three authors use the exact same source for their raw data: Walker's *Metrology of the Roman Silver Coinage*, and yet each author selects, arranges, displays and, of course, interprets these data in different ways. In each case, there is an observable congruency between the choices made about data selection and presentation, on the one hand, and the narrative which contextualizes the data, on the other. Data perform both an empirical and a rhetorical service.

The fact that the same data can and often do generate radically different and even opposing interpretations represents a real crisis for the empiricist enterprise. How does a reader determine whether Harl, Duncan-Jones or Howgego most accurately 'heard' what the evidence "spoke'? The philosopher Karl Popper argued that claims induced from empirical evidence are logically absurd because "observation is always selective. It needs a chosen object, a definite task, an interest, a point of view, a problem."[23] Indeed,

[19] Ibid., 126. [20] Duncan-Jones (1994), 225. [21] Ibid., 14–6.
[22] Howgego (1995), 116; Rathbone (1996a), 327; Christiansen (1988), I:87; Walker (1978), III:141.
[23] Popper (1963), 61.

for Popper, all forms of theorizing contained "an irrational element" or a "creative intuition."[24] Even induction arbitrates between facts and non-facts through prior assumptions – these assumptions are merely informal, unstated or in some cases under-developed. Even the naïve inductivist – exposed by Collingwood and discredited by the postmodernists – investigates through *a priori* concepts. The aim of theorists, therefore, according to Popper, should not be to create purely logical claims; instead, theorists should concentrate only on *testing* and *refining* claims. Thus, Popper crafted his 'critical rationalism' – a perspective which demands that *all* scientific claims be 'tested' against empirical observations. Falsified claims are discarded while non-falsified claims endure to be refined through continued criticism and falsification. The unique feature of Popper's critical rationalism is that claims are never 'confirmed'; rather, non-falsified claims continue in use unless/until they are falsified. An interesting consequence of this approach is that claims never achieve permanence, infallibility or universality. Popper's criticisms of induction continue to generate controversy among philosophers and theorists, as do other aspects of his critical rationalism.

These philosophical discussions bear strongly upon the work of Roman economic historians, where empirical and especially inductivist studies of the Roman monetary system are prevalent. One reason for this prevalence is obvious: numismatic evidence, compared to several other kinds of evidence, is particularly durable, visible and valuable. The relatively high survival rate of numismatic evidence, however, has not prevented historians from deriving very different and sometimes contradictory interpretations: a kind of Popperian trap. Hopkins was aware of this problem. He perceptively described the endurance of diametrically opposed views on the Roman economy as "not so much a problem of fact and evidence, but rather a problem of preference, of a general sense of how the Roman world worked, and of the balance of probabilities and plausibilities."[25] Some scholars may insist that the evidence alone informs their claims but, in reality, pre-existing hunches, preferences and ideologies *always* shape scholars' selections, observations and interpretations of the sources. All human beings, for example, including scholars, are biologically trapped by their own 'motivated reasoning' – a term psychologists use to describe the universal cognitive justification strategies humans use to seek out information which confirms their pre-existing beliefs while simultaneously avoiding, ignoring or dismissing

[24] Ibid., 8. [25] Hopkins (2002), 224.

facts which undermine their worldview.[26] Historians' so-called inductive investigations are likely – whether intentionally or subconsciously – oriented toward confirming prior convictions or ideologies. Historians, because they are human, do not simply discover and report historical facts.

None of what I have said in this section is meant to dismiss close and careful readings of the empirical evidence. The sources are in fact crucial to redirecting economic theory toward understanding the Roman monetary system. Neither do I advocate the relativistic excesses of postmodernism and its reckless rejection of *a priori* knowledge (as will become clear in the following chapter). What I reject is the naïve belief that inductive empiricism is sufficient for understanding Roman economic history. In fact, Popper's suggestion that claims be deductively 'tested' against evidence is equally problematic for Roman economic historians.

Deductive Empiricism

Some Roman historians have expressed concerns about inductive and abductive empiricism. Their proposed alternatives are often deductive approaches, especially those that draw upon formal economic theories. Willem Jongman, for example, encourages Roman historians to abandon the "cult of the particular" in favor of what he calls "proper economic analysis."[27] Enter cliometrics and its deductive, formal 'tests' of mathematical and logical models by means of statistics and aggregates drawn from the empirical evidence.[28] Does such a formalist methodology – one amicable to Popper's 'critical rationalism' because of the centrality of deductive tests against experience – offer a way for Roman historians to break the habit of induction? Friedman, for example, calls for an economic history methodology which closely follows Popper's agenda:

> Viewed as a body of substantive hypotheses, theory is to be judged by its predictive power for the class of phenomena which it is intended to 'explain.' Only factual evidence can show whether it is 'right' or 'wrong' or, better, tentatively 'accepted' as valid or 'rejected'. . . . the only relevant test of the validity of a hypothesis is comparison of its predictions with experience. The hypothesis is rejected if its predictions are contradicted ('frequently' or more often than predictions from an alternative hypothesis);

[26] Kaplan, Gimbel and Harris (2016); Friesen, Campbell and Kay (2015); Hahn and Harris (2014); Kahan (2013); Kunda (1990).
[27] Jongman (2014b), 32, 34. [28] Davidson (2012).

> it is accepted if its predictions are not contradicted; great confidence is attached to it if it has survived many opportunities for contradiction. Factual evidence can never 'prove' a hypothesis; it can only fail to disprove it, which is what we generally mean when we say, somewhat inexactly, that the hypothesis has been 'confirmed' by experience.[29]

Friedman proposes that hypotheses which do not yield "frequently" correct predictions (an ironically inexact qualification, it must be said, for a so-called 'objective' approach) must be rejected. Friedman also, like Popper, avoids 'justification' or 'proving' hypotheses. Instead, economic historians should attach "great confidence" (another woolly term) to hypotheses which are not contradicted by experience.

Philosophers Martin Hollis and Edward Nell offer a useful sketch of the cliometric approach – a sketch I have modified below (Fig. 3.1).

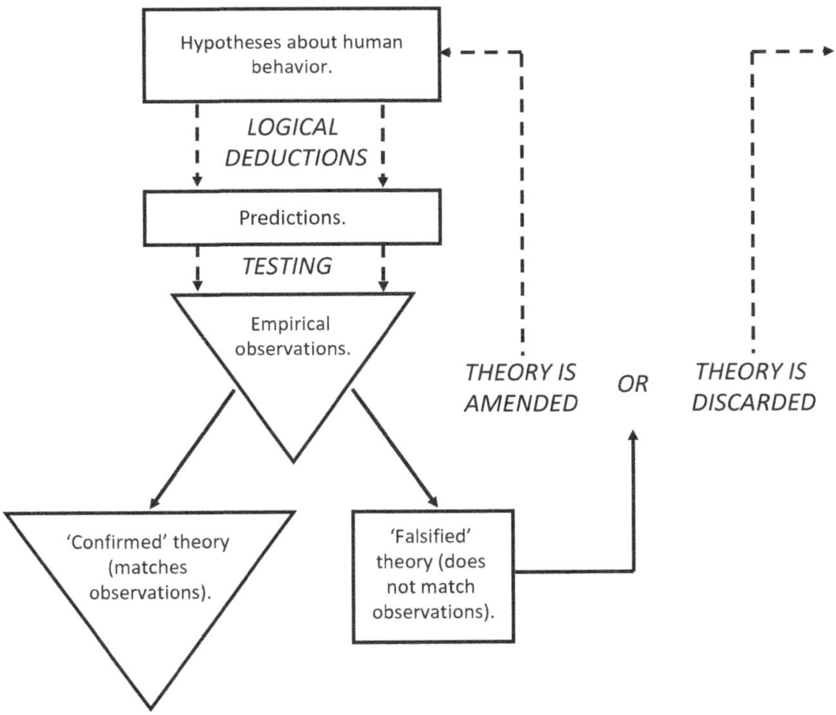

Fig. 3.1 A sketch of the positivist method.
After Hollis and Nell (1975), 9.

[29] Friedman (1953), 8–9.

The widespread use of the cliometric approach has given economic historians a diverse, but ultimately incoherent collection of empirically tested propositions, equations, predictive statements and assumptions which can seemingly be deployed with impunity anytime, anywhere.[30] Under such a totalizing methodological regime, the history of any society functions as a laboratory set up to serve economic models. As Roman historians continue to generate quantitative data, they simultaneously create an attractive testing ground for cliometric analysis. North argues that quantitative data are essential for doing economic history:

> It is impossible to analyze and explain the issues dealt with in economic history without developing initial hypotheses and testing them in the light of available evidence. The initial hypotheses come from the body of economic theory that has evolved in the past 200 years and is being continually tested and refined by empirical inquiry. The statistics provide the precise measurement and empirical evidence by which to test the theory. *The limits of inquiry are dictated by the existence of appropriate theory and evidence* . . . The evidence is, ideally, statistical data that precisely define and measure the issues to be tested.[31]

Roman historians now have both a set of pre-fabricated economic hypotheses and data ready-made for such testing.

A growing number of studies of the Roman economy test models and hypothetical-deductive statements against evidence in order to confirm or falsify them. Temin, for example, uses the Antonine plague as a means for testing the nature of labor in the Roman Empire. Rather than inductively proceeding from evidence to generalizations, Temin builds the deductive framework of neoclassical labor market theory and its logical relationship to wages, equilibrium and the rationality of workers. Only after outlining the model in the abstract does Temin say something (briefly) about the historical Antonine plague itself:

> in a functioning labor market, wages increase as the number of laborers decreases because of the competition to hire them; workers are more productive when fewer of them are available to work. It is hard to know of small changes in Roman labor supplies, but plagues led to rapid, large falls in the pool of available labor. Egyptian wages doubled after the major Antonine plague of 165–175 CE. *This clearly is the standard labor-market response* to a sharp decrease in the supply of labor. It demonstrates that wages in the early Roman empire moved to clear markets, in this case to allocate newly scarce labor.[32]

30 Ibid., 38. 31 North (1973), 1–2. Emphasis in original.
32 Temin (2004), 519. Emphasis added.

What Temin does here is simple, yet powerful. After outlining how a "functioning labor market" operates, he observes that there was in fact a doubling of (some) wages in Egypt after the Antonine plague. According to the hypothetical-deductive model, this doubling of wages fits into the model's assumed market clearing and labor reallocation; thus it can be said that Roman labor markets were 'functioning' according to the model or, rather, that the model 'predicts' the market-oriented nature of labor in the Roman world. Historians have consumed gallons of ink inductively assessing the economic impact of the Antonine plague through close analysis of inscriptions, papyri and literary texts. Discussions of the nature and practical function of labor in the Roman Empire have been even more voluminous. In a remarkable illustration of both the power and the peril of cliometrics, Temin's swift application of the neoclassical labor market model seemingly resolves several long-standing debates with but a few strokes of the pen. In Temin's defense, the neoclassical model *does* fit the facts. The problem, however, is with the model itself and the circularity which underpins it. It was *the model* which first dictated which facts were to test it and which facts were to be omitted and ignored.

In the cliometric approach, empirical facts not only formulate economic theories, but the facts ultimately have the ability to overturn theory.[33] Thus, even the deduction practiced by adherents of the new economic history fits within an empiricist epistemology. This is a point which confuses some substantivist critics of cliometrics. Much of the new economic history makes deductive use of oversimplifying and in some cases patently false assumptions to make empirical predictions which are subsequently either falsified or 'confirmed' (insofar as they are *not falsified*; see Friedman above) by the 'experience' found in historical sources. The new economic history, therefore, is as empiricist as some of the more traditional approaches used by economic historians. 'Inductive empiricism' and 'deductive empiricism' are two sides of the same epistemological coin. Roman economic historians who embrace cliometrics and neoclassical economics have merely exchanged one kind of empiricism for another.

Cliometric assumptions may be internally consistent, but are they historically applicable? Most if not all neoclassical and new institutional theories, for example, contain simplifying assumptions about markets, market-like substitutes and/or universal economizing rationality among actors. Critics of cliometrics see such assumptions as fundamentally anachronistic. The cliometrician, however, can argue that their theories

[33] Friedman (1953), 14–5.

have withstood falsification via repeated tests against phenomena in other historical periods. A cliometrician thus reasonably believes that she is operating on firm ground when she applies such theories one-off to selected episodes from the Roman world. She is doing the initial work of establishing the validity of cliometric models by repeated testing, the only difference is the pre-industrial context. The problem that substantivists rightly point out, however, is that models which have been created, refined and tested in market economies – real or imagined – carry that context with them to the ancient world by assumption alone. The implied presence of such assumptions is one reason why Finley, for example, argued that "to speak of a 'labour market' or a 'money market' is immediately to falsify the situation."[34] Maucourant points out that the teleology of such appropriations enslaves history to (American) capitalism.[35]

The term 'economics imperialism' describes economics' perceived colonization of the research performed within other disciplines.[36] Some see economists as aggressively "*trespassing* on the territory of antiquity."[37] Those most concerned about economics imperialism aim many of their attacks disproportionally at Temin. Therefore, whether or not the case against Temin is entirely fair, his work is necessarily the starting point for evaluating the presence and impact of economics' alleged colonialization of Roman economic history. Temin has spent much of his career analyzing the economic history of nineteenth-century and 1930s America. Interestingly, he began his foray into Roman economic history just around the time that von Reden declared that "modern economic and monetary theory is now regarded by most scholars as unhelpful for understanding money in the ancient world."[38] Temin's presence in the field has made a seismic impact. Under the established dichotomies, Temin's approach and conclusions are formalist and modernist. Bang, for example, places him in the pedigree of modernizers such as Rostovtzeff, Jean Hatzfeld and Jean Rougé.[39] Erdkamp states that "Temin's view is as un-nuanced as Finley's, overstating his case and missing the necessary shades of grey."[40]

Unquestionably, Temin's matter-of-fact modernism is partly responsible for the lukewarm reception of his work and, according to his

34 Finley (1985b), 23.
35 Maucourant (2012), 197. See also Morley (2006a); Harris (2007), 528–9.
36 Fine (2002); Fine (1999); Maucourant (2012).
37 Boldizzoni (2011), 72. Emphasis added.
38 Temin (1969); Temin (1976); Temin (2001). Quotation from von Reden (2002), 142.
39 Bang (2007), 5. Similarly, Aarts (2005), 3, 9.
40 Erdkamp (2014), 226.

recollections of his early forays into Roman economic history, outright ridicule.[41] His bold assertions about the dominance of market exchange in the Roman world shock scholars used to more subtle approaches to the old debates. Temin, in words that seem to echo early modernizers such as Rostovtzeff and Meyer, unambiguously labels the Roman economy "a market economy" which "functioned as part of a comprehensive Mediterranean market."[42] He asserts that the Roman Empire featured "an economy where most resources are allocated by prices that are free to move in response to changes in underlying conditions. . . . markets in the early Roman Empire typically were equilibrated by means of prices."[43] In his *The Roman Market Economy*, Temin boldly proclaims that "the market for land in the Roman empire worked approximately like the land market today."[44] Dogmatic primitivists have predictably reacted to such statements with resistance and even outright hostility.

Temin's formalism also generates critical reactions. His deductive use of economic theory runs contrary to what Hopkins identified as the "traditional techniques of patient, inductive empiricism" embedded in Roman historiography broadly.[45] Regressions and econometric models, however, are far less controversial among economists and economic historians of other periods. Some historians see Temin as a radical, but his approach comes from the mainstream of economics, where his work has helped define the new economic history. As with his modernism, however, Temin's formalism dismantles the idea that ancient historians are 'beyond' the old binaries.[46] Temin's work asks (and answers) a serious methodological question: do ancient peoples' inability to fully grasp the nature of the market or lack of technical means to quantify their own interactions and exchanges preclude modern historians from using formal economic theory to study their economic actions?[47]

Ancient historians' reaction to Temin's rather conventional formalism shows that Roman economic historians remain deeply embroiled in old polemics, despite many claims to the contrary.[48] Temin has since found some key allies. Jongman declares, as he has for much of his career, that Finley's primitivism must not haunt Roman historians. The ghost of Finley continues to stoke irrational fear of economic theory and a

[41] He relates that colleagues went so far as to laugh at his work early on: Temin (2013), viii, 95.

[42] Temin (2001), 169.

[43] Temin (2013), 6; Temin (2001), 170; Temin (2014), 204. Criticism in Bang (2007), 25 n. 59; Haley (2003), 11–12.

[44] Temin (2013), 139.

[45] Hopkins (2018), 288.

[46] Temin (2012a), 45.

[47] Temin (2001), 180–1.

[48] Temin (2006), 133 n. 1.

"romantic dislike for numbers."[49] The irony, of course, is that Jongman's warnings appear within an edited volume dominated by economic theory, computer modeling and quantitative arguments for a market-oriented, even modernistic Roman market economy. While Temin is sometimes unfairly held up as the avatar of modernism and formalism run wild, he is merely one among a collection of scholars who incorporate modern economic analysis into their research agendas – a movement which in fact predates Temin's arrival in the field. Hopkin's approach to measuring growth in the Roman Empire, for example, was unmistakably Keynesian in flavor.[50] Classicist Mary Thornton and economist Robert Thornton used Keynesian modeling in their discussions of the fiscal policies and building programs of Augustus, Tiberius and Nero.[51] Alfred Wassink, too, seemed to see the fiscal policies of emperors in Keynesian terms.[52] Economist Morris Silver has been a steady proponent of the use of economic theory in the study of ancient economies for nearly four decades. David Hollander's balanced investigation of the monetary system of the Roman Republic drew upon economic logic and equations to make some of its most novel claims.[53] Scheidel's pathbreaking research on demography, disease and now inequality is deeply rooted in economic modeling.[54] A sizeable group of Roman historians embrace the agenda of new institutional economics.[55] The recent publication of *Economic Theory and the Ancient Mediterranean* introduced ancient historians to modern economic theory in unsurpassed detail.[56] In 2006, Temin claimed that "ancient historians have typically not incorporated economics into their analysis."[57] Now, more than a decade later, the deductive empiricism of economics occupies an established space in the field of Roman economic history.

A wider knock-on effect of these developments is a noticeable turn toward modernistic descriptions of the Roman economy in the scholarship, even in works which do not employ formal economic theory. It is now common to encounter a Roman economy characterized as permeated by long-distance trade networks, an abundance of specialized urban

49 Jongman (2014a), 169. See also Jongman (2003), 182.
50 I am not the first to characterize Hopkins' model in this way. See Bang (2007), 6; Scheidel, Morris and Saller (2007), 7.
51 Thornton (1971); Thornton and Thornton (1983); Thornton and Thornton (1989); Thornton and Thornton (1990). Thoughts on their approach in Elliott (2015), 274–6.
52 Wassink (1991), esp. 490.
53 Hollander (2007).
54 Scheidel (2009); Scheidel (2010a); Scheidel (2014); Scheidel (2017).
55 A few examples will have to suffice: Lo Cascio (2006); Kehoe (2007); Manning (2011); Lyttkens (2012); Kehoe, Ratzan and Yiftach (2015a); Bresson (2015).
56 Jones (2014).
57 Temin (2006), 133.

markets, a robust entrepreneurial class, widespread monetization, low transaction costs and labor-saving technologies. The combined efforts of the Roman state and its wealthy, economically rational elites underpinned the "high-level equilibrium of urbanization, market integration, agricultural specialization, and prosperity for many" in the economy of the Roman Empire.[58] Such characterizations still avoid the brazen anachronisms of early twentieth-century modernizers, but a constellation of congruities – the arrival of new institutional economics, the adoption of deductive empiricism, the rise of quantitative studies of the Roman economy (whether or not economic theory is consulted) which seek to identify and collect 'data', an increasingly modernistic tone in recent histories of the Roman economy – are no accident. Morley rightly observes the "tendency for many quantified models to assume without question two of the basic tropes of modernity, that more is always better, and that resemblance to modern economic and social structures is always good."[59]

The influence of Finley and his followers continues to recede.[60] A subtle but strong modernist undertow is observable in the rhetoric of the current wave of Roman economic historians. One scholars speaks of how the Roman economy lacked the fossil fuels, modern science and radical growth of industrial capitalism, but it nevertheless enjoyed a kind of pre-modern proto-capitalism:

> Peace, law, and transportation infrastructure fostered the capillary penetration of markets everywhere. The clearing of piracy from the Mediterranean in the late Republic may have been the single most critical precondition for the burst of commercial expansion that the Romans witnessed; risk of harm has often been the costliest impediment to seaborne exchange. The umbrella of Roman law further reduced transaction costs. The dependable enforcement of property rights and a shared currency regime encouraged entrepreneurs and merchants. Only lately have we come to appreciate the stunning advances in the Roman credit system. Roman banks and networks of commercial credit offered levels of financial intermediation not attained again until the most progressive corners of the seventeenth-eighteenth century global economy. Credit is the lubricant of commerce, and in the Roman empire the gears of trade whirred . . . All the same, there are no signs that the Romans threatened to induce accelerating breakaway growth, such as we take for granted in the modern world. The great liftoff only occurred when science was hitched to economic production and when fossil fuel

58 Jongman (2014a), 185. 59 Morley (2014), 38.

60 A useful summary of the current state of the field is offered by Tedesco and Banaji (2017).

> sources of energy, like coal, were exploited at scale. So, it does no discredit to the Romans to admit they had not transcended the basic mechanics of pre-modern economies.[61]

Scholars carried by the new modernist tide do not deny Rome's pre-industrial nature. Above, however, there is a kind of rhetorical modernism which analogizes the Roman economy to an industrial machine with "lubricant" and "gears." Such subtle rhetorical devices are easier to notice when compared with more primitivist rhetoric. Bang, for example, tells of the Roman Empire's "merchants and traders" who "oil the wheels of the agricultural economy and tribute extraction."[62]

Modernizing metaphors and analogies are also used to discuss Roman money, whether in the way the state administered the monetary system or even in descriptions of the monetary system more generally. When Temin and David Kessler say that the "single currency area" of the Roman Empire was "like the euro zone today," they certainly mean no harm – but is it responsible to analogize the Roman monetary system of coins, commodities and gift-exchange (let alone the embedding contexts of these media) to the modern regime of ubiquitous euro banknotes, credit instruments and widely used banking and financial institutions?[63] Similarly, there may not have been central bankers in antiquity, but in AD 33 Tiberius apparently *acted like* one by providing "liquidity through interest-free loans . . . functionally the same as what we would call quantitative easing."[64] It is true that the literary accounts of the crisis of AD 33 describe a financial intervention, but "quantitative easing" implies a set of structures, policy agendas and mentalities that seem conspicuously absent in the early Principate.[65] Such rhetorical anachronisms, even when used to describe a single episode, can become normalized as part of the institutional or cognitive context of an entire historical period. Even if, for example, historians can take for granted that Tiberius' motives were purely economic in that he only aimed at rescuing the financial system, can historians subsequently argue that emperors in general supervised the monetary system in order to promote market exchange?[66] Historians should be cautious not to let literary devices, metaphor and analogy overcome the very sources meant to be illuminated.

All of these factors combined – the use of deductive economics, quantitative studies, increasingly modernistic characterizations of the Roman economy, etc. – constitute economics imperialism. Institutional boundaries

61 Harper (2017b), 37–8. 62 Bang (2008), 121. 63 Temin and Kessler (2008), 159.
64 Kay (2018), 170. See also Temin (2013), 142. 65 See Chapter 4, pp. 90–6.
66 Katsari (2011), 53, 71, 143–4, 154.

in the academy, however, act as a countervailing restraint. It is, after all, Classics and History departments which still train new generations of Roman historians, not Economics and Political Science departments. Graduate students are far more likely to encounter critical theory than economic theory. Not too much has changed in the decade and a half since Morris wrote:

> The vast majority of specialists on ancient Greece are educated in humanistic university departments ... nearly all their teachers work in liberal humanistic styles. Once they have completed a gruelling Ph.D. programme, overseen by these same professors, they will seek jobs from like-minded employers... On balance, individuals who are predisposed to want to contribute to large, comparative analyses ... in which discussion of empirical data may be subordinated to debates over theory and method, are less likely to persevere in classics than those who find particularism and empiricism congenial ... they will tend to exit the game early. And those who do not exit ... may find the professional rewards for speaking the language of neoclassical economics meagre by comparison with those for entering the fray in philology or cultural history.[67]

Classics departments in liberal arts colleges and smaller universities, as well as small Classics departments within large research universities, must necessarily ensure that faculty are able to teach the essential courses in languages and classical civilization demanded by their students. There are few places in these institutions for ancient historians who have chosen to specialize in economic theory and methodology over the themes and approaches that Classics students expect to encounter. Economics imperialism may indeed have arrived in Roman economic history, but the institutional mechanisms of self-replication as well as the professional incentives in fields such as Classics and Ancient History ensure that the 'colonization' which has thus far occurred will never blossom into an outright 'assimilation' of the field.

Should historians worry about the economics imperialism which has already taken place? Assessing the situation as it is, not as it might be after a continuous slide down a slippery slope, helps critics avoid hysterical thinking. Even the term 'economics imperialism' is problematic; it implies an 'empire' – and many reductionist polemics against economics treat the discipline as a menacing monolith. Economics, however, is a diverse, complex and often internally adversarial discipline. Even neoclassical

67 Morris (2002), 23–4. My own experience on the academic job market in the 2010s aligned with Morris' observations! See also Bagnall (1995), 1–2.

economics represents a combination of somewhat antagonistic traditions – in this case, traditions mostly rooted in Keynesianism and monetarism. Keynesianism has itself split into various sub-schools over the years, although these are generally united by an emphasis on the role of 'demand' – an aggregation of all spending in an economy – in creating economic cycles which affect money, trade, production and labor, among other elements. Monetarist ideas which influence neoclassicals are mostly methodological, such as the positive economics approach already discussed in this book's introduction – a quasi-Popperian testing of supposedly value-free economic models against empirical evidence in order to produce more refined, 'scientific' theories.[68] Monetarist thought also emphasizes the role of the money supply (hence, the name) on prices, production and economic cycles. Some critics also place new institutionalism in the neoclassical tradition.[69] It is true that some new institutionalist analyses seem indistinguishable from neoclassicism, but new institutionalism is really post-neoclassical due to its extended analysis of political, legal and social rules and norms and the 'friction' these institutions create in economies.[70] Nevertheless, even if new institutionalism is merely a branch of neoclassicism, its presence would only strengthen my argument that it is mistaken to dismiss economics as a uniform and systematic collection of anti-historical dogma. If anything, because of its complex intellectual and methodological history, economics as a whole represents an almost incoherent mix of theories and postulates – some of which are contradictory. Economic theories and concepts, therefore, should be criticized individually on the basis of whether they help or harm historical understanding.

The wide range of economic schools and styles also suggests that there are underutilized alternatives to neoclassical and new institutional economics which might be of use to Roman economic historians. Beyond the so-called 'mainstream' approaches are a range of 'heterodox' schools – many of which are antithetical to the kinds of discourses, assumptions and techniques found within the neoclassical synthesis. Adherents of many of heterodox schools follow intellectual traditions which branched away from the paths taken by the founders of monetarism and Keynesianism. Also, there is no reason to believe that the present dominance of the neoclassical synthesis is the result of a meritocratic process. Historians can, and in some cases already have, investigated heterodox alternatives to neoclassical and

68 Hill (1968), 259–60. 69 Boldizzoni (2011), 18–53.
70 Kehoe (2007), 31. See also discussion in Chapter 1, pp. 10–8.

new institutional economics. A few Roman historians, for example, now dabble in the emerging field of 'complexity economics', which uses computer simulations to study and model systems which are self-organizing, adaptive to their environments and show global properties which are substantially different than the simple sum of their parts.[71] Advocates see complexity economics as an improvement over the rough, arbitrary aggregates of traditional neoclassical economics, as modern computers can run hundreds of thousands of simulations with slight changes to numerous variables in order to cope with uncertainty, learning, adaptability and relationships between heterogeneous agents.[72] As with any exercise in modeling, the devil is in the detail. Models which assume markets will tend to confirm markets, and vice versa. Complexity-based models may be good tools for stimulating new thinking on old problems, but historians need to resist the temptation to use computers to make simplifying predictions about historical phenomena.

In contrast to developing new approaches, it is also possible to revive or reform pre-neoclassical economics. Marxian economics, for example, retains some influence among Roman economic historians. The Marxian tradition – to be differentiated from the political and ideological hard line of 'Marxism' – tends to focus upon the identification and distribution of surplus (products, value, capital) as well as the role of class and class struggle in economic systems. Marxian ideas, especially through Weber, influenced Finley and several others, even those who are not strictly primitivists. Many discussions of class, surplus, labor and 'modes of production' in the ancient world owe their terminology if not their conceptual frameworks to Marxist historiography.[73] At the same time, apart from works like Geoffrey Ernest Maurice de Ste. Croix's *The Class Struggle in the Ancient Greek World*, few exclusively Marxian treatments have appeared.

Another economic school with a rich pre-neoclassical tradition is the Austrian School. Although Menger was one of three economists to discover marginal utility and usher in the neoclassical revolution, the early neoclassicals largely abandoned him.[74] Mises and Friedrich Hayek, however, preserved and expanded upon Menger's legacy during the twentieth century. Austrians reject cliometrics, positive economics and most other

[71] Verboven and Poblome (forthcoming); Lavan (forthcoming).

[72] Barbieri (2013), 51–2; Poblome (2015).

[73] Harris (1988); Samson (1989); Wickham (2005).

[74] An important exception is Robbins (1932).

econometric approaches. They only embrace a small selection of neoclassical microeconomic theory. Austrians use theory deductively, but are anti-positivist – a methodological combination which prevents any reconciliation or synthesis with neoclassical economics. Austrian theory is based upon what might be called 'rationalism' in the philosophical or epistemological sense of the term; economic principles are deduced from the cognitive process shared by all human beings, but which are also independent of empirical observation.[75] Austrians also make use of the meta-theoretical concepts of methodological dualism, methodological individualism and, ultimately, the subjective value preferences of individuals.[76]

I bring up these selected 'heterodox' schools and approaches – and many others could be mentioned – to demonstrate the diversity in economics. Reducing this diversity into a monolith for purposes of stereotyping and dismissing the use of all economic theory is disingenuous and facile. Some schools of economics are indeed colonizing Roman economic history, but characterizing *all* or even most methodological experimentation with economics in this way is not particularly helpful nor is it sustainable. The answer to the presence of economics imperialism and anachronism in neither polemics nor a retrenchment into a naïve substantivism which automatically rejects economic theory. If all economics were inherently modernizing, then yes, formal economic theory would need to be rejected whole cloth. Modernism and economic theory, however, are not synchronous, nor does it *automatically* follow that the use of economic theory necessarily produces modernistic historical narratives or even modernistic teleologies. It is true that such overlaps have occurred, especially recently, but this is not evidence of a methodological or ideological truism. Some approaches to economics, especially some sociological expressions prior to and outside of the neoclassical synthesis, are compatible with both a 'primitive' Roman economy as well as some of the approaches more amicable to substantivists. The final section of this chapter discusses one such meta-theoretical construct: 'methodological dualism'. Methodological dualism offers historians a foundational framework for redirecting the use of economic theory toward understanding Roman monetary history.

75 See discussion in Chapter 4, pp. 87–9.

76 Selgin (1988). A discussion of different views of methodological individualism is found in Chapter 4, pp. 87–9.

Understanding and Methodological Dualism

Modern neoclassical and new institutional economics is methodologically 'monist'. Methodological monism is an epistemological position, after Popper, in which "all theoretical or generalizing sciences [should] make use of the same method, whether they are natural sciences or social sciences."[77] Many sociologists and economists of the early twentieth century, however, segregated the methods of the social sciences from those of the natural sciences. German philosopher Wilhelm Dilthey was one of the first to draw a methodological boundary between what he called the human sciences and the natural sciences.[78] This anti-positivist 'methodological dualism' evolved in the writings of Dilthey and especially Weber to encompass the idea that *Geisteswissenschaften* ('mental sciences') should be studied differently from *Naturwissenschaften* ('natural sciences').[79]

Methodological dualism is a practical division for purposes of study; it does not claim that the natural world and the subjective world are actually separate, only that the limits of human understanding require natural and subjective phenomena to be studied differently.[80] Natural phenomena operate according to observable, constant, determinate and comparatively simple properties. The actions of human beings – especially in a social context – are, however, highly variable, complex, ideological and will-oriented. While it is true that questions of causality are common to both the natural and social sciences, the way in which cause and effect are studied must differ depending upon the extent to which the subjectivity of human choice is involved in causality.[81] Natural phenomena are easier to model and predict. Social phenomena – despite the claims of positivist economists – are not constant and therefore thwart prediction by so-called economic or social 'laws'. To paraphrase the American philosopher Michael Martin: human beings are purposeful; nature is not.[82]

Dilthey argued that the approach most useful for studying *Geisteswissenschaften* was something he called *Verstehen* ('understanding'): "the process of recognizing a mental state from a sense-given sign by which it is expressed."[83] Dilthey observed that human beings seem to have the ability to intuitively infer and interpret the meanings of the actions of other human beings ("we explain nature, but understand mental life").[84]

77 Popper (1957), 120. See also Blaug (1980), 42–8; Dusek (2008). 78 Dilthey (1910).
79 Addleson (1995), 17; Weber (1968), 78; Nafissi (2005), 144. 80 Hayek (1952), 179.
81 Weber (1947), 88; Mises (1957), 92–93. 82 Martin (2000), 9. 83 Dilthey (1976b), 247.
84 Dilthey (1976a), 89.

This ability, nevertheless, is fallible and notoriously difficult to systematize into a methodological process which allows outside observers to effectively relate to the culture being observed. Weber applied *Verstehen* by demonstrating how observers might create theoretical constructs by abstracting selected characteristics of observed phenomena in 'ideal types':

> An ideal type is formed by the one-sided accentuation of one or more points of view and by the synthesis of a great many diffuse, discrete, more or less present and occasionally absent concrete individual phenomena, which are arranged according to those one-sidedly emphasized viewpoints into a unified analytical construct (*Gedankenbild*). In its conceptual purity, this mental construct (*Gedankenbild*) cannot be found empirically anywhere in reality. It is a utopia. Historical research faces the task of determining in each individual case, the extent to which this ideal-construct approximates to or diverges from reality . . .[85]

Ideal types focus upon a particular element of society which can be typified – certain categories of actors (peasants, priests), actions (prayers, sacrifices), processes (exchange, worship) or social structures (cities, tribes) – thus enabling observers to focus on fundamental social relationships as well as causal phenomena. Historians can use ideal types to categorize and understand the primary sources and vice versa, as the complexity of the sources refines and improves the resolution of ideal types.[86]

Collingwood conceived a related but slightly different approach to *Verstehen* compared to Weber. His view was that historians can understand historical individuals by 're-enactment': "[the historian's] main task is to think himself into this action, to discern the thought of the agent."[87] In much the same way as Austrian rationalist philosopher Alfred Schütz distinguished between the "inner" and "outer" meanings of human action, Collingwood argued that historians needed to move beyond the study of "mere events" on "the outside" and instead attempt to understand the "inside" thoughts of historical actors.[88] Historians can (and must) use their own subjectivity as a means of accessing the subjectivity of the historical persons under study.[89] Collingwood's *Verstehen* process assumed that the historian's thought process was fundamentally the same as the subject's. This internal (or "inside") "*a priori* imagination" was prior to the external (or "outside") evidence.[90] Because, in fact, the historian's agency comes

[85] Weber (1949), 90. [86] Weber (1922), 216. See also Reibig (2001), 248.
[87] Collingwood (1994), 213. [88] Ibid., 118; Schütz (1967), 134; Long (2009), 7–8.
[89] Munslow (2000), 62. [90] Collingwood (1999), 152; Collingwood (1994), 245.

before both interpretation and the evidence itself, the historian *makes* evidence: "[The historian] cannot use [evidence] unless he comes to it with the right kind of historical knowledge . . . evidence is evidence only when someone contemplates it historically."[91]

This "*a priori* imagination" may sound mystical to an empiricist, but Collingwood believed that human beings think and act according to universally identifiable and also "publicly accessible standards of logical reasoning": "the philosophy of history . . . is the exposition of the transcendental concept of history, the study of history as a universal and necessary form of mental activity."[92] Thus, the methodological dualism which framed Collingwood's approach to *Verstehen* was, according to philosopher Giuseppina D'Oro "a methodological dualism (or pluralism) that rests on the acknowledgment of Kantian-inspired transcendentals or categories."[93] The process of *Verstehen*, therefore, need not merely rest upon ideal-typical abstractions from the evidence, but deeper universal process of human thought: "what the historian imagines, in so far as he does his work aright, is what he *must* imagine."[94] From their unique synthesis of rationalism and Marxism, Hollis and Nell identify the power of transcendent universal knowledge: "If there are necessary truths stating relations which are bound to hold among whatever in fact falls under certain concepts which can be understood *a priori*, then we can break out of [the circularity of empiricism] by appeal to *a priori* foundations for all knowledge."[95] Methodological dualism, therefore, may offer economic historians access to true *a priori* knowledge. If so, it may be possible to break away from the imperialistic and circular reasoning of *a posteriori* cliometrics and truly understand the thinking of those who participated in the Roman monetary economy.

Conclusions

Verstehen connects the abstract world of theory and the empirical world of history. Is, however, a *Verstehen* application of economic theory – one aimed at understanding and explaining the choices of ancient peoples – available to Roman historians? Weber argued that one such application was 'ideal-typical' economic theory: observers could use economic theory

[91] Collingwood (1994), 247. [92] Rizzo (2015), 369; Collingwood (1994), 357; Long (2009), 20.
[93] D'Oro (2002), 126. The relevance of Kant's epistemological categories is discussed in more detail in Chapter 4, pp. 82–4.
[94] Collingwood (1999), 152; Collingwood (1994), 383–4, 390, 435, 475–6.
[95] Hollis and Nell (1975), 159.

to understand the thinking of individuals whenever certain conditions – whether external, internal or both – are/were present. Collingwood, however, argued that *Verstehen* is possible through re-enacting the cognitive process shared by all human beings – a process which occurs *prior* to experience, and thus prior to the empirical evidence. Is there a way to formally define and subsequently use this universal *a priori* cognition? How do embedding contexts dictate the articulations of *a priori* cognition in historical societies? The next chapter defines and studies a rationality which is *a priori* in origin but bounded by embedding contexts in history. Without the historian's craft, therefore, it is impossible to use economic theory to understand historical societies.

CHAPTER 4

Rationality, Purposefulness and Action

> Actors do not behave or decide as atoms outside a social context, nor do they adhere slavishly to a script written for them by the intersection of social categories that they happen to occupy. Their attempts at purposive action are instead embedded in concrete, ongoing systems of social relations.
>
> Mark Granovetter[1]

A lasting work on rationality in the Roman world, even now more than twenty-five years since its publication, is Rathbone's *Economic Rationalism and Rural Society in Third-Century* AD *Egypt*. In his book, Rathbone engaged and even anticipated many of the central issues most important to the historiography of the Roman economy: market integration, financial sophistication and economic decision-making.[2] The book's methodology also demands discussion. Rathbone's appraisal of accounting and financial management techniques in the papyrological archive of the Appianus estate favors induction and abduction; because of this – both in style and approach – Rathbone makes a legitimate claim to empirically observing economic rationality in Roman Egypt (if not the Roman Empire broadly).[3] Rathbone's source material suggests to him the clear presence of an agricultural 'enterprise' which rigorously measured profitability – implying an underlying mentality of utility maximization and financial self-interest.[4] Thus, Rathbone comes to somewhat 'modernist' conclusions without anachronistically 'modernizing' his subject and sources through deductive 'testing':

> [The accounts of the Appianus estate] contained much data which could have been used as the basis for making economically rational decisions about future activities and practices. Whether they were used for these

[1] Granovetter (1985), 487. [2] Snooks (1996), 195–6. [3] Rathbone (2002), 166.
[4] Rathbone (1991), 385–7, 394; Hitchner (2002), 80; Rathbone (2002), 166–7.

> purposes cannot be proved, but the presentation of the information in a logically structured format which facilitated its analysis and the more general evidence for the attitudes and practices of the management of the Appianus estate imply that its accounting system was designed and used as an aid to economically rational management of the estate.[5]

If 'economic rationalism' can be induced from ancient sources, then Roman historians can legitimately deflect allegations that they are deductively 'mapping' neoclassical rationality anachronistically onto the Roman world. *The evidence* reveals how Appianus and those with whom he interacted behaved. Rathbone even avoids bringing a prefabricated definition of economic rationality to his sources. In an assessment, however, which Rathbone calls "the most substantial and thought-provoking critique of my book," Maucourant and Jean Andreau interpret Rathbone's 'economic rationalism' as meaning profitability calculation, profit maximization, cost reduction, risk-minimization, economies of scale, and these regardless of any social, political or cultural factor.[6] Later, Rathbone provided an explicit definition of what he meant by economic rationalism: "that where and when the Appianus Estate had a choice, it was interested in efficiency, productivity, profitability."[7]

Scholars engage the topic of economic rationality in the Roman world through a variety of means, some less direct than others. Some, like Rathbone, look for the presence of certain techniques and practices (e.g. double-entry bookkeeping, banking, recording-keeping or budgeting) in the sources.[8] Others, especially those interested in institutions, investigate broader policies or legal frameworks (e.g. monetary policy, economic planning, private property rights).[9] Some have asked whether certain scientific or theoretical developments had occurred to ancient Romans, especially the discovery and/or definition of formal economic theories (e.g. quantity theory of money, the law of exchange or subjective value).[10] Interestingly, microeconomic rationality (e.g. profit maximization, pursuing "rational self-interest," making "as much money as possible"), with few exceptions, are sometimes assumed.[11] Some historians are comfortable

5 Rathbone (1991), 387.

6 Andreau and Maucourant (1999), 50: "un calcul de rentabilité . . . la maximisation du gain, de la réduction des coûts, de la minimisation des risques – indépendamment de tout autre facteur, social, politique, culturel, etc. . . . elle permet des économies d'échelle." Summary and translation mine. For Rathbone's comments, see Rathbone (2005), 262.

7 Rathbone (2005), 267.

8 Verboven (2012), 604.

9 Bransbourg (2011); Kessler and Temin (2007), 321; Zuiderhoek (2009), 47.

10 Katsari (2011), 36; Andreau (1999), 109; Lo Cascio (1981).

11 Andreau (1999), 24–6.

using evidence for one kind of economic rationality, say evidence that elites planned endowment funds for public goods, to speculate about broader phenomena, such as the presence of "a wider, substantial, and sophisticated market for credit and investment capital" unregulated by the state.[12] Or, for example, if a scholar argues that Roman authorities followed a liquidity-promoting monetary policy, it may seem reasonable to suggest – even without much evidence – that these same authorities also had ways of quantifying the money supply and understood at least basic dynamics of money supply and prices. The issues at stake in such discussions are not merely semantic, but methodological and even ideological. Some definitions and uses of economic rationality carry inescapably modernistic and, less charitably, anachronistic baggage: assumed behaviors, policy aims, institutional frameworks and knowledge, all of which require a higher standard of justification and examination than is often provided.[13]

Some Roman economic historians are, however, overtly skeptical of economic rationalities which explicitly impose capitalism-centric value-judgments based upon expected or even predicted sets of (arbitrary) results. Bang critiques such 'mapped' rationalities by pointing out that "observations that Greeks and Romans structured their thinking about estate management on other principles than those at the core of modern accounting and management theory, are taken as making an implicit statement about their cultural shortcomings or lack of rationality."[14] Bang, however, also identifies a related problem: how do Roman historians define and locate these "other principles" by which Romans structured their economic thinking? Should Roman historians study rationality as a phenomenon exclusively 'locked' inside the minds of individuals, or is it possible to study rationality as something at least influenced or even determined by collectivized social and cultural structures (or embedding contexts)? Structures of meaning framed the creation of the artifacts historians study. Furthermore, historians themselves, as outside observers of past societies, interpret historical sources through their own meaning structures – even when historians claim to be inducing interpretations from the historical evidence alone. Yet again, it would seem that the gulf between antiquity and modernity is substantive, and perhaps even unbridgeable.

Near the end of the previous chapter, I alluded to Collingwood's idea that observers' cognitive process comes before their observations of

12 Hoyer (2018), 19. 13 Bang (2008), 32–3; Aarts (2005), 38. 14 Bang (2008), 32.

historical evidence. Some postmodernists have taken this insight as validation for rejecting all *a priori* arguments. Collingwood himself, however, made no such error. In this chapter, I argue that Collingwood's suggestion that observers and subjects share the same *a priori* cognitive process opens up new opportunities for understanding the thinking of ancient peoples. First, I define this cognitive process, after Weber and especially Mises, as 'purposefulness' and defend its *a priori* epistemological status. Then, using Weber's insights on ideal types, I discuss how purposefulness articulated in history is necessarily always embedded.[15] Finally, I combine these arguments into an experimental heuristic process for understanding the purposeful actions of historical individuals by comparing their historical choices against both ideal-typical economic theory and unchosen counterfactual choices.

Rationality Located: Purposefulness

The discussion of rationality in the opening chapter of Weber's *Economy and Society* is a faithful wellspring for sociologists' investigations of rationality over the past century.[16] Weber's methodological dualism shines through in this section, as all of Weber's forms of rationality see action as an articulation of a prior mental state. Weber's insights represent a useful starting point for discussing the intersections between rationality, purposeful action and embeddedness. Weber identified four overarching categories of rationality:

(1) "Instrumental" rationality (*Zweckrationalität*): "rational consideration of alternative means to the end, of the relations of the end to the secondary consequences, and finally of the relative importance of different possible ends."
(2) Value rationality (*Wertrationalität*): in which action is "bound" with a larger ethical, aesthetic or religious "cause."
(3) "Affectual" or emotional rationality: in which action is governed by the actor's "specific affects and feeling states." Weber believed that this type of rationality "stands on the borderline of what can be considered 'meaningfully' oriented."
(4) "Traditional" rationality: a rationality which governs action which is habitual – and which is also on the edge of "meaningful" rationality.[17]

[15] Granovetter (1985), 487. [16] E.g. Mueller (1979). [17] Weber (1968), 24–6.

The most studied of Weber's forms is *Zweckrationalität*, the rationality of the Protestant ethic.[18] *Zweckrationalität* also, however, bears the mark of the Austrian economists and Menger specifically, as it is the rationality of post-marginal-utility capitalism. Hence, Weber emphasized the role of individual subjective valuation using marginal utility (a term he himself uses) in *Zweckrationalität* as a way of distinguishing it from *Wertrationalität*, which "from the view of [*Zweckrationalität*], is always irrational."[19]

Weber was, nevertheless, unsure of the firmness of his own categories. He admitted, for example, that probably more than one form of rationality governed most human action.[20] Some sociologists now affirm that, at least in concept, Weber's *Zweckrationalität* is a kind of archetypical rationality which subsumes the other three forms. *Zweckrationalität* is, according to Polish social theorist Zygmunt Bauman, "the only framework in which sociological study as an activity aimed at the objective understanding of human behavior can take place."[21] Weber's friend Mises saw *Zweckrationalität* in similarly broad terms, calling it "purposefulness" – the use of means to attain chosen ends. Mises, and many of his followers in the Austrian School, continue to use purposefulness as the basis of their economic analyses. Although not drawing explicitly upon Mises, Collingwood used a nearly identical form of purposefulness as the basis of his "re-enactment," arguing that historians in fact *only* studied acts done "on purpose." "If they were not," he claimed, "there can be no history of them."[22] For Collingwood, ever the dualist, the historian does not study natural products and processes, but *rational* ones: history of mind.[23] It is the mind which allows human beings to use reason to pursue chosen ends – or, in other words, to act purposefully:

> The processes of nature can therefore be properly described as a sequence of mere events, but those of history cannot. They are not processes of mere events but processes of actions, which have an inner side, consisting of processes of thought; and what the historian is looking for is these processes of thought. All history is the history of thought.[24]

The purposefulness described by both Collingwood and Mises is articulated in human action; in fact, the action of human beings *must* originate in a prerequisite purposefulness.[25] Collingwood called such action "purposive action" while Mises called it "human action":

[18] Whimster (2007), 190. [19] Weber (1968), 26. [20] Ibid.
[21] Bauman (2010), 54. See also Levine (2005), 123 n. 40. [22] Collingwood (1994), 310.
[23] Collingwood (1999), 46. [24] Collingwood (1994), 215. [25] Ibid., 309–13.

> Human action is purposeful behavior. Or we may say: action is will put into operation and transformed into an agency, is aiming at ends and goals, is the ego's meaningful response to stimuli and to the conditions of its environment, is a person's conscious adjustment to the state of the universe that determines his life.[26]

Mises argued that purposeful action is congeneric with purposefulness as a manifestation of several cognitive conditions: (1) a "felt uneasiness" born of a desire "to substitute a more satisfactory state of affairs for a less satisfactory," (2) the ability imagine a better situation than that of the present, and (3) "the expectation that purposeful behavior has the power to remove or at least to alleviate the felt uneasiness."[27] Purposeful action follows after choice; as Hollis summarizes, "a man's reasons for acting can explain his actions."[28] Choice requires a chosen end as well as unchosen alternatives – otherwise there is no choice. When purposeful action takes place, therefore, one or more counterfactual actions do not. Why is one action chosen instead of the other(s)? Yet one more chain of deductive reasoning informs Mises' answer: the purposeful action taken is ranked higher in the mind of an individual than the action(s) not taken. Therefore, by studying the purposeful actions of individuals dualistically – as products of human choice and subjective preference – observers can learn something about their subjects' perceptions of value.

Both purposefulness and purposeful action maintain the Weberian notion of value-freedom and do not evaluate any particular means used or ends pursued. A peasant, therefore, who employs "magic rites" to grow his crop is no less rational than one who employs better fertilizer, because

> the concept of action does not imply that the action is guided by a correct theory and a technology promising success and that it attains the end aimed at. It only implies that the performer of the action believes that the means applied will produce the desired effect.[29]

All human *behavior*, however, is not purposeful action. Any human behavior or experience which is instinctive, reactive, unwilled or lacks what Schütz called an "antecedent project," for example, is not purposeful action by definition.[30]

Why are the insights of Weber, and especially Collingwood and Mises relevant to Roman economic historians? Purposefulness opens up non-anachronistic ways of using economic theory to think about and understand

[26] Mises (1949), 11. [27] Ibid., 13–4. [28] Hollis (1977), 12. [29] Mises (1949), 37.
[30] Schütz (1967), 239.

the Roman monetary economy, its embedding contexts and the economic choices made by inhabitants of the Roman world. Unlike the mapped, passive rationality of *homo economicus*, purposefulness is applicable to real human beings who inhabit a real world of absolute scarcity. Polanyi and other substantivists are correct that the social values which override economizing behavior in some societies negate what we might think of as *relative* scarcity – the scarcity that arises from subjective human wanting in specific instances. The anthropologist Marshall Sahlins' famous study of 'stone age' aboriginal groups reveals an economy characterized by non-intensive and under-utilized labor, goals of self-sufficiency and the dominance of redistribution and gift exchange as a means of forming social ties, acquiring power and meeting the material needs of family members and neighbors, among other things.[31] Sahlins' fieldwork shows that "it is possible for there to be vast resources and scarce wants," upending the universality of *homo economicus*.[32] It is true – that the ever profit-maximizing *homo economicus* is a false construct. Nevertheless, in being bounded to mortal physical bodies with inescapable physical needs while simultaneously inhabiting a physical world which requires the consumption of time to meet these needs, real human beings must always face *absolute* scarcity. Even if human wants for a particular good are met (relative scarcity), there are *always and everywhere* temporal and spatial limits upon choice (absolute scarcity). These limits, which necessarily bound purposefulness, do not negate it.

Hollis in his *Models of Man* argued that social scientists need to substitute their passive and deterministic ideal types of human agency for an 'autonomous man' ideal type – a man who acts purposefully, attempts to understand his environment, makes decisions, uses means and achieves ends.[33] Autonomy of choice does not immunize an individual from society, cultural values, emotions, traditions or habits and therefore the other (subsumed) forms of rationality described by Weber.[34] In fact, to Hollis' (and Mises') point: because human beings are inescapably embedded in society, humans' purposeful actions are unmappable, unpredictable and ungoverned by constant, time-invariant laws.[35] Human beings must not be modeled; they must instead be understood.

Weber's rationalities are ideal-typical in that they are generally true but not necessarily always and everywhere true. Mises, on the other hand, claimed that the purposefulness which governs human action is universally

[31] Sahlins (1974). [32] Hodgson (2002), 277. [33] Hollis (1977), 12.
[34] Weber (1968), 24–6. [35] Mises (1949), 646.

present in all human beings. A historian who wishes to use these ideas to adjudicate competing historical claims, according to Collingwood, must engage in a kind of philosophizing which

> reflects on the actual practice of historians and in doing so can guide historians in their reading of the relationship between past and present, and in their interpretations of historical evidence. Philosophy in rethinking the principles of history establishes the coherence of principles with one another and hence can rule out inappropriate historical assumptions and procedures.[36]

Mises' case for purposefulness, for example, is philosophically rationalist and in many respects specifically neo-Kantian, although Mises never cited Kant directly. A brief discussion of Kant's basic categories of knowledge helps frame the epistemological position of purposefulness and the purposeful action which follows from it, in contrast to ideal-typical forms of rationality, including those assumed by some schools of economic thought.

Kant proved the existence of what he called synthetic *a priori* statements – logically constructed statements (timeless, person-less and abstract) which simultaneously speak about real things in the real (external) empirical and historical world. The synthetic *a priori* is defined by the intersection of two binaries in Kant's writing.

The first binary is the analytic–synthetic distinction. Analytic judgments are tautologically true merely by virtue of the self-contained logic of their constituent verbal parts. Synthetic judgments, on the other hand, are true only by reference to a relationship external to the objects themselves. 'All bachelors are unmarried' – an analytical statement – is self-referentially true because the term 'bachelor' contains the idea of being unmarried. 'All bachelors are unhappy', however, is a statement in which 'happy' is not self-evidently contained within the idea of 'bachelor'; some kind of external knowledge must be referenced if the statement is to be validated.

Kant's second dichotomy is between *a priori* and *a posteriori* arguments. *A priori* arguments are deduced through logic and reason and cannot be proven or disproven by experience. The mathematical statement 2 + 2 = 4 is aprioristically true. Alternatively, we might again think about the statement 'all bachelors are unmarried', only this time as an *a priori* judgment. It would be pointless to search the entirety of the real world in all

[36] Browning (2004), 76.

	Analytic	Synthetic
A posteriori	*Analytic a posteriori* judgements are absurd; if analyzing the logic of a proposition is enough to validate it, then there is no need to seek out *a posteriori* knowledge. Example: 'Water is H_2O'.	*Synthetic a posteriori* judgements are purely empirical. Concepts within these statements can *only* be related to one another by appealing to experiential knowledge found the real world. Example: 'All bachelors are unhappy'.
A priori	*Analytic a priori* judgements define terms and statements of verbal logic; they require no external knowledge, whether empirical or otherwise. Example: 'All bachelors are unmarried'.	*Synthetic a priori* judgements apply to the empirical world, but are not derived from it. Instead, reason alone supplies the external knowledge which makes these propositions true. Example: 'The sum of all the angles within a triangle must equal 180 degrees'.

Fig. 4.1 A summary of Kant's epistemological categories
Arguments for the existence of analytic a posteriori have, nevertheless, been advanced by Kripke (1980), 107, 128. Kripke argues that 'water is H_2O' is an example of a tautology which is only known through experience. Similar arguments are made by Block (2003), 65–6.

times and places for a married bachelor – the verification of the statement comes *before* any real-world observations. *A posteriori* arguments, on the other hand, *require* an empirical examination of the real world to determine their validity. If one suggests that 'all bachelors are unhappy', one must go out and discover whether this is experientially true because there is no rationally self-evident connection within the elements of the proposition.

Just as with the dichotomies discussed in Chapter 1 (primitivism/modernism and substantivism/formalism) and Chapter 2 (chartalism/metallism), Kant's binaries overlap in interesting ways (Fig. 4.1).

The most important intersection among Kant's binaries for understanding the epistemological status of purposefulness is the synthetic *a priori*. These judgments require external knowledge for validity, and yet this external knowledge is derived independent of or *before* experience. Kant's examples of synthetic *a priori* judgments in *Critique of Pure Reason* come from mathematics and the natural sciences.[37] The geometric principle that the sum of all angles within a triangle equal 180 degrees must be validated by knowledge which originates outside of the definition of the words used in the statement's construction; that is, it is synthetic. At the same time, the statement can be validated without any need to measure every triangle which has ever been created in the real world; it is therefore *a priori*. Reason alone proves the statement.

Kant's influence on philosophy is well-known; his ideas have also filtered into the methodologies of economics, but in less obvious ways. Hollis speaks of "a class of truths whose denial is impossible" and includes among these not only mathematics and logic, but also some of the statements of microeconomics.[38] Kant's synthetic *a priori* was formally extended to economics by Mises' proposition: "humans act" – by "act" Mises means "act purposefully" or "employ means to attain ends."[39] "Human" does not automatically contain "act" or "action"; any relationship between the terms can only be understood synthetically. This synthesis, however, cannot be validated through observation because the "action" (or "choosing") performed by human beings happens in the mind; the mere observation that a human body moves does not automatically indicate that the movement is directed by *choice*. Mises argued that the connection between "human" and "action" was understandable only through rational intuition. Hollis argues that "some beliefs are universal. There are, because there have to be, precepts and concepts shared by all who can understand each other, together with judgments which all would make and rules of judgement which all subscribe to."[40] Those convinced by the synthetic *a priori* nature of purposefulness defend it by noting that it is impossible to argue against purposefulness without acting purposefully – a performative contradiction.[41] Similarly, some of Nietzsche's critiques of Kant are dismissed by neo-Kantians because Nietzsche, in his critique of rationality, was himself abiding by its precepts. Likewise, empiricists who reject the synthetic *a priori* must in fact formulate the meta-theoretical rules of their approach in synthetic *a priori* terms.[42]

Some scholars, especially in light of postmodernism, may reject an *a priori* purposefulness insofar as they reject universal categories of thinking altogether. The Marxian tradition, for example – a tradition far more coherent on the structure of rationality than Marx himself was in his writings – tends to make much of the idea of class-based 'logic'. In reaction

[37] Kant, *CPR*, B14–18. [38] Hollis (1977), 171. [39] Mises (1949), 13.
[40] Hollis (1996), 229. [41] Selgin (1988), 22. [42] Johnson (1960).

to Ricardo's universalizing economic logic, Marx himself sometimes vaguely referenced 'proletarian logic' or 'bourgeois logic', as if social class could determine logic itself. Nietzsche, of course, managed to give a sense of rigor to the idea that aprioristic statements were in fact the products of ideology, culture, class etc., a view which many historians accept.[43] In his *Framing the Early Middle Ages*, Wickham, for example, helpfully discloses to readers his perspective that "different modes of production have different economic logics."[44] It is clear from reading Wickham's analysis in context that "logics" has less to do with philosophy and instead is more or less a synonym for the 'rules' which govern particular modes of production. The rules of the 'peasant mode of production' ideal type, for example, uniquely channeled the economy of the early Middle Ages into structures which were distinct from those produced under the 'feudal mode', and utterly alien to the structures of the 'capitalist mode'.[45] 'Modes', at least in broadly Marxian historiography, are 'forms of production' (*Produktionsweisen*) which describe the unity of social relations, power dynamics and legal frameworks governing production and the means of production (technologies, tools, infrastructure, materials, labor types) in a particular economic system. Wickham's analytical approach to 'logics' here is in fact complementary to an approach based upon *a priori* purposefulness. The mode of a given economy will no doubt channel the thinking and choices of individuals. Even if a 'logic' of which "the maintenance of social relationships is its express intention" characterized many early Middle Ages societies, for example, individuals constrained by such a mode still used purposeful action to achieve ends. Even as Polanyi explains that "man's economy, as a rule, is submerged in his social relationships," he nevertheless draws implicitly upon purposefulness to make his point:

> man's economy, as a rule, is submerged in his social relationships. He does not act so as to safeguard his individual interest in the possession of material goods; he acts so as to safeguard his social standing, his social claims, his social assets. He values material goods only in so far *as they serve this end.* Neither the process of production nor that of distribution is linked to specific economic interests attached to the possession of goods; but every single step in that process is geared to a number of social interests which eventually *ensure that the required step be taken.* These interests will be very different in a small hunting or fishing community from those in a vast despotic society, but in either case the economic system will be run on noneconomic motives.[46]

43 Munslow (2000), 22. 44 Wickham (2005), 695. 45 Ibid., 535–41.
46 Polanyi (1944), 48. Emphasis added.

What Polanyi here calls "noneconomic" motives are nevertheless still "purposeful" motives. Actions taken as the result of such motives, by virtue of the antecedent means–ends process which generates them, are necessarily purposeful actions.[47] Both Weber and Mises observed that the ends–means calculation performed in religious prayers and sacrifices was identical at a fundamental level to the rationality of an entrepreneur in the modern world.[48] The embedding contexts of such purposefulness, however, dictate radically different purposeful actions.

Another objection to a synthetic *a priori* purposefulness may come from those who see 'mentality' (or more specific to the *Annales* tradition, *mentalité*) as more meaningful or even prior to logic. Schiavone declares, for instance, that modernity and antiquity "are separated by insurmountable qualitative factors, which reflect their drastically divergent *mentalities*, customs, behaviours, and material and cultural circumstances."[49] Sociologist Niklas Luhmann argues that when the market *developed* (note that it was not ever-present) it brought "its own natural law, its own regulations, its own *logic of decision-making*."[50] Bang observes that "[the Greeks and Romans] *organised their thought* in a fashion different from some patterns which have been gaining ground since the birth of modern capitalism."[51] Finley, whose primitivism was far tamer than some his detractors have characterized it, merely spoke of the embedded economy's "disincentives to change" and how "over-riding values" inhibited the choices of ancient peoples.[52] For the same reason that purposefulness accommodates different 'modes' of logic, however, it also subsumes mentalities. In fact, the 'thin' nature of purposefulness – which does not dictate how it must be channeled – makes it amicable to a variety of humanistic approaches to historiography and, conversely, hostile to any kind of economics imperialism. Purposefulness – as a philosophical construct – does exactly what Collingwood said that philosophy could do for historians; it helps observers adjudicate between competing ideological views of the same phenomena or even the same specific event in history.

This should be welcome news for Roman historians, even those who are disposed toward substantivism. Purposefulness allows for embedding contexts – whether they be social, cultural, political or of some other nature – to shape and influence the thinking of individuals. At the same

47 Schütz (1967), 239; Mises (1949), 18.
48 Weber (1968), 424; Mises (1949), 37; Kalberg (1980), 1148.
49 Schiavone (2000), 176. Emphasis added.
50 Luhmann (1982), 200. Emphasis added. See commentary in Love (1991), 216–22.
51 Bang (2008), 32. Emphasis added.
52 Finley (1985b), 60, 115. See also Kehoe (1997), 18.

time, however, it follows from the logic of purposeful action that *choice* itself can only be meaningfully taken by individuals – a view which is summarized as 'methodological individualism'. Unfortunately (yet again!), here is another term which inherited a warped meaning in the century following the *Methodenstreit*, and some untangling is necessary. At twenty-five years old, Schumpeter published his first book *Das Wesen und Hauptinhalt der theoretischen Nationalökonomie*, a work heavily influenced by Austrian-school economists such as Menger and Eugen Böhm von Bawerk. Schumpeter, however, soon abandoned his early predilections for Austrian economics, and allowed neither an English translation of the book nor even a second printing in the original German. Nevertheless, the book's sixth chapter, "Der methodologische Individualismus," articulated the concept of 'methodological individualism' – a metatheory which is indispensable to both Weberian sociology and Austrian economics.[53] The following year, in an article published in *Quarterly Journal of Economics*, Schumpeter argued that the study of society must begin with the study of individuals because "only individuals can feel wants," whereas "society as such, having no brain or nerves in a physical sense, cannot feel wants and has not, therefore, utility curves like those of individuals."[54] In its Schumpeterian form, methodological individualism describes a seemingly *a priori* reality: collective entities – e.g. families, religious groups, social classes etc. – do not ultimately take action as a single unit nor do they have a consciousness or mind; therefore, they cannot *act* in the strict economic sense of the word.[55] Schumpeterian methodological individualism was one of the core concepts Weber drew upon to formulate his interpretive sociology. For Weber, *Verstehen* itself depends upon methodological individualism:

> for sociology, such concepts as "state," "association," "feudalism," and the like, designate certain categories of human interaction. Hence it is the task of sociology to reduce these concepts to "understandable" actions, that is, *without exception*, to the actions of participating individual men.[56]

Weber's unequivocal adherence to methodological individualism divides him from Marx, Émile Durkheim and historicists who treat social classes and nation-states as the "real subjects of history."[57] As a value-free sociological construct, methodological individualism seemingly enables social

[53] Schumpeter (1908), 88–100. [54] Schumpeter (1909), 214–5. [55] Elster (1989), 11.
[56] Weber (1946), 55. Emphasis added. [57] Camic, Gorski and Trubek (2005), 8.

scientists to locate and study rationality, human action and meaning, even in complex societies because rationality is "without exception" restricted to individuals.[58]

This (*geisteswissenschaftlich*) form of methodological individualism was, however, an early casualty in the post-*Methodenstreit* era of economics.[59] One of the early canonical texts of the Chicago School, for example, Frank Knight's *Risk, Uncertainty and Profit*, presents a methodological individualism much different to that used by Schumpeter and Weber. Here "every member of society *is to act* as an individual only, in entire independence of all other persons ... free from social wants, prejudices, preference, or repulsions, or any values which are not completely manifested in market dealings."[60] Knight and many other early neoclassicals transformed methodological individualism into an imperative – the way man "is to act." In so doing, real people were transformed into what Hollis calls "plastic men" whose rationality is the "effect of causal antecedents."[61]

As neo-liberalism and what might be called rational choice imperialism began its ascent in the mid-twentieth century, otherwise value-free methodological individualism was infused with the neoliberal political ideology to create a kind of ontological individualism.[62] Real people became "consumers" or "market actors." Michel Foucault observed in the late 1970s that "American neo-liberals apply, or at least at any rate try to apply economic analysis to a series of objects, to domains of behavior or conduct which were not market forms of behavior or conduct ... to marriage, the education of children, and criminality, for example."[63] Many Western governments, but especially those of the United States and the United Kingdom, walked back central planning in favor of policies of deregulation, privatization and tax cuts – the assumption being that rationally self-interested consumers would create better outcomes for society compared to state officials, civil servants and legislators. Such a climate made it seem reasonable for British Prime Minister Margaret Thatcher to offer that infamous atomistic assertion that "there is no such thing as society."[64]

The enthusiasm with which many British conservatives in the 1970s and 80s embraced such an unrealistic and value-laden methodological

58 Weber (1968), 15, 18, 26.
59 On the varieties of methodological individualism, see Zouboulakis (2002).
60 Knight (1921), 78. Emphasis added. 61 Hollis (1977), 25.
62 Mirowski (2002), 439–47; Koppl (2002), 35. 63 Foucault (2008), 268.
64 Thatcher (1987).

individualism is a little puzzling because some of their Austrian-school influences were entirely opposed to the idea.[65] Mises, for example, retained a value-free Schumpeterian methodological individualism in his 1949 treatise on economic theory *Human Action*:

> Society is concerted action, cooperation. Society is the outcome of conscious and purposeful behavior ... The actions which have brought about social cooperation and daily bring it about anew do not aim at anything else than cooperation and coadjuvancy with others for the attainment of definite singular ends. The total complex of the mutual relations created by such concerted actions is called society. It substitutes collaboration for the – at least conceivable – isolated life of individuals. Society is division of labor and combination of labor. In his capacity as an acting animal man becomes a social animal.[66]

Hayek, through his founding of the Mont Pelerin Society, exerted an even stronger ideological influence upon both British conservatives and their supporters in the academy compared to the more dogmatic Mises. Hayek shared Mises' adherence to Schumpeterian methodological individualism, declaring at length in the pages of *Economica* that methodological individualism must begin with the unmapped and unpredictable subjectivity of individual choice "and not from the results of their theorising about their actions"; this, Hayek argued, "is the characteristic feature of *that* methodological individualism which is closely connected with the subjectivism of the social sciences."[67] Any arguments that economists should return to *that* (*Geisteswissenschaftlich*) approach to methodological individualism, however, were ignored by neoclassicals and their political allies.

Collingwood, too, seemed to believe that methodological individualism was central to the work of the historian: "the idea of history is the idea of action as individual."[68] Methodological individualism informs the study of the Roman monetary economy by demanding that any action supposedly taken by 'the Roman state', 'the military', 'laborers', 'elites' or any other supra-individual group or class be disaggregated for purposes of study into individual action(s). In order to understand the meaning of economic action in history, therefore, historians must consider the motives and choices of individuals as well as the embedding contexts that shaped those choices.

65 Gane (2013), 5. 66 Mises (1949), 143, 41–3. 67 Hayek (1942), 286. Emphasis added.
68 Collingwood (1995), 157.

Rationality Contextualized: The Crisis of AD 33

It is possible to briefly illustrate how purposefulness, methodological individualism and embedding contexts intersect in the case of the financial crisis which occurred under the emperor Tiberius in AD 33.[69] Several recent expositions of the crisis – narratives which seem to be themselves products of a society accustomed to boom–bust capitalism – compare Tiberius to a modern central banker because

> he used a technique that we still use two millennia later, known since 2000 as the 'Greenspan put'. (The chairman of the American Federal Reserve flooded the market with money after crises to help maintain the value of financial assets – similar to land in Roman times.)[70]

Crawford, however, who wrote (only briefly, unfortunately) on the crisis in the context of the ascendency of primitivism, viewed Tiberius' action in starkly different terms: "[money] was supplied not for economic reasons, but, as we might expect, in order to preserve social status."[71] Crawford's comments on the event are often ignored; instead, the episode is frequently cited as evidence of the Roman government's quasi-capitalistic monetary and fiscal management.[72] Tiberius' purposeful actions, however, resulted from a combination of individualized motives and embedding contexts, especially Roman elite notions of patronage. Roman elites understood money as one of many *beneficia* that cemented social relationships and defined social hierarchies.[73] Money distributions elicited the loyalty of armies, expanded the emperor's client base, legitimized his position and enhanced his status against other members of the elite class.[74] Weber defined "the spirit of patrimonial administration" as interested in "public peace, the preservation of traditional means of livelihood and the satisfaction of the subjects"; it "is alien to and distrustful of capitalist development, which revolutionizes the given social conditions."[75] Were Tiberius' actions consistent with Weber's "spirit of patrimonial administration" and, if so, what does this say about the emperor's purposeful action?

Land was the primary measure of status and political power in the Roman system. The Roman elites who both produced and consumed the histories of their society often fixated upon land.[76] The Roman

[69] Elliott (2015). [70] Temin (2013), 142. [71] Crawford (1970), 46.
[72] Thornton and Thornton (1990); Katsari (2011), 53; Temin (2013), 141–2; Kay (2018).
[73] Saller (1982), 58. [74] On monetary modes see Verboven (2009).
[75] Weber (1968), 1109, 1366. [76] Garnsey and Saller (2014), 91–108.

political and social system effectively subsidized the land market. Elites and those aspiring to elite status would have needed to retain and, in many cases, augment their landholdings, regardless of interest rates and prices. Such constraints could not break the power of supply and demand to determine prices, but price movements must have been inelastic and 'bound' by such social and cultural motivations on the part of individuals who made choices to buy and sell land. In Tacitus' full commentary on the crisis – an account which doubtlessly bears the author's well-known spin – it is clear that status (*dignitas* and *fama*) was *the* critical component in both the crisis and its solution:

> Meanwhile a great host of accusers assailed men who grew their money by lending it, contrary to the law of Caesar regulating the nature of loans and property ownership in Italy – a law long since neglected, private profit taking precedence over public good. True, the evil of money-lending was inveterate at Rome. It was seditions' and disputes' most frequent cause, and therefore restricted, even under ancient and less degraded mores. First, a Twelve Tables rule that no one lend at more than one-twelfth. (Exactions were formerly made at the whim of the rich.) Later the rate was reduced to half that by tribunician law. Finally, paying interest was forbidden. There were many laws providing obstruction to chicanery – so often checked but rising again in astounding practices. On this occasion Gracchus, the praetor to whom the relevant court was allotted and overwhelmed by the number of defendants, brought it before the senate. The senators, alarmed since from this guilt none was exempt, sought the Emperor's indulgence – granted. The next year and a half were given for everyone to arrange their finances in accordance with the law.
>
> The result was a money shortage, given the simultaneous disturbance to everyone's debts and the fact that, with so many convictions and foreclosures, cash was detained in state and imperial treasuries. In addition, the senate had stipulated that people invest two-thirds of their capital in Italian land, but creditors demanded full payment and it was not respectable for those dunned to fail their pledge. Thus, first, there were scrambling and entreaties, then a clamour at the praetor's tribunal. What had been devised as a remedy, selling and buying, turned into the opposite, since lenders had placed all their cash in land purchases. With depreciation following the glut of selling, the more someone owed the more he was subject to distraint. Many were toppled from riches. The overturning of fortunes sent statuses and reputations headlong until Tiberius brought help: 100 million sesterces banked for three-year, interest-free loans if the borrower gave the people twice the value in estates as guarantee. Thus was credit re-established, and gradually private lenders, too, were found. Nor was the sale of land conducted to the requirements of the

> senatorial decree – vigorous the beginnings, as so often in such matters, careless the end.[77]

While Tacitus carefully describes particular financial and economic phenomena, these elements serve a proximate position in his larger narrative. They are symptoms of an overarching problem which is summarized just before Tiberius' intervention: "the overturning of fortunes sent statuses and reputations headlong" (*dignitatem ac famam*). Even here, in the midst of a passage filled with financial terminology, we see the subsuming presence of the embedded economy. The account suggests that the economic elements mentioned by Tacitus are meant to be seen as symptoms of the social upheaval that defined the age of Tiberius.

Before any discussion of the economics of the crisis, and especially before any use of economic theory, the episode needs to be *understood.* Historians need to ask: why did Tiberius spend so lavishly to save members of the body he seemed to despise? As Catharine Edwards has shown, the *princeps* – as the capstone at the top of the Roman social pyramid – was deeply invested in perpetuating and solidifying the stability of the nobility, even if only for appearances.[78] Tiberius' predecessor Augustus was the financial patron of eighty senators who needed funds to maintain the minimum wealth requirements of their social class.[79] Augustus himself had previously raised these requirements, perhaps in part so that he might then act as a patron to his former peers.[80] There were multiple occasions where Tiberius followed the lead of his predecessor. He donated to the senator Aurelius Pius after the Senate rejected his plea for financial relief after constructing a public aqueduct and highway.[81] Tiberius gave one million sesterces to ex-praetor Propertius Celer and many other unnamed senators who were down on their luck.[82] Tiberius' actions in AD 33 were consistent with precedent and thus reinforced his status as *princeps*.

The cultural context paints a fuller picture of the crisis' true nature. Tacitus records, for instance, that the initial cause of trouble was social strife between money-lenders and their clients. Consistent with other elite authors who declaimed usurious money-lending along with several other commercial activities, Tacitus signals his elite virtues by naming money-lending a "disease" (*malum*) and the most frequent source of discord and

77 Tac. *Ann.* 6.16–17. The financial terminology is effectively translated by Damon (2013).
78 Edwards (1993), 185–6. 79 Dio Cass. 55.13.6. 80 Dio Cass. 54.17.3.
81 Tac. *Ann.* 1.75.1. 82 Tac. *Ann.* 1.75.1, 2.37.1.

dispute among his peers.[83] For cultural reasons, therefore, interest was regulated by Roman officials, although perhaps increasingly for appearances only. Augustus, for example, regulated usury among equestrians.[84] It was an open secret that many elites did their lending indirectly through banks, freedmen and other intermediaries – a strategy which both ensured compliance with law and custom while also allowing elites to avoid breaking social taboos against certain forms of money-lending.[85] Tacitus even ties a sense of guilt or criminality (*culpa*) to senatorial money-lending, one of many indictments the author levies against senators in the age of Tiberius.

Because of their ruinous reliance upon the unsavory practice of usurious money-lending, members of the Senate were subsequently thrust into another dependent relationship – in this case with the Emperor Tiberius. The account of the crisis is yet another Tacitean anecdote meant to exemplify the moral desperation of the times by showing how the Senate moved from the patronage of one set of immoral masters (usurious money-lenders) to a single disinterested, impotent and wicked one (Tiberius). The vices of money-lending and enslavement (through the monetary rescue) to an inferior patron entrapped those whom Cicero once called the "guardians of the Republic."[86] Elsewhere, Tacitus distinguishes between senators who had fallen on bad financial luck and those who followed their own vices into destitution.[87] Tacitus describes economic causes and effects so clearly for a cultural purpose: the economic situation in AD 33 is yet another example of the ongoing moral and social crisis among Rome's elite. Tiberius' remedy to the crisis is similarly both economic and social, accomplishing two purposes. The injection of new money re-established credit. It also preserved and upheld the social status of members of the Senate, although by a mechanism unsavory to Tacitus and other moralists. Ultimately, the story uses a detailed description of financial crisis to map the dysfunction in the Roman social order under Tiberius.

In no way does the historical context allow historians to suggest that Tiberius acted or intended to act as an 'economically rational' central banker. The monetary injection was aimed at and indeed could only accomplish a strictly limited purpose: to make the land portfolios of elites align to the law. Tiberius used scarce means to achieve ends; he acted

83 After Woodman's commentary; see Woodman (2016), 154–5. The broader topic of elite concerns with money lending is addressed in Cic. *Off.* 1.47, 1.150, 2.24; *Verr.* 5.167; Cato *Agr.* Preface 1–4. See also Morley (2007), 83–4.

84 Suet. *Aug.* 39. 85 Von Reden (2012), 280–2. 86 Cic. *Sest.* 137. 87 Tac. *Ann.* 2.48.3.

purposefully. The emperor loaned out money to elites during a cash shortage so that they could avoid the shame of defaulting on their loans and also maintain the minimum landholdings required to retain their senatorial status. There certainly is no substantial fiscal or monetary stimulus here: an injection of 100 million sesterces (= 25 million *denarii*), to take the number we are given by Tacitus literally (if indeed we should grant him the benefit), represents maybe one one-hundredth of the total money stock of the Roman Empire at the time.[88] Such a relatively small injection had little or no impact upon general prices, interest rates or land prices. Indeed, it is unclear whether the emperor redistributed old republican *denarii*, minted new coin or, in fact, offered a simple nominal credit guarantee from the *fiscus*. William Harris, for example, resting upon Tacitus' emphasis on the role of established banks (*mensae*), suggests that coinage was not involved at all.[89] Duncan-Jones, however, observes a noteworthy correlation: precious metal coin production may have increased in the later years of Tiberius' reign.[90] Kay seems convinced that the surge in *denarius* and *aureus* minting implied in the numismatic record was a direct result of Tiberius' rescue package.[91] Kevin Butcher and Matthew Ponting, however, urge caution because these new coins were produced in Lugdunum and distributed in regions outside of Italy. Tiberius' "monetary injection," therefore, may have in fact been a "monetary redistribution" of existing Republican *denarii*.[92] Butcher and Ponting's argument seems especially plausible when considering that Tacitus specifies that "coined silver" (*signatum argentum*) was locked in the *fiscus* before the injection.[93] Nevertheless, despite its relative abundance of economic detail, Tacitus' account of the crisis still lacks the information necessary to perform an econometric analysis. What the account *does* tell historians, however, is that the rescue package, no matter how it was paid out, targeted a specific class of people (elites) for reasons largely congruent with cultural norms (establishing Tiberius' patronage and salvaging the status of those who received the loans).

At the same time, Tiberius' response to the crisis of AD 33 was a purposeful choice, not an automatic behavior or instinctual impulse. An embedded, overriding cultural, social and even ideological framework

88 Following the highly speculative estimate of Goldsmith (1987), 36–42. Another approach is to compare the figure to reasonable estimates of senatorial wealth, an exercise which also moderates interpretations of the injection's impact; see Martin (2001), 135–9.
89 Harris (2006), 12. Contra Verboven (2009), 122 n. 126.
90 Duncan-Jones (1994), 11, 25, 250–1.
91 Kay (2014), 263.
92 Butcher and Ponting (2015a), 184. Contra Martin (2001), 141.
93 Tac. *Ann.* 17.1.

helped determine the values of certain actions in his mind, but Tiberius still selected his chosen end by means–ends calculation. Those sympathetic to primitivist readings of this episode, therefore, would be right to reject any superimposition of *homo economicus* upon Tiberius or anyone else involved. At the same time, there is equally no justification for rejecting the rationality of choice – and all that it implies – in the episode either. Purposeful action does not mandate that actors, whether acting in the present or the past, pursue financial gain; they must merely use scarce means to pursue chosen ends. I discuss the crisis of AD 33 here merely to show that such a claim does no violence to historical understanding. Identifying purposefulness in history requires neither the use of value-judgments to evaluate the objects which were pursued (financial gain, social connections, reciprocation, status, patron–client relationships) nor to evaluate the means by which such objects were pursued (self-interest, religion, patron–client networks). Identifying purposefulness is first concerned with determining whether an object was *pursued* at all.[94] This may seem banal to some, but the humanistic work of the historian is in fact *the* crucial prerequisite to economic history and even the use of economic theory. It is the task of the historian – whether through ideal types, induction, abduction or some other approach – to locate the intersection between the wider matrix of embedding contexts and individualized purposefulness in order to identify and explain its significance.

Purposefulness' broader contribution to Roman history is to enable theory-driven analysis of the Roman economy on its own unique and embedded terms, as purposefulness assumes neither (internal) market-oriented rationality nor (external) market institutions. Purposefulness, therefore, passes through the polemics of the modernist/primitivist debate entirely. There is no requirement for particular institutions, capitalism, neoclassical theory or predictions; the only *a priori* assumption is that human beings use scarce means to obtain chosen ends. Purposefulness equally motivates non-market modes of exchange (e.g. reciprocity, gift-giving, patronage) as it motivates what might be thought of as 'capitalist' modes (e.g. market exchange, profit maximization, self-interest).[95] In fact, because human beings assign value to goods based upon bounded subjective preferences, not quantifiable measurements or comparable objective criteria, the meanings and values of goods and services can and must

[94] Mises (1933), 92. [95] O'Connor (2002), 8–9.

change depending upon the social context in which individuals' act upon their subjective values.[96]

Rationality Applied: Counterfactual Ideal Types

Purposefulness is a 'thin' concept. Why would such a construct, one discarded long ago by main mainstream economists, be useful to Roman economic historians? Purposefulness offers Roman historians several benefits. First, it demands that the statistics and data, which cliometric studies often tear from their social and cultural context, remain historically embedded. It follows from purposefulness and purposeful action, for example, that prices, wages and other "quantitative" artifacts of the Roman economy are "products of human thought" rather than inert or instinctual products of impersonal "market forces" or the outputs of mechanical, mapped rationalities and "economic laws."[97] Such information, therefore, cannot be surgically amputated from embedding contexts and inserted into cliometric equations and models to posit simple cause-and-effect connections; as Boldizzoni writes: "regression should not be a substitute for interpretation."[98] Rather than ask "do these prices confirm/falsify the existence of a capitalistic labor market?" for example, scholars might instead seek to identify and understand the factors which shaped the value preferences of the individuals who made exchanges at a certain prices at specific times, in specific places and within specific cultural and social contexts. In other words, the *a priori* presence of purposefulness and purposeful action *requires* historical investigation into the meaning(s) that governed economic choices.

In contrast to economic rationality and its standard uses, purposefulness thwarts attempts to make 'laws' out of subjective means–ends choices and helps historians to avoid subordinating such choices to modeled rationalities.[99] Instead of assuming certain means and ends are normative – a mapped rationality which easily drifts into a kind of economics imperialism – and then testing history for the evidence of such elements, *a priori* purposefulness frees historians from any other assumptions and encourages interpretation through *Verstehen*. Perhaps this is why Mises' approach won over Polanyi himself, who, despite his affinity for historicism, recognized the extent to which purposeful rationality fundamentally liberated economic analysis from "atomistic rationalism."[100]

[96] Mises (1953), 52–3. [97] Selgin (1988), 22. [98] Boldizzoni (2011), 151.
[99] Selgin (1988), 18–9. [100] Dale (2010), 101–3.

The *a priori* position of purposefulness in the larger process of historical inquiry *necessitates* the work of the historian – work which defines the sorts of limits, boundaries and material conditions through which purposefulness flowed. Unlike deductive empirical approaches, which ignore the agency, ideology and motivated reasoning of the observer, historians can and should direct their economic historical inquiries toward the contextualization and understanding of purposefulness. Collingwood argued that historians must *assume* purposeful action. It follows from this argument that historians' crucial task is to *understand* how action was influenced by and ultimately articulated within the social and cultural context of their subjects' historical world. Historians are thus able to use the universally shared and publically available notion of purposefulness as an empathetic device. Purposefulness, therefore, enables generalized study of both the 'internal' perspective of historical individuals and the 'external' world in which they lived.

The remainder of this chapter outlines an experimental process for 'bounding' or otherwise historicizing purposeful action through ideal-typical and counterfactual comparisons. This process is not itself a formal model as such, but a kind of map for organizing and understanding economic historical models. It is not unlike, and indeed it draws upon, the ideal types of Weber. Ideal types are "concepts which transcend contexts" – generalizations derived from history which show differences and similarities across various historical systems.[101] Ideal types are not themselves hypotheses, but they offer "guidance to the construction of hypotheses."[102] At the same time, because ideal types distill "utopias" from concrete historical phenomena, they are ultimately empirical *a posteriori* constructs derived from historical sources and comparative history.[103] Weber believed that economic theory was ideal-typical:

> [Economic theory] offers us an ideal picture of events on the commodity-market under conditions of a society organized on the principles of an exchange economy, free competition and rigorously rational conduct. This conceptual pattern brings together certain relationships and events of historical life into a complex, which is conceived as an internally consistent system. Substantively, this construct in itself is like a utopia which has been arrived at by the analytical accentuation of certain elements of reality. Its relationship to the empirical data consists solely in the fact that where market-conditioned relationships of the type referred to by the abstract

[101] Kennedy (2005), 363 n. 32. See also Chapter 3, pp. 71–3.
[102] Weber (1949), 89.
[103] Camic, Gorski and Trubek (2005), 8.

> construct are discovered or suspected to exist in reality to some extent, we can make the characteristic features of this relationship pragmatically clear and understandable by reference to an ideal type. This procedure can be indispensable for heuristic as well as expository purposes. The ideal typical concept will help to develop our skill in imputation in research: it is no 'hypothesis' but it offers guidance to the construction of hypotheses. It is not a description of reality but it aims to give unambiguous means of expression to such a description.[104]

For Weber, "laws," including those found in economic theory, "cannot be the *end*, but only the *means* of investigation."[105] Economic theories are heuristic devices to aid in the earliest stages of research. Whether investigating human action in the present or the past, observers can use the assumptions of economic theory to understand the meaning that actions had to the actor.[106] Weber believed that economic theories were ideal-typical in that their premises and assumptions were *usually* true but not necessarily *always* true. He had harsh words for those who saw economic theories as *a priori*:

> The extreme free-traders, however, conceived of [economic theory] as an adequate picture of 'natural' reality, i.e. reality not distorted by human stupidity, and they proceeded to set it up as a moral imperative – as a valid normative ideal – whereas it is only a convenient ideal type to be used in empirical analysis.[107]

Weber observed that the "perfect" economic rationality of *homo economicus*, for example, assumes both capitalism ("a society organized on the principles of an exchange economy") as well as "rigorously rational" conduct – a rationality Weber called "errorless" and "optimal."[108]

Like Weber, Mises believed that ideal types were required for all historical investigations: "no historical problem can be treated without the aid of ideal types."[109] Mises, however, maintained that some economic propositions followed logically from an *a priori* purposefulness. Hence, while both Weber and Mises were anti-positivists and proponents

[104] Weber (1949), 89–90.
[105] Weber (1922), 178. "Wo immer die kausale Erklärung einer 'Kulturerscheinung' – eines 'historischen Individuums', wie wir im Anschluß an einen in der Methodologie unserer Disziplin schon gelegentlich gebrauchten imd jetzt in der Logik in präziser Formulierung üblich werdenden Ausdruck sagen wollen – in Betracht kommt, da kann die Kenntnis von Gesetzen der Verursachung nicht Zweck, sondern nur Mittel der Untersuchung sein."
[106] Koppl (2002), 27. [107] Weber (1949), 44. [108] Ibid., 90, 42, 43.
[109] Mises (1949), 60.

of *Verstehen*, Mises remained skeptical of Weber's "historicization" of economic theory.

> It was a fundamental mistake of the Historical School of *Wirtschaftliche Staatswissenshaften* in Germany and of Institutionalism in America to interpret economics as the characterization of the behavior of an ideal type, the *homo economicus*. According to this doctrine traditional or orthodox economics does not deal with the behavior of man as he really is and acts, but with a fictitious or hypothetical image. It pictures a being driven exclusively by "economic" motives, i.e. solely by the intention of making the greatest possible material or monetary profit.[110]

Mises rejected both *homo economicus*' perfect rationality as well as *homo economicus*' usefulness to historians. Indeed, it seems absurd to create models, ideal types or tests which assume an 'economic man' because this man has never existed in history. Attempts to 'humanize' *homo economicus*, such as in Ayn Rand's *The Fountainhead* or *Atlas Shrugged* produced preachy demi-gods – the Howard Roarks and John Galts whom Rand obtusely called 'heroic' (and who were, therefore, ironically not real people). Rather than constructing ideal types out of anti-historical absurdities such as *homo economicus*, Mises advocated ideal types created from "an understanding of the motives, ideas, and aims of the acting individuals and of the means they apply."[111] It is my contention that it is possible to combine Weber's ideal-typical approach with Mises' notion of *a priori* purposeful action to create processes for using economic theory to understand economic history.

Historians might approach such a task in several different ways. In my view, a preliminary step is a dualistic evaluation of any economic theories used. The *a posteriori* elements of theories must be segregated from *a priori* elements. Ignoring this necessary step is likely to produce fundamental errors in the analysis. If *a posteriori* conditions are mischaracterized as *a priori* assumptions, for example, then history becomes the victim of imposed artificial economic constructs. The first casualty whenever history is subordinated to "rational choice," for example, is, ironically, *choice* – as human beings become automatons who merely react to external stimuli using their pre-programmed economizing instincts. Similarly, if apodictic statements are treated as hypothetical *a posteriori* statements, then "economic laws become contingent rather than necessary" and are thus no longer free "from the defects of positivism or historicism" – neutering their full analytical potential.[112]

[110] Ibid., 62. [111] Ibid., 60. [112] Selgin (1988), 20.

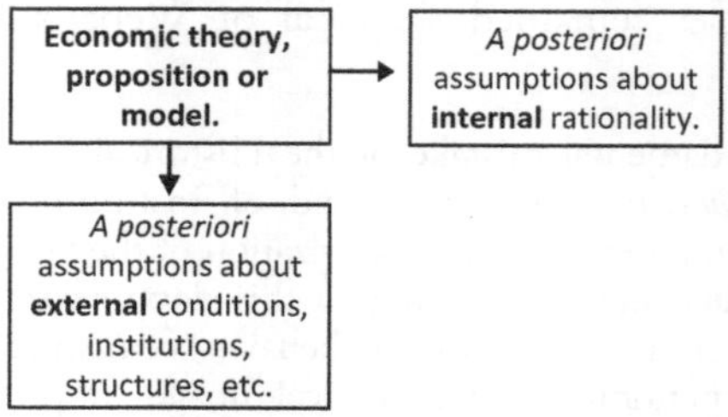

Fig. 4.2 Dualistic separation of 'external' and 'internal' assumptions of an economic theory

Historians will be caught in the Popperian trap I described in Chapter 3, pp. 56–8. Collingwood discussed these problems in some detail:

> all rational beings do, and must, act on the same principles: the principles which define what rationality is. It is necessary therefore to distinguish between two kinds of principles: these universal and necessary principles, apart from obedience to which there is no such thing as action at all, and others, which may be called empirical principles, which can be changed without such consequence ... Two complementary errors are therefore possible: the error of regarding as necessary what is really optional, and the error of regarding as optional what is really necessary.[113]

An epistemological shortcoming of the new economic history is its methodological monism, which regards as necessary that which is really optional (and vice versa). As many critics of neoclassical and new institutional economics have already observed, many economic models and concepts are themselves historically and culturally embedded. Boldizzoni rightly states, for example, that "profit itself is a value."[114]

Historians then should, after Collingwood, divide the *a posteriori* elements of an economic theory into (1) assumptions about the 'external' environment (conditions, institutions, structures, etc.) and (2) assumptions about the 'internal' rationality of actors (Fig. 4.2).

Consistent with Weberian sociology, any *a posteriori* conditions concerning 'external' structures, institutions and other phenomena – all of which exist outside the minds of individuals – can be formulated into ideal types. These 'conditional' ideal types, however, should not pass into the historical narrative unmodified by historical evidence; they must be limited to time and space (i.e. they cannot, by nature, be thought of as universal).

[113] Collingwood (1994), 476. [114] Boldizzoni (2011), 99.

This book has already discussed several different approaches for doing this. Cliometricians, for example, usually treat *a posteriori* conditions as simple deductive hypotheses to be confirmed or falsified by empirical evidence. Other approaches, such as Hopkins' "taxes and trade" model, combine various hypotheses – whether deduced from theory or induced from evidence – into what he called "wigwam" arguments.[115] Boldizzoni also argues for a combined synthesis, although his approach prioritizes a kind of informal or intuitive induction ("historians will not allow themselves to be led by some prefabricated theory") to create "meta-theoretical" models which are limited to specific periods and places.[116] Regardless of the exact approach used to identify and formulate embedding context, this context nevertheless transforms the *a posteriori* abstractions of an economic theory into what we might think of as a theoretically conceived but historically 'bounded' ideal type – a model which generalizes at some level beyond the historical sources but which is also still tethered to them. The historical specificity of embedding contexts, therefore, restricts the theory's *ceteris paribus* conditions. To take an obvious example: an application of the *a posteriori* logic of Gresham's law to the historical context of the third-century AD Roman Empire prohibits 'good' and 'bad' money from being paper banknotes. An ideal-typical model of Gresham's law for the Roman world will probably be restricted to coins and assessing the specific historical conditions (differences in metal content? different emperors on the obverse? different uses?) which made coins 'good' or 'bad'.

Such ideal types, because they present, through generalization and abstraction, an alternative structural reality from the historical past itself, have counterfactual properties. They also obtain counterfactual properties from their genesis in economic theory, unlike approaches which are uninformed by formal economics (Fig. 4.3).

Alternative histories suggest comparisons and counterfactuals. In the case of these counterfactual ideal types, however, the comparison is not between two historical narratives per se, but between historical narratives and a historically bounded theoretical alternative.[117] Economists, especially new institutional economists, have previously advocated modifying theories in similar ways to create what cliometrician Robert Fogel called "hypothetical-deductive" models.[118] Whereas, however, cliometricians *test* such counterfactuals as hypotheses against evidence for purposes of *predicting* or *explaining*, I propose *comparing* them as ideal types for purposes

[115] Hopkins (1978), 19–20; Elliott (2016), 1–2. [116] Boldizzoni (2011), 150–2.
[117] Hawthorn (1993), 19–20. [118] Fogel (1966).

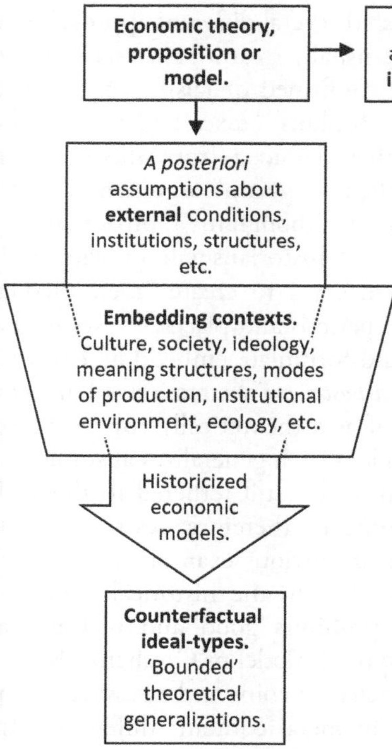

Fig. 4.3 Embedding contexts 'bound' economic models and create counterfactual ideal types

of *understanding*. This difference probably requires some explanation. Fogel argued that economic historians should 'test' and 'verify' counterfactual propositions by determining (1) "whether the proposition asserted follows from its logical premises" or (2) "whether the assumptions of the model are empirically valid."[119] Cliometrics' hypothetical-deductive models rest upon simple assumed relationships, ensuring that only certain variables are tested by specific sets of empirical evidence. The counterfactual possibilities are thus restricted to clear and concise conditions. There is, however, a trade-off: a simple model is more likely to be a historically vague model; historical analysis is necessarily particular and complex. Cliometric counterfactuals, for example, are unfit to account for the historically specific meanings of empirical evidence. It may be possible to show that wheat prices were higher in Rome than they were in

[119] Ibid., 655–6.

Alexandria, and even to create a counterfactual mathematical model to test whether distance accounts for the differences in prices.[120] Such a model, however, says *nothing* about both the subjective preferences of the individuals who made an exchange at certain prices or about the larger embedding contexts that necessarily influenced these subjective values. The simplicity of cliometric counterfactuals may lend them a certain rigor, but this simplicity is only achieved by assuming *both* a counterfactual 'external' world and a counterfactual 'internal' rationality. Imagining a perfectly rational Roman as well as separating him from his social context and cultural influences may make testing, quantifying, programming and perhaps even predicting specific behaviors in simple economic scenarios easy. Such deductive tests, however, assume (away) so much historical context and *all* human choice that their epistemological weaknesses make them of limited use (at best) to historians.[121] Finley rightly observed that "every man except Robinson Crusoe has his freedom limited in one way or another in consequence of living in society. Absolute freedom is an idle dream."

What about the 'internal' *a posteriori* assumptions of economic theory? If it is not yet clear, I see little usefulness in mapped assumptions about rationality for economic history. Historians should discard these assumptions entirely, as they assume away the very phenomena historians seek to understand. In the place of such assumptions, historians should insert purposefulness, which is unmapped and yet also *a priori* to all acting humans. Here is where many Austrian School economists, including Mises, would exit historical analysis because their approach to economics concerns deductions from the logic of choice, and does not investigate *meaning*.[122] The epistemological status of purposefulness, however, benefits economic historians in at least three ways. First, for the reasons mentioned previously, historians can safely assume an *a priori* purposefulness exists in historical people. Second, because purposefulness follows merely from *being human*, historians can place it before the embedding contexts that shape individual choices. Finally, the value-free nature of purposefulness protects these same historical people from the violent *a posteriori* rationalities of historians and other observers. Purposefulness, however, does not necessarily equate to 'clean' abstraction; understanding purposefulness requires historians to get their hands 'dirty' with the evidence.[123] Unlike *homo economicus*, for example, purposeful individuals

120 Kessler and Temin (2007); Temin and Kessler (2008).
121 Sahlins (2000), 39.
122 Mises (1949), 47; Greenfield and Salerno (1983), 45.
123 Hirsch, Michaels and Friedman (1987).

are not autonomous from the real world they inhabit. Individuals are members of and identify within larger social, cultural and economic groups which constrain their choices and values. Even the implausible lone individual must nevertheless grapple with physical and ecological barriers to action.

Whatever the historical constraints on purposefulness may be, economic historians *must* investigate them. So, as with 'external' *a posteriori* assumptions of economic theory, *a priori* purposefulness and the purposeful action that follows it cannot be understood apart from an embedding context. Again, to use Gresham's law as an example, historians cannot assume that all Roman coin-users knew about differences in coins' metal content or even that coin-users assigned any value to precious metal at all. Historians can assume, however, that coin-users acted purposefully; but to understand whether "obtaining precious metal" was a desired end and "holding high-fineness coins back from exchange" was a chosen means requires historical investigation. Embedding contexts dictate the ways in which purposefulness obtains meaning through observed behaviors and actions. The previous section, for example, discussed how Tiberius' means–ends rationality was channeled through the culturally specific mode of Roman patronage. Distributing wealth reified Tiberius' dominant position in the social hierarchy and protected the (subordinate) elites who legitimized his social position. Tiberius' purposeful action, at least as Tacitus presents it, reveals that acting as a central banker or saving the financial system was not the determinant goal (if it was a goal at all) in his ends–means calculation, although financial motives were clearly present and there were economic consequences to his actions. Ultimately, as purposefulness passes through an embedding context, it should be better *understood.* My admittedly simple historical narrative of the crisis of AD 33, nevertheless explains how a cultural and social context (investigated *a posteriori*) channeled Tiberius' (*a priori*) purposefulness and concomitant purposeful action. Historical narratives must investigate the meanings of purposefulness. Naturally, historical narratives do not merely include purposeful actions; they may be mostly or even wholly dedicated to supra-individual structures (classes, nations, societies etc.) or even the physical environment. Wherever humans are involved, however, purposefulness is also present, and purposefulness can only be meaningfully understood at the level of the individual. Historical 'bounding' of purposefulness is also limited to purposeful action – or, more specifically, the evidence of purposeful action. Historians cannot examine purposefulness as it occurred inside the mind, but, after Collingwood, they can use purposeful action (history) as a means of accessing the minds of historical people.

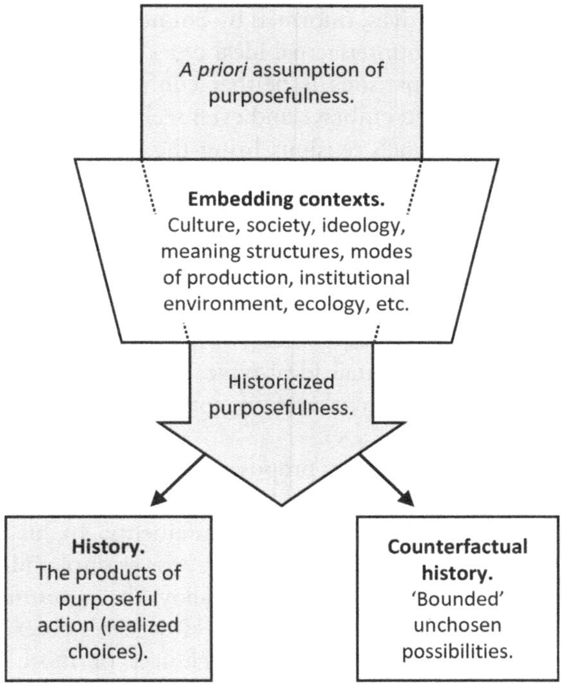

Fig. 4.4 Embedding contexts 'bound' purposefulness, creating history and unchosen counterfactual history

Purposeful action is a chosen means selected from a set of lesser-ranked unchosen alternatives. These unchosen alternatives are, as Schütz observed, also "typifications" – prefabricated definitions and generalizations based upon past experience and knowledge.[124] Real people, as opposed to theoretically modeled people, do not make choices based upon perfect knowledge, but by limited or 'bounded' knowledge dictated by the individual's own experience and social context. After the moment of choice, other choices become counterfactual choices, or in the case of past choices, they become counterfactual history. Moreover, these counterfactual choices are not infinite, but are also strictly bounded in context by the actor's experience, knowledge and culture. The existence of historical persons with the power to choose means and ends – even if those choices are limited – necessarily implies the existence of counterfactual alternatives (Fig. 4.4).

[124] Schütz (1970), 111–22; Kim and Berard (2009).

These historical narratives, informed by bounded purposeful action, can be compared with the counterfactual ideal types I described earlier. Again, the point of such comparisons is neither confirmation nor falsification. Instead, historians should embrace and even seek out any tension between theory and history, as such tensions bring the distinguishing features of historical purposeful action into sharper focus. The approach ultimately generates questions that promote understanding. Where does the counterfactual ideal-typical model fail and why? How do cultural, social, emotional, habitual contexts – the sorts of complexities which humanistic approaches are best equipped to interpret and understand (and which positivistic economics ignores) – create disparities between the historical narrative and its counterfactual ideal-typical alternative? The rationale of introducing economic theory, therefore, completely changes from prediction to understanding (Fig. 4.5).

The counterfactual ideal types proposed here are more complex than the economic theories that form them, but they can be used to amplify and understand even very simple historical statements. In his discussion of coinage debasements in the Roman Empire, for example, Howgego states that debasements at Rome were used "to allow the government to spend more *than it could otherwise have done*."[125] Howgego's observation implies unseen counterfactuals based upon the choices of those in charge of minting Roman currency (if we think of "the government" through the lens of methodological individualism). The choice to debase coinage and its resulting consequences can be evaluated against the counterfactual choice of *not debasing*. In a counterfactual world, if Roman officials (or perhaps the emperor?) wished to spend more money than they had on hand without lowering the currency standard, then some alternative needed to be pursued to make up the budgetary gap such as increasing revenues, reducing spending or some combination of these. Did revenue and spending need to be reconciled? Was some form of 'default', along with its concomitant effects, a legitimate counterfactual consequence? Against all of these counterfactual scenarios, the actual choice that metallurgical evidence indicates (coin standards were lowered) is better understood. Thus, underneath Howgego's almost offhand statement about debasement is a web of counterfactual historical questions, any of which may conceivably support further investigation. Was it realistic (or even possible) for Roman officials to reduce spending or generate new revenue (through raising taxes or property confiscations perhaps)? Could the

[125] Howgego (1995), 125. Emphasis added.

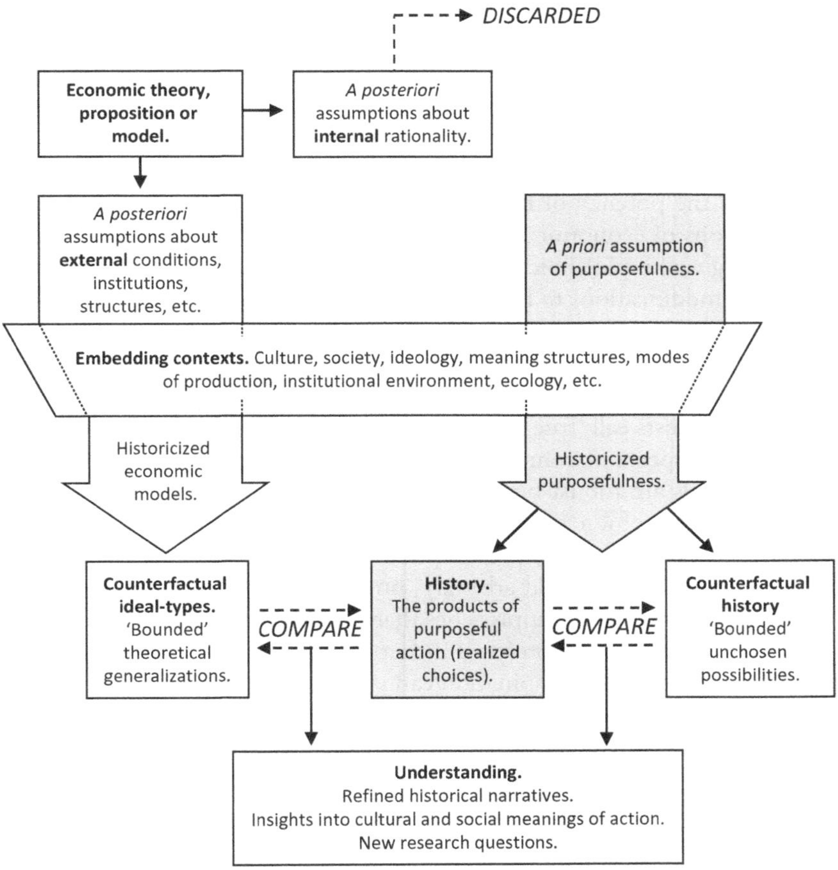

Fig. 4.5 An approach for using *a posteriori* economic theory, *a priori* purposefulness and embedding contexts to understand economic history

Roman state have 'defaulted'? – the word may be anachronistic, but is the concept exclusive to the capitalism or proto-capitalism of more recent eras? My point is that even simple counterfactual statements challenge historians to explore certain causal economic relationships and their context. Historians, however, need a process for organizing and evaluating the theories and models that they use to explore such relationships. Historical study is an essential component of all counterfactual analysis, but so is economic theory and purposefulness.

Conclusions

Purposefulness is neither derived from empirical evidence nor is it ideal-typical; rather, it is both synthetic and *a priori*. What can such a deductive and otherwise 'clean' concept accomplish for the comparatively 'dirty' research that historians perform? An *a priori* purposefulness both increases the potency of humanists' existing methodologies and channels applications of economic theory toward understanding purposeful action, including economic choices. An analytical framework derived from choice requires modifications to both the structure and use of economic theory in historical analysis. In some limited cases, where economic historians previously deployed *hypothetical* knowledge, they may now use *apodictic* knowledge. Historians can move beyond 'competing fictions' and work with what rationalists call 'true knowledge'. They can build counterfactual ideal types for purposes of comparative analysis and, ultimately, understanding. Such models are robust because their workings derive from the apodictic pivot of purposeful action rather than imagined, speculated or abstracted fictions. The aggregated, presumptive models of mainstream economics alone will necessarily yield arbitrary, unreliable historical analyses. Equally unreliable, however, are approaches that deny or ignore the aid of apodictic economic principles. *Verstehen* is in fact compatible with aprioristic theory; if done carefully, the combination can yield reliable, productive analyses of historical phenomena.

The discussion in this chapter offers merely a general and somewhat experimental framework. I suspect many readers will need to see how it might work in practice. How does this framework interact with some of the monetary theories commonly used by Roman historians? The remaining chapters of this book argue that even theories dominated by *a posteriori* conditions can be made both historically bounded and infused with purposefulness. Such modified theories better reveal the unique social and cultural framework of the Roman economy compared to standard uses of unmodified economic theories. An *a priori* and yet bounded purposefulness demands histories in which real people – whether they were officials, merchants, coin-users or autarkic peasants – were not slavishly following mapped behavior, but instead used means to achieve subjectively determined ends within frameworks of social and cultural meanings. Why did those who participated in the Roman monetary system – whether they used coins, credit instruments, supervised the system or enforced state interventions – make the choices they did and what were the consequences of their choices? What alternative actions were available to them and why did they not pursue these alternatives? In the remaining two chapters of this book, I apply the approach outlined in this chapter to monetary phenomena in the Roman world. The investigation modifies two theories – the quantity theory of money and Gresham's law – and redeploys them as counterfactual ideal types.

CHAPTER 5

Money Quantity and Quality

> ... the quantity theory of money: you cannot prove it, it's useless for us, what can we make of it, or with it? it's past, it's finito, it's no more ... you must not be overwhelmed by an economic theory of the past.
>
> Marcello de Cecco[1]

Historians are aware that money neither falls from the sky, as in Friedman's famous "helicopter money" parable, nor is it created "by miracle," as in David Hume's scenario in which "every man in Great Britain should have five pound slipped into his pocket in one night."[2] In the Roman world and even in modernity, patronage, for example, plays a crucial role in determining the timing and quantity of changes in the money supply. In most historical monetized societies, new money was distributed by means of a network of favored elites and privileged institutions. Roman money was as much a medium for redistributing political and social capital as it was a medium of economic exchange. Some Roman historians rightly resist "theories which imply a simple relationship between the coin supply and prices."[3] Few scholars, however, reject the basic economic logic of what many economists call "the quantity theory of money." As a logical statement, divorced of its econometric augmentations, the quantity theory of money describes an automatic relationship between money supply and prices in a monetized economy. According to the theory, if the supply of money increases (monetary inflation), then *ceteris paribus* the aggregate price level of all goods and services in relation to money will rise (price inflation). If the supply of money decreases (monetary deflation), then the prices of goods and services in relation to money will fall (price deflation). This frequently used rendering is a tautology which is of little use to monetary historians and may, in some

[1] De Cecco (2000), 271–2. [2] Friedman (1969). Hume, *Of Interest* 2.4.9.
[3] Howgego (1995), 123.

cases, derail the process of historical inquiry and *Verstehen*. Mises called it "nothing but a mathematical expression of the – untenable – doctrine that there is proportionality in the movements of the quantity of money and of prices."[4]

Quantity theory's logic was first formulated into a mathematical equation by the proto-monetarist Irving Fisher.[5] The equation – often called the 'Fisher equation' or 'equation of exchange' – however, was never meant to take the central place in economic analysis that it now occupies. Fisher developed the equation to push his 'compensated dollar' – "a piece of social engineering," according to Schumpeter, in which the gold-weight of the dollar would be changed once a month to keep prices stable.[6] The United States never adopted the 'compensated dollar', but Fisher's equation nevertheless survives to the present day as a major tenet of monetarism. In the Fisher equation, an aggregated money supply [*M*] is multiplied by the velocity [*V*] with which this nebulous money supply moves through the economy (i.e. how often currency is spent). The product of *M* and *V* is equal to the total output [*Q*] of goods and services in the economy multiplied by the aggregate price level [*P*]:

$$MV = PQ$$

If solving for P ($MV/Q = P$), then a higher value for *M* (monetary inflation), assuming the other values remain constant, necessitates a proportionally higher value for *P* (price inflation). Higher prices, however, could also be the result of higher values for *V* (velocity) or lower values for *Q* (output). Velocity of money is practically impossible to measure, so neoclassical economists typically assume that it is constant – one of the many assumptions which pose significant problems for any real-world application (present or past) of the Fisher equation.[7]

In a 2010 article published in *American Journal of Numismatics*, Scheidel illustrates how the Fisher equation both can and cannot aid the historian in dealing with complex historical monetary puzzles. As part of a broad attack on "nominalist" (i.e. chartalist) views of Roman money, Scheidel slots some hypothetical numbers into the Fisher equation in order to provide alternative explanations for an apparent permanent doubling of prices in Egypt between the middle and late second century AD. If, for example, all variables are valued at 100 in, say, AD 160, then *P* – to represent a doubling of prices – must double to 200 by, say, AD 190. The equation

[4] Mises (1949), 396. [5] Fisher (1911); de Cecco (1985), 814–5.
[6] Schumpeter (1954), 1103; Fisher (1913). [7] Mises (1949), 396; Howgego (1992), 12.

would then be imbalanced, as 100 × 100 [$M \times V$] = 10,000 but 200 × 100 [$P \times Q$] = 20,000; at least one of the other variables must be changed. Scheidel speculates that the lingering demographic effects of the Antonine plague may have reduced the aggregate output of goods in the economy proportionally (so Q becomes 75 instead of 100) and might have raised the velocity of money because "the plague and other dislocations interfered with credit arrangements and privileged transactions in coin" (so V becomes 150 instead of 100).[8] With these new hypothetical numbers, $MV = PQ$ balances, as 100 × 150 (MV) and 200 × 75 (PQ) both equal 15,000. If money supply also increases, then changes in the other variables can be moderated. If, for example, money supply (M) became 125 by AD 190, then velocity (V) would only need to increase to 120 instead of 150. Scheidel's conjectural and ultimately counterfactual use of quantity theory successfully discredits any *a priori* chartalist reading of the Egyptian (if not the Roman) monetary system on grounds of counterfactual logic.

Scheidel wisely refrains from making the Fisher equation do anything more than generate hypotheses. Bowman rightly remarks that the Fisher equation is "a good tool to think with, but it is very uncertain what numbers should be plugged into it."[9] It may be correct to go further and say that *any* numbers which are used in the equation are arbitrary, speculative and empirically meaningless. Italian economist Marcello De Cecco called the equation "useless."[10] The complexity of the Roman monetary system, as I argue in this chapter, cannot be expressed in a tautological and highly aggregated equation. What kinds of 'money' compose M, for example – circulating cash, hoarded cash, credit, securities, money-like commodities? Furthermore, the supply of money and the velocity with which it moves through a real economy – as well as the demand for money, for that matter – are always subject to various institutional mechanisms, the dynamics of culture and the subjective values of individual money-users. Not only are there insufficient data to quantify the numbers, but the numbers are themselves products of human choice rather than of constant and mechanistic phenomena.

The overarching problem with quantity theory is that it looks only "at the total supply of money in the *Volkswirtschaft* and not at the actions of the individual men and firms."[11] Rather than assume that prices, money supply, velocity of money and economic output are sterile variables formed and changed by naturalistic processes or 'forces', historians must understand these elements as products of purposeful action and a unique

[8] Scheidel (2010b), 107. [9] Bowman (2009), 289. [10] De Cecco (2000), 271–2.
[11] Mises (1949), 402.

embedding context which bounded purposeful action. This chapter, therefore, investigates changes in the quantity and quality of Roman money *historically* – that is, as operating in time, space and society. Money in the Roman world was largely physical; it occupied certain spaces and not others. Even credit money was limited to certain accounts held by certain individuals in certain locations where it could be obtained. Were there consequences when new money appeared in one place and not in another? Time is also involved. New money – however it was created or distributed – was used by some people *before* it was used by others. While it is erroneous to assume that velocity is constant, it is equally if not more problematic to assume that velocity is insensitive to temporality. Finally, what did new money *mean* to those who received it and received it before others? How did people respond to changes in their stock of money? What choices were available to them if they wished to spend, save, invest or give away money? What effects did these choices have on the 'real' structure of the Roman economy? New money could be used to obtain things, to be sure, but receiving and giving money in the Roman world had social consequences apart from exchange.

Money Neutrality, Briefly

Mainstream theoretical analysis of monetary systems typically avoids the complexity caused by physicality and temporality by assuming 'money neutrality' – the idea that changes in the supply of money only affect 'nominal' variables (variables measured in money: prices, wages, exchange rates) in the long run. The 'long run' is the time it takes for market prices to clear – hence, money neutrality is also premised upon the assumption that markets equilibrate to reflect supply and demand – almost like the law of gravity.[12] The equilibration process further assumes that actors in the market make choices according to a mapped profit-maximizing form of rationality, rather than their subjective preferences and embedding contexts. If money is non-neutral, however – as some economists in both the post-Keynesian and Austrian traditions believe (for *very* different reasons, however) – then changes in the money supply have permanent effects on 'real' factors (e.g. production, labor, credit markets, etc.) in historical economies.

[12] A succinct discussion is provided in Jones (2014), 315.

Post-Keynesians typically treat money as 'endogenous' to an economy. New money is created when lenders respond to the demand for money and extend credit. Therefore, changes in the money supply have 'real' economic effects.[13] Low interest rates, for example, will convince economically rational debtors to demand more credit and thus create more money. Austrian School economists, by contrast, reject money neutrality on more fundamental grounds. Austrians think of money as a good – "the most marketable good which people acquire because they want to offer it in later acts of interpersonal exchange."[14] The value of money, therefore, is a function of purposefulness and methodological individualism. Individuals' subjective values of their supply of money, demand for money and their time preferences are unique: "on a market there are only individuals or groups of individuals acting in concert."[15] The subjective individual preferences of those who hold or desire to hold such goods also dictate the way in which money interacts with other economic goods. Additionally, Austrians believe it is irresponsible to theorize in terms of aggregates such as those found in the Fisher equation. *Q*, for example, is abandoned in favor of a disaggregated view in which a good's properties and value may be different depending upon its position in the stages of its production.[16] Thinking of goods as having a history, and hence temporality, allows economic historians to factor time into their analysis of purposeful action – i.e. how changes in the money supply might alter the values of goods at different stages of the production process. The timing and location of changes in the money supply affect the structure of production in an economy in uneven ways, creating asset bubbles, redirecting investments and favoring certain individuals against others because of their ownership over or exploitation of specific types of assets.[17] Such 'malinvestments' cannot be identified and analyzed unless *Q* is disaggregated and thought of as a process which unfolds over time.[18]

Weber too was a proponent of non-neutral money. In his criticisms of Knapp's *State Theory of Money*, Weber observed that

> it is not possible to estimate quantitatively the effect on prices – revolutionary or gradual increase, or perhaps a decrease – of currency expansion or contraction over a certain future period. To do this, it would, in cases of [monetary] inflation ... be necessary to know ... the channels the

[13] Howells (1997); Howells (1995); Moore (1988); Kaldor (1986). [14] Mises (1949), 398.
[15] Ibid., 397. [16] This was first accomplished in Hayek (1967), 32–68.
[17] Mises (2000); Mises (1949), 411. [18] Horwitz (1996), 293.

inflationary process would follow, that is, who would be the primary and subsequent recipients of newly-issued money.[19]

Weber, as he sometimes did, yields to the Austrian view of money non-neutrality. He describes inflation not as the mere rebalancing of a sterile tautological equation, but rather as a process that is both historicized and disaggregated in time and space. Weber here suggests disaggregation by identifying specific "channels" through which new money moves. Weber also, crucially, places money supply changes in time by observing that some groups receive money first while others receive money later. Weber was no doubt referring to the phenomenon economist Mark Blaug calls "Cantillon effects," after Richard Cantillon, the early eighteenth-century Irish-French economist who first observed the importance of such 'channeling' in money supply changes.[20] Early recipients of new money – in addition to receiving the money itself – also receive temporal and spatial *privilege* compared to those who receive money later because the price structure of the economy has not yet adjusted to the fact that the new money exists. These early recipients therefore obtain economic power to promote their interests, whether these interests are economic, social or political.

The relatively few economists who study Cantillon effects in the modern economy attempt to identify such early recipients of new money. In the present regime of central-bank capitalism, such first users are easily identifiable: the commercial banks with accounts held by the central bank as well as national governments who sell bonds to the central bank to allow for new spending without the burden of generating new revenue (presumably through taxation). Large corporations and other financial entities with close political and economic connectivity to these well-networked financial and governmental institutions – ties which are not always disclosed or traceable – also benefit disproportionately. By contrast, wage-earners, typically in the working classes, and those on fixed incomes are unlikely to see wage increases until well after the 'real' economy has adjusted, putting these later recipients at an economic disadvantage.[21] Expansions in the money supply do not ripple evenly across even modern economies – despite the fact that many economic models, including quantity theory, often assume neutrality. Even the analogies used by economists to explain the workings of monetary stimulus, such as when Friedman said that

[19] Weber (1968), 188. A thoughtful take on Weber's reading of Knapp is found in Swedberg (1998), 76–7.

[20] Blaug (1997), 21. See also Spengler (1954a); Spengler (1954b).

[21] Easterly and Fischer (2001).

central-bank expansion of the money supply was like dropping money from a helicopter, obscure the inequalities inherent in money distribution in the modern monetary system.[22] Abandoning money neutrality, however, opens up new ways of studying not only prices and production, but also social relationships and systemic inequalities.

As for historical monetary systems, Cantillon effects complicate any mapped application of quantity theory with its unwieldy aggregates, lack of temporality, commensurate assumptions about economic rationality among money-users as well as the ecological conditions of the economy. Analyses of changes in the supply of money in the Roman monetary system must therefore, whenever possible, account for Cantillon effects and avoid assumptions of neutral and atemporal monetary injections. Wealth transfers through changes in money supply and prices are difficult to model for the modern economy, let alone the Roman economy. While the Roman world did not have central banks and their modern client network, there was nevertheless a monetary authority with a semi-monopolistic hold on the money supply. It is probably safe to speak of an imperial center, for example – whether the emperor himself, and/or a small group of elites or clients who managed the coinage. Beyond this imperial center, it may be difficult to consistently identify and model what Weber called "primary" and "subsequent" recipients because these appear to have changed from regime to regime based upon both the personal whims of emperors and larger social and economic trends as the Principate evolved. Emperors usually surrounded themselves with their own unique favorites: family members, freedmen, generals, politicians and favored clients. In rare cases, the sources record payments to this tier that immediately surrounded the imperial center. Quantities of such payments in ancient sources – such as the 2.2 billion sesterces Tacitus claims that Nero distributed to his friends and favorites – are often unreliable. Still, these sources provide historians with information about what Saller calls "proximity" – the position of a person or group along the channel of imperial *beneficia* – as well as monetary flows in the social networks of the imperial elite.[23] Septimius Severus, for example, famously (and perhaps fictitiously) told his son Caracalla to "enrich the soldiers, scorn all other men."[24] Indeed, over time, emperors seem to have channeled more and more new money

22 Friedman (1969).

23 Tac. *Hist.* 1.20.1. See also Suet. *Nero* 30. "Proximity" is discussed throughout Saller's book on Roman patronage, but most especially see Saller (1982), 63–9.

24 Dio Cass. 73.14.3.

toward the military, in terms of both salary increases and *donativa*. The increasing bureaucratization of imperial administration also promulgated a body of state employees who must have benefited from their relatively early position in the flow of new money, but civil servants' distance from the center was presumably greater than that of the imperial household or the military.[25]

In addition to the geography of imperial patronage, physical geography – via the location of mints, the areas where any new coins were spent and almost certainly the presence of the emperor himself – must have produced real economic distortions. Lo Cascio, for example, notes the geographic dimension to monetary injections under the Principate:

> most of the new coinage was injected into the economic system by public expenditure … it was discretely and differently localized in the various areas of the empire which determined the different degree of monetization and availability of coinage in different times and places … Thus the economy of the *limes* was heavily influenced by payments to the army and the spending of them by the recipients, even if the number of soldiers was not, in comparison with the level of the whole population, really substantial.[26]

Beyond Lo Cascio's astute observation here, few scholars (if any?) have identified let alone formally studied Cantillon effects in the Roman world. Understandably, existing methodological paradigms – especially money neutrality – marginalize such efforts. Moreover, the sources rarely provide historians with information about the geographic or political flows specific influxes of new money followed. Finally, uncertainty and debate regarding the integration of the Roman monetary system makes it impossible to quantify the speed and impact of new money as it moved (or did not move) through the Roman economy.[27] There are, unfortunately, few opportunities to map monetary flows in the Roman Empire.

Money in Time and Space: A Case Study from the Roman Empire

Only very rarely do primary sources from the Roman world refer to changes in the money supply. A well-known money supply change, however, occurred at the beginning of the Roman Principate.[28] Upon defeating Mark Antony and Cleopatra at the Battle of Actium in 31 BC,

[25] Whitby (2004), 180; Lo Cascio (2000), 80; Duncan-Jones (1994), 176; Rodewald (1976).
[26] Lo Cascio (2000), 80–1. [27] Howgego (1994), 6; Bedford (2007), 325.
[28] Another is under Tiberius in AD 33. See Elliott (2015).

Octavian returned to Rome two years later in the summer of 29 to celebrate a triumphal procession of unprecedented splendor in which "the Romans forgot all their unpleasant experiences" of the preceding decades of civil war.[29] Octavian's triumph not only featured the typical grandiose displays of war trophies and captured spoils, but because he seized the accumulated treasuries of the Ptolemies, as well as the war chest of his rival Antony, the triumph was accompanied by massive monetary pay-outs. Cassius Dio's early third-century AD history says that "so vast an amount of money, in fact, circulated through all parts of the city alike, that the price of goods rose and loans for which the borrower had been glad to pay twelve percent could now be had for one third that rate."[30] Suetonius' version of the event includes additional details:

> by bringing the royal treasures to Rome in his Alexandrian triumph [Augustus] made ready money so abundant, that the rate of interest fell, and the value of real estate rose greatly ... He often gave largesse to the people, but usually of different sums: now 400, now 300, now 250 *sestertii* a man; and he did not even exclude young boys, though it had been usual for them to receive a share only after the age of eleven. In times of scarcity too he often distributed grain to each man at a very low figure, sometimes for nothing, and he doubled the money tickets.[31]

This monetary expansion appears to have been more than literary exaggeration because the sources include in their descriptions some purported knock-on effects: reduced interest rates and rising prices. Increases in the supply of money, according to quantity theory, put downward pressure on the price of money: interest rates.[32] The simple *a posteriori* logic here is that lower interest rates would have made borrowing easier and, hence, generated greater demand and higher prices in general.[33] This is indeed what we observe in Dio's account. A cliometrician might, therefore, claim that the post-Actium economy 'confirms' the operation of quantity theory.

How does the approach to economic theory I advocate in this book enhance or even change the way historians understand an episode like this one? The most important difference is accounting for context, firstly time and place. The problem is that although Octavian's post-Actium monetary

[29] Dio Cass. 51.21.4. Octavian was awarded the title of 'Augustus' on January 16, 27 BC. Hence, this book uses 'Octavian' when discussing events which took place before this formal change. In the context of events from 27 BC onward, or to discuss the person of Augustus himself, 'Augustus' is used after modern convention.

[30] Dio Cass. 51.21.4–5.

[31] Suet. *Aug.* 41.

[32] Strictly speaking, the price of money *in the present*. See Mises (1949), 523–9.

[33] Lo Cascio (1981), 82, 86.

expansion is mentioned in several literary sources, these sources do not help illuminate the channels through which money was distributed. Suetonius provides the most useful information by isolating price increases in the category of investment for which elite Romans typically borrowed money – property purchases. The aim of the biographer in his discussion of Octavian's triumph, however, is neither to show economic causality nor catalogue statistical data, but to demonstrate that the emperor's *liberalitas* (his noble generosity) extended "to all the orders" (41.1.).[34] Suetonius' examples for various cash distributions lack concrete dates and figures except that "[Augustus] *frequently* provided distributions to the people . . . sometimes 400, sometimes 300 and on occasions 250 sesterces."[35] Augustus' self-glorifying record of his great deeds, his *Res Gestae*, despite its propagandizing purpose and style, nevertheless fills in some details which literary accounts lack. The *Res Gestae*'s figures for monetary distributions may tempt economic historians to make quantitative estimates but, after Saller's notion of proximity, the most valuable information for understanding the patterns of monetary distribution are the places in the *Res Gestae* which signal which groups received new money, the source from which the money came and the year in which money was distributed. Amounts in the *Res Gestae* are always recorded in sesterces – the main unit of account at the time – but the payments themselves were almost certainly issued in silver *denarii*, whether newly minted from Egyptian bullion or, more likely, they represent a redistribution of Antony's Eastern-minted *denarii* which were captured after Octavian's final victory.[36] In either case, the money mentioned in the *Res Gestae* should be thought of as 'new' (to the Italian economy) because it had hitherto been regionalized to the East – locked up either in the Ptolemaic treasury or in Antony's war chest. Finally, Octavian's gifts at first appear to benefit those at the lower and lower middle end of Rome's socio-economic spectrum – the Roman plebeians and veteran legionaries – something the *Res Gestae* makes much of. In fact, the situation is far more complicated.

To what extent did these monetary gifts alter the real economy of the city of Rome and the Italian countryside? A cliometrician might treat the

[34] Wardle (2014), 309–10.

[35] Emphasis added. The HS 250 figure is probably either fictitious or stylized, as it cannot be made from *denarii*. On stylized figures, see Scheidel (1996).

[36] No new *sestertii* were minted until almost a decade after Actium. Also, Greek inscriptions sometimes use δηνάρια. See Scheid (2007). On Octavian reusing Mark Antony's 'legionary' *denarii*, see Dillon (2007).

figures in the *Res Gestae* as roughly reliable 'statistics' – at least for purposes of making estimates – and perform some simple mathematics. The cash gifts listed in the *Res Gestae*, whether given to soldiers or to the population of Rome, total 2.4 billion sesterces. This figure could then be compared to one of several guestimates for the size of the Roman money supply in the early Principate – many of which hover between two to four billion sesterces.[37] From such comparisons – taking into account that not all the money circulating in the Roman world was isolated to Italy – it would be reasonable to deduce that, on aggregate, Octavian's post-Actium cash gifts in the *Res Gestae* alone could have conceivably doubled or even tripled Italy's money supply.

I suggest, however, that we think more qualitatively and historically about how substantial injections of new money changed the social and economic position of specific groups of people within the network of distribution. The *Res Gestae* mentions, for example, that an unknown number of plebeians (*plebei romanae*, not merely the *plebs frumentaria* which Augustus restricted to 200,000 qualified persons in 2 BC) were given 400 sesterces each "from the spoils of war" during the year of Octavian's Alexandrian triumph (29 BC).[38] Elsewhere in the *Res Gestae*, Augustus claims that each dispersion to the plebs, including this one, was given to at least 250,000 men. Again, one approach here is to argue that 100 million sesterces (= 25 million *denarii*) was injected into the city's monetary economy. The more important historical question in my view, however, is how this new money – however much it was in actuality – helps us understand the choices made by those who received it. Since most urban plebeians lived at or near subsistence, their material conditions probably tempted them to consume most of the money they received from the handout on food purchases. Rome's male plebeians were eligible for a monthly dole (five *modii*) of free grain from the state – enough to feed an individual for a month, but more was needed to feed adult or underage dependents. The doled grain was unmilled (and thus inedible); it could be crudely crushed with stone instruments and boiled into an edible although unappetizing porridge. Some urban poor may have occasionally had the luck to obtain a little money to hire the services of a miller or even a bread-baker.[39] A *modius* of ordinary milled flour (the amount an adult male might consume in a single week) sold in Rome for twelve sesterces according to Pliny, about six sesterces more than what unmilled seems

[37] E.g. Harris (2006), 21; Goldsmith (1987), 41. [38] *RG* 15. [39] Holleran (2012), 133–6.

to have typically gone for in Rome.[40] The difference between these figures alone implies that the annual costs of milling grain could have easily reached 300 sesterces; baking costs, whether to rent the use of an oven and/or a baker, would have been in addition to this amount. Alternatively, for roughly the same amount of money, an urban plebeian could obtain a year's supply of unmilled grain for family or other dependents. Either choice seems more valuable to a plebeian living at or near subsistence compared to other consumption options obtained in what Claire Holleran calls the "flexible and low-cost modes of distribution, such as markets, street trading, and hawking" available for urban plebeian spending. Thus, Octavian's post-Actium gift of 400 sesterces per Roman plebeian may have temporarily flushed Rome's poor neighborhoods with cash, but considering the tremendous consumption needs among those who received this gift, most of this money probably ended up in the hands of those who sold, milled and baked grain over the course of the next year.

Military veterans are also favored in the *Res Gestae*'s account of post-Actium monetary distributions. Again in 29 BC, Octavian "gave from my war-spoils to colonies of my soldiers each 1,000 sesterces per man"; this amount is roughly equivalent to a year's salary for a Roman legionary at the time.[41] The *Res Gestae* goes on to say that "about 120,000 men in the colonies received this triumphal public gift." As above, the figure of 120 million sesterces (= 30 million *denarii*) taken at face value from the source and used as a statistical aggregate does little for historical understanding. Again, the more pressing question is a historical and relational one: *where* and *how* did such a large distribution of new money bring about changes in the choices made by individuals? The post-Actium colonies for Octavian's veterans were located exclusively on Italian soil. Some of these colonies were concentrated in the Po Valley, but otherwise the distribution of veterans was spread across Italian regions.[42] Post-Actium money distributed to veterans likely provided the most immediate stimulus outside of Rome. The *Res Gestae* mentions that 120,000 veterans received this distribution (120,000), but Octavian's active army contained less than half that number eligible for retirement. This distribution probably also went to those who had already been settled since the battle of Philippi in 42 BC (all in Italy)

40 Plin. *HN* 18.90. 41 *RG* 15.
42 Gurval (1998), 59; Dillon (2007), 41; Keppie (1983), 78–9.

and perhaps even Antony's surviving retirees (many settled outside of Italy).[43] A second post-Actium gift mentioned in the *Res Gestae* also appears to benefit veterans in Italian colonies. Augustus claims that he sent the largest amount of money by far – 600 million sesterces (= 150 million *denarii*) – to Italian landowners to pay for the land confiscated in 30 BC to create veteran colonies.[44] Dio, who also says that this massive gift was given right after Actium in 30 BC, should be trusted on this particular point, as Octavian would have been desperate to demonstrate faithfulness to Italian landowners on whom he imposed sudden and severe property and income confiscations in 31 BC to pursue his war against Antony.[45]

At first glance and certainly in the most direct terms, these gifts benefited military veterans, as the money both provided a year's salary and enabled around 100,000 veterans to become small landowners.[46] Even after these distributions, however, Roman elites disproportionately held Italian land, and these holdings were vast. The accumulation of Italian land by elites was not merely driven by economics, but by a wider set of political, social and cultural conditions. Landed wealth of at least 400,000 sesterces was a prerequisite for equestrian status.[47] A law of Julius Caesar required that a majority of this landed wealth be held in Italy specifically.[48] Moreover, Italian land – especially land with easy transport access to urban markets – was arguably the most stable and secure financial investment during the late Republic and early Principate.[49] Because of its secure value, Italian land commonly served as collateral for elite borrowing. Changes in the value of land, therefore, directly affected the amount of credit available to landowners. From the mid-second century BC onward, Italian land was exempted from the land tax (*tributum soli*).[50] Finally, Italian land was valuable for its patrimonial function: it was a physical manifestation of wealth, social status and political opportunity which could be passed down from generation to generation with greater reliability compared to

43 Cooley (2009), 173. Antony's veterans seem to have been settled mostly outside of Italy; see Keppie (1983), 79–80.

44 *RG* 16. 45 Dio Cass. 50.16.3, 51.4.6. See Dillon (2007), 41–4. 46 Suet. *Jul.* 26.

47 Although there was no explicit minimum property requirement for senators until about a decade after Actium, senators likely maintained at least (and often in abundant excess) of the equestrian qualification; see Lintott (1999), 71–2; Garnsey and Saller (2014), 136.

48 Kay (2018), 167; Hopkins (1978), 47 n. 65.

49 Garnsey and Saller (2014), 72; Roselaar (2010), 189.

50 Cic. *Off.* 2.76. See also Lavan (2013), 28; Potter (2014), 54.

cash or fiduciary assets. These embedding contexts necessarily bounded elite thought, causing elites to value land investments higher than other more economically profitable opportunities. Demand for Italian land among elites, therefore, was steady and otherwise inelastic. Membership in the landed elite and especially the Roman Senate, remained the exclusive privilege of the super-rich who could afford such real estate prices.

In quantitative terms, the gifts to or on behalf of veterans after Actium alone amounted to over half a billion sesterces of direct stimulus into the Italian real estate market. Whatever the figures actually were, the *Res Gestae* suggests that Augustus' distributions to elite landowners were orders of magnitude greater than those given to all other groups combined. Cultural-political factors ensured that much of this cash quickly found its way into landed wealth as formerly dispossessed elite, if they desired to maintain membership in the Roman aristocracy, were required to take their cash compensation and invest it back into purchases of Italian land, driving up prices in this asset class against others. This feedback cycle would have especially benefited those politically networked elites who had *not* had parts of their landholdings confiscated for veteran colonization and had otherwise maintained their estates or portions thereof during the civil wars of the previous decades. The post-Actium monetary injection would have raised nominal values of this elite landed capital *without any change in its real value*. Suetonius, of course, mentions surging land prices as a corollary of Octavian's triumphant return to Rome in 29 BC. A disaggregated and historicized approach – yet one which also pivots upon economic theory – helps us understand some broader meanings of these prices.

Therefore, while the post-Actium surge in new money allowed the urban poor in Rome to afford a little more grain, or perhaps subsidized the conversion of their inedible grain into a more palatable form – benefits experienced for perhaps a year at most – the patrimonial elite saw the value of their most important asset – Italian real estate – rise higher than it would have absent the emperor's beneficence. The post-Actium monetary expansion was both a short-term windfall and more crucially, a longer-term stimulus to the types of assets that sustained the social and economic privilege of these elites. Although elites dedicated small portions of their landholdings to self-sufficiency or for gardens and parks, an overwhelming amount of elite-owned Italian land produced grain, oil and wine for sale, as

Cato's handbook suggests.[51] Italian land, therefore, in addition to providing social and cultural capital, also functioned as economic capital. It is also possible to think about how the post-Actium monetary injection improved the status of land as economic capital. If the Italian agricultural production structure is both disaggregated into stages and also placed in time, then land (as capital) would exist at or near the beginning of the production chain. Roman estate owners typically sold or auctioned their produce privately, usually well ahead of the harvest, rather than taking it directly to markets (*nundinae*) themselves.[52] This practice allowed landowners to pass the risk of bad harvests onto intermediaries as well as to avoid the practical matter of transporting and marketing produce.[53] Elites distanced themselves (nominally, at least) from the sordid dealings of markets and instead entertained supplicant buyers and auctioneers as though they were clients.[54] Those who purchased goods (especially *argentarii* and *coactores argentarii*) and subsequently used these assets, whether in physical or virtual form, to extend credit to borrowers, were also near the earlier stages of the production process.[55] Further down the chain were wholesalers, then urban retailers and ultimately urban consumers.

As new money moved down the production and distribution process in the Italian land market, those who owned assets near the beginning of the process gained real wealth at the expense of those involved in later stages of production (Fig. 5.1).

The process I describe here is generalized and simplified for purposes of analysis, but it is a way of historicizing and disaggregating the 'capital function' of land (again, one of many functions of land, depending upon the context) into a series of ideal-typical stages which end in consumption.[56] Roman landowners, for example, regularly used their land as collateral for borrowing. Higher land values therefore extended landowners' access to credit, allowing them to pursue new investment opportunities *before* those who held other forms of capital. Such investments may not have been economic, but were perhaps what we might call 'social investments' – consumption of goods and services which enhanced social status or political opportunities. Cicero's writings, for example, are filled with such motivations.[57] The artificial boom to land values which followed from the post-Actium monetary injection shifted real economic resources

[51] Cato *Agr.* 2.7. [52] Marzano (2007), 82; Morley (2000a), 216.
[53] Verboven (2009), 117; Morley (2000a), 217–8. [54] Morley (2000a), 219.
[55] Howgego (1992), 15; Erdkamp (2005), 113; Andreau (1999), 149–50.
[56] Erdkamp (2005), 141. [57] Koedijk (forthcoming).

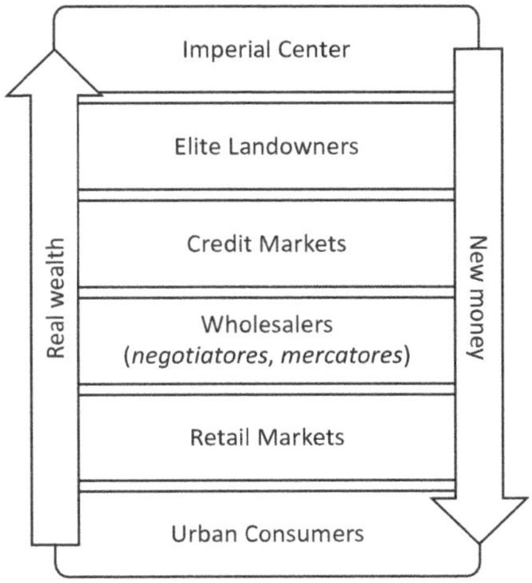

Fig. 5.1 Money and wealth flows in the Italian land market after Actium

(labor, land and ultimately future consumption as the new investments moved down the chain of production) toward servicing elite economic and social power. Moreover, I want to emphasize that the shift happened *before* the new money went through the long-run market-clearing process and hence became reflected in the overall price structure. Thus, those who owned Italian land enjoyed a period of time in which the spending power of their cash, their access to credit and/or the returns on their capital silently transferred real wealth away from those further down the chain. Even with the information in the *Res Gestae*, the amounts are unquantifiable. What my approach shows, however, is that Italian landowners gained against a counterfactual scenario in which money was not distributed or was distributed into assets which were not disproportionately held by elites. The first indication of such a shift would have been changes in interest rates, which are reduced when investors move their money away from short-term capital assets and into long-term capital assets, or, to put it another way, from capital assets late in the production process to those at or near the beginning. Interestingly, both Suetonius and Cassius Dio mention rapid and punctuated falls in interest rates in their accounts.

Context frames the larger meaning of these phenomena. Membership into Rome's patrimonial elite was made all the more difficult, not only by high land prices as a result of the monetary surge of 29 BC, but, a year later, by Octavian's formal 'review of the Senate' (*lectio senatus*) which saw between 20 and 40 percent of members purged from the Senate.[58] Subsequent actions by Augustus – too many to list here – sought to further clarify and reinforce the boundaries between Roman social classes, especially of the elite. At or before the time of his second review of the Senate, which would take place in 18 BC, for example, the minimum real estate investment required for membership in the Senate was fixed at either 1,000,000 sesterces (according to Suetonius) or 1,200,000 sesterces (according to Dio).[59] For roughly eighty senators, these requirements were too onerous, and so Augustus himself drew from his private fortune to make up the difference. It was a happy coincidence for Augustus and the most socially and economic powerful senators that the prices of Italian land cooperated with the rest of the agenda of the emperor – an agenda aimed at reinforcing and in some cases reinventing the divisions within the Roman social hierarchy (*discrimina ordinum*) generally, and the propertied aristocratic class especially. Augustus, as the patron of so many senators, not only legitimized his status as the first man in Rome in culturally understood patron–client terms, but also in the practical sense that members of the senatorial order were dependent upon the regime and its success for continued sustainability.

Coin Quality and Prices

Accounting for time and space is but one way to reconfigure quantity theory for purposes of understanding. It is also possible to think a little differently about the theory's supposed automatic link between prices and money supply. Previous studies of Roman money, many of which focus upon coin debasements in the second and third century AD, tend to take this relationship for granted. Scheidel, for example, assumes that debasement and money supply increases "were logically linked and predicated upon one another."[60] Ramsay MacMullen notes that "inflation, *of course*, arose principally from the government minting more and more coins."[61] Harl speaks about the proportional relationship between debasements and prices: "since the population accepted the baser coins, prices and wages seem to have risen only in proportion to each debasement."[62] Scholars sympathetic to chartalism, such as Kay Ehling below, tend to criticize the

58 The low number is Evans (1997), 85. The high number is Lintott (2009), 86.
59 Suet. *Aug.* 14.1 and Dio Cass. 55.13.6, respectively.
60 Scheidel (2010b), 100. See also, for example, Hopkins (1980), 117 n. 48.
61 MacMullen (1988), 37. Emphasis added.
62 Harl (1996), 141.

notion that debasements *automatically* led to decreases in the purchasing power of coinage:

> Da sich die Legionsantoniniane qualitativ aber nicht weiter von den vorausgehenden und nachfolgenden Emissionen unterscheiden, muß man daraus den Schluß ziehen, daß die Geldempfänger und -benutzer den Wert des Geldes durch den Staat als münzprägende Institution garantiert sahen. Letztlich bürgte dafür das Porträt des Kaisers auf der Münzvorderseite. Es ist deshalb ein metallistischer Irrtum anzunehmen, daß jede Absenkung des Silberfeingehalts sich 'automatisch' negativ auf die Kaufkraft des Münzgeldes ausgewirkt und damit ein Ansteigen der Preise für Waren und Dienstleistungen hervorgerufen hätte.[63]

Chartalists are correct to critique the naïve metallism which sometimes appears in narratives of a third-century crisis. It would be equally naïve, however, to assume that the power of the state's stamp and tendency to take coins in taxes nullified coin-users' preferences for precious metal. Unfortunately, unlike either the money supply increase after Actium or the proportionately smaller monetary injection under Tiberius in AD 33, literary sources provide little indication of how coin debasements were incorporated into the valuations of Roman coin-users.

Chartalists pounce upon this silence in the sources. No third-century author mentions general price inflation – the expected consequence of such rapid and pronounced changes in coinage standards. The little evidence which has been assembled, furthermore, seems to contradict the metallist paradigm. A passage in Cassius Dio, in fact, suggests that the nominal exchange rate between *denarii* and *aurei* remained in effect in the early third century AD.[64] While the most dramatic silver debasements did not come until after Dio's time, the *denarius* was already a half-silver coin under Septimius.[65] Non-literary evidence also casts doubt upon any money-supply-caused price inflation, as known Egyptian prices – regionalized and numerically limited as they are – hint that price inflation may not have occurred until the monetary reform of Aurelian in the AD 270s.[66]

Figure 5.2, for example, shows wheat prices that can be graphed (without misleading readers, as many prices and dates are unconfirmed).[67] Prices seem permanently higher in the third century compared to the second, although these third-century prices are more erratic, ranging from

63 Ehling (2008), 853. 64 Dio Cass. 55.12.4–5.
65 Gitler and Ponting (2003); Butcher and Ponting (2012). 66 Rathbone (1997).
67 Although there are other wheat prices, I explain elsewhere why they cannot be included on graphs such as this one. See Elliott (forthcoming). A complete graph of all prices, including those which have unconfirmed prices and dates, is found in Rathbone (1997). See also Harper (2016a).

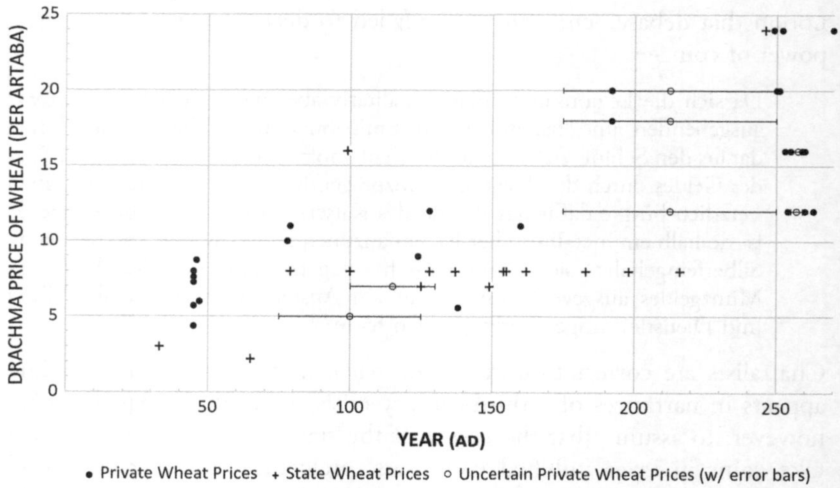

Fig. 5.2 Wheat prices in Roman Egypt (confirmed and dated), AD 1–270.
Data sources: Rathbone and von Reden (2015); Rathbone (1997). Chart after Elliott (forthcoming).

a low of twelve *drachms* an *artaba* to twenty-four. Wheat is merely one good money could purchase – and there are plenty of possible explanations for price changes (or price stability) in a single good which have nothing to do with monetary changes. Rathbone attempted to correct for this problem by also including some prices for wine and donkeys – information which might give a more generalized picture of price movements in Egypt. Prices (all eight of them) of adult female donkeys, for example, rise discernibly from the mid-second through the early third century AD as do the (five) prices for young female donkeys. Male donkeys, both young and adult, do not seem to fetch increasingly higher prices over the same period, although one young male donkey sold for 500 *drachms* in AD 219 – a price well above the range of 120 to 340 *drachms* within which the other (five) prices fall. Wine prices range between five and twelve *drachms* per *keramion monochoron* (a measure of roughly seven litres) in the second century.[68] After a half-century gap in the data, wine in the mid-third century fetches between eight and twenty-one *drachms*.

Even if these few wheat, wine and donkey prices reflect a generalized price inflation in the late second century followed by a period of price stability in the third century, is it methodologically sound to treat such

[68] On the *keramion monochoron* see Rathbone (1991), 469.

prices as having a mechanistic relationship with an aggregated money supply? Rathbone answers in the negative, but in a way which in some respects upholds methodological monism. His explanation is that the use of coined money increased so rapidly during the second and especially the third century so as to absorb money supply increases.[69] In other words, aggregate demand for money increased enough to counteract the inflationary effects of increases in aggregate money supply. The demand-for-money argument is mathematically captured in the Fisher equation's cousin, the Cambridge equation – named after a group of influential early twentieth-century economists affiliated with the University of Cambridge who sought to improve the Fisher equation. Their revised equation substitutes k (money demand) for the Fisher equation's V (money velocity). Replacing money velocity with money demand gets around the absurdity of a constant velocity – an improvement to be sure. It is also possible to use demand theory to think about purposeful action, as Hollander does in many respects, by asking not only how much money was demanded by individuals in the middle and late Roman Republic but *why*?[70] Unfortunately, the Cambridge equation, like the Fisher equation, fails to account for the fact that monetary value and the prices of goods and services occur in time and space (money non-neutrality) and are subjectively determined (*a priori* purposefulness). When demand and supply are two sides of an atemporal mechanistic equation, it is true that they neatly balance out. In historical time and space, however, when, say, money supply increases before demand rises, the 'real' economy changes (as in the Italian land market after Actium) as resource allocation shifts because of purposeful action. A subsequent increase in money demand does not mechanistically 'undo' the real economic changes brought on by the earlier increase in supply. It is more accurate to say that in fact a *second* wave of disaggregated change sweeps through the economy. Even if money supply and demand 'canceled out' in the long-run general price level, real structural changes will have been caused as individuals adjusted their preferences and purposeful actions based upon their changing (or unchanging) values. A money demand argument may explain the dissonance between third-century debasement and prices at the most aggregated, general level; indeed, perhaps coincidentally on balance the money demanded by individuals increased roughly proportional to any increases in the money supply brought about by debasements (unless debasements triggered

69 Rathbone (1996a). 70 Hollander (2007), 141–55.

hoarding, and money supply decreased).[71] A disaggregated approach to money quantity, however, encourages historians to think about what changing prices and money supply meant to the individuals whose choices ultimately *made* these prices. Narrowing the study in both temporal and spatial terms helps historians better understand the thinking of historical individuals. So the most important question is not: did money supply/demand increase or decrease? It is, instead, better to ask: are there particular economic, social, cultural or even ecological factors which influenced the way in which Egyptian residents or those who made exchanges with them valued local commodities (especially wheat) or the monetary objects in which the value of commodities was quantified? Did the coinage itself change, for example? Did coin acceptability change? Did changes in coin quality affect coin acceptability?

The first of these questions may be the most crucial. Just as geography channeled the effects of post-Actium changes in money quantity, Egyptian prices are local to *Egypt* and they must not be divorced from their spatial context. Egyptian prices are not only regionalized geographically, but the monetary system of Egypt was itself to some degree separated from the imperial system used in many other parts of the Roman world. Some argue that the difference between the two systems was merely nominal, and the Egyptian *tetradrachm* was "the local version of the imperial silver coinage."[72] It is true that the existence of fixed exchange rates between *denarii* and Egyptian *tetradrachms* may justify such a view. Alternatively, the nominal equivalence between *denarii* and *tetradrachms* may have been complicated if not undermined by local factors – especially the mechanism by which the Egyptian mint obtained silver, the time of year coins were minted and the year-to-year variation of the grain harvest. These local factors nevertheless all revolve around Egypt's importance to the larger Mediterranean grain trade and tribute network. The abundance of grain enjoyed by the agrarian regions of Egypt – the Nile Delta, the Nile Valley and the Fayyum – was cleverly exploited for bullion through the workings of the closed currency system.[73] All foreign coins – and Roman coins were treated as foreign – were exchanged for Egyptian coins, providing a net inflow of precious metal to Egypt. Simply put: grain went out, silver and gold came in. Some quantity of precious metal also entered the province through the luxury trade.[74] While the amounts of this trade are difficult

71 The relationship between debasements and hoarding is discussed throughout Chapter 6.

72 Rathbone (1996a), 326.

73 Summarized with references in Lorber (2012), 212–3.

74 Strabo 17.1.7–31, for example, was impressed by the level of trade in the early first century AD.

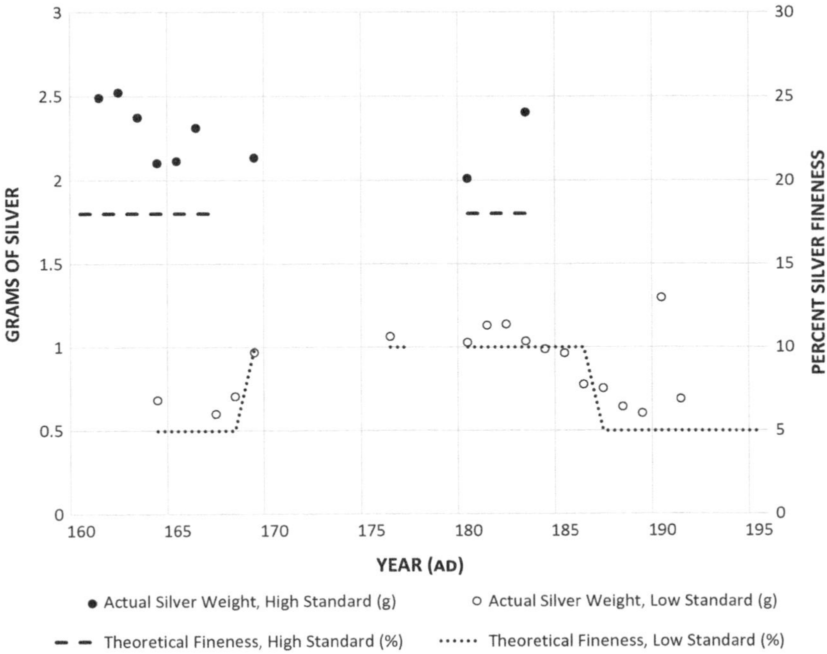

Fig. 5.3 Egyptian *tetradrachm* silver fineness and weight, AD 160–195. Elliott (forthcoming). Raw data from Howgego, Butcher and Ponting (forthcoming).

to quantify, most scholars suspect that they were certainly orders of magnitude smaller than the precious metals imported via the grain trade.[75]

The closed currency system ensured that Egyptian grain was ultimately purchased with *tetradrachms* (whether in physical form or by accounting convention) rather than imperial *denarii*. Did any changes in the *tetradrachm* occur during the second or third centuries AD? An as yet unpublished paper by Howgego, Butcher and Ponting provides weight and fineness figures for the *tetradrachm* in the middle and late second century.[76] I have compiled these data into Figure 5.3; its initial impenetrability perhaps fittingly reflects the confusing behavior of the Alexandrian mint during the AD 160s through 190s.

[75] Tchernia (2016), 48–50; Rathbone (2007), 710–11; Young (2001), 47–71; Greene (1990), 29.
[76] Howgego, Butcher and Ponting (forthcoming).

Through AD 166/7, most *tetradrachms* were produced at a standard similar to the one used as early as Nero's reform, with the fineness levels of individual coins falling between 12 and 20 percent. The average weight of silver in each of these *tetradrachms* was around 2.3 grams. After 166/7 most but not all *tetradrachms* were produced on a much lower standard which seems to have been initially set around 4 to 5 percent fineness (based upon a single coin, however) in 164/5 before improving to 8 to 10 percent fineness. Then, under Commodus, the standard declined incrementally back down to near the 5 percent benchmark. As late as 183/4, it appears that at least a small number of *tetradrachms* were produced on the old, higher standard. In addition, there is a noteworthy gap in production across most of the 170s, although coins were again minted during a single year (176/7). Howgego et al. offer a few reasonable and not mutually exclusive explanations for the odd activities of the Alexandrian mint during this period. Different workshops may have used different standards, old coins may have been reminted using new dies without changes to the standard or perhaps the mint experimented with depletion surface silvering, testing the low threshold for the metallurgical technique, which was at or just below 10 percent fineness.[77] Either way, it was impossible for ancient mint workers to preserve a silver appearance on the surface of alloyed coins with such low silver fineness.

Unmodified quantity theory can explain some of what occurs in the numismatic record. Does the substantial and easily perceptible drop in the silver content from the AD 160s through 190s, for instance, represent a quantitative increase in the money supply which triggered price inflation according to quantity theory's tautological logic? Christiansen, along with numismatist Joseph Milne before him, guessed that it did.[78] If we arbitrarily assume for illustrative purposes only that the Alexandrian mint used the same amount of silver to mint coins in 167/8 as was available the year before, the reduced standard would have allowed the mint to as much as quadruple coin production over the previous year. If something like this happened in all four years of the reduced standard prior to the minting hiatus which began in 170 – and again, this is merely a speculative exercise – then the long gap in production during the 170s is benignly explained by full monetization; no coins were needed, so the mint did not produce them. In this scenario, the stand-alone issue of 176/7 represents a shot in the arm – perhaps to compensate for coin loss – which carried the monetary system through to the resumption of regular minting on the new

[77] Beck et al. (2004); Scott (2011), 37.

[78] Milne (1971), xxii. Contra Rathbone (1996a), 328.

standard in the 180s. A hypothetical-deductive use of quantity theory thus offers historians a ready-made narrative into which selective pieces of evidence can be inserted – a methodological shortcut which, although superficially attractive, is nevertheless deeply problematic. Unstated in the explanation above, but nevertheless present, is the (assumed!) idea that the Alexandrian mint both had the necessary information and financial motivation to plan and execute a benevolent market-friendly monetary policy. Rathbone's 1996 piece rightly affirmed, however, that 'monetarist theory' tends to oversimplify rather than clarify; the analysis should therefore go further.[79]

Scheidel's aforementioned *AJN* article brought up the crucial issue of money *quality*. The quantity theory of money, because of the supposed proportional relationship between money supply and prices, ignores the issue of money quality. The same can be said of the chartalist paradigm, but for different reasons: the power of the state's fiat declarations of value and the state's consistent acceptance of whatever object(s) the state deems as money in tax payments is supposed to be sufficient to override any alternative value preferences among money-users – including preferences based upon money quality.[80] Metallist viewpoints, by contrast, attach meaning to the quality of money because it may affect the value preferences of individual money-users.[81] Metallists would tend to ask, for example, whether *tetradrachm* debasements under Marcus and Commodus were obvious to coin-users and whether coin-users cared about such changes. Christiansen, for example, was firmly convinced that the change was "quite evident to everyone ... anyone ... can tell the difference."[82] The new *tetradrachms*, lacking a silver-enriched surface, took on a noticeable brown hue. From the point of view of those who used the coinage to buy and sell grain, it must have appeared as though copper coins had replaced silver ones. The debased coins are also measurably thinner, wider and lighter; anyone holding the coins in hand could discern that a major change in standards had occurred.[83] Whether there were more, less or the same amount of coins in aggregate floating around in Egypt seems less important at the level of the individual coin-user. It is more meaningful to ask whether such an obvious alteration in quality prompted grain

[79] Rathbone (1996a), 322.

[80] Semi-chartalist or otherwise hybrid approaches include Bransbourg (2011); Bransbourg (2013); Katsari (2011), 244–53; Haklai-Rotenberg (2011). Chartalist or chartalism-dominant: Lo Cascio (1996); Rathbone (1996a); Rathbone (2009).

[81] Elliott (2014); Scheidel (2010b). [82] Christiansen (2004), 108.

[83] Howgego, Butcher and Ponting (forthcoming), 10, esp. fig. 2.

merchants to charge more for purchases made in the new 'copper' coins as opposed to the older 'silver' *tetradrachms*. Another, related question: did the change in the appearance of physical coins affect the way that coin-users used the *tetradrachm* as a unit of account?

To understand coin-users' reactions to the altered Egyptian currency standards, I again wish to emphasize the local nature of both the numismatic and papyrological sources. The Egyptian context and its unique social, cultural, economic and even geographic features bounded the means–ends choices of local coin-users. Christiansen's careful die studies, for example, reveal that the Alexandrian mint adhered to a discernable seasonal pattern when it came to coin production. *Tetradrachms* were minted in higher numbers in late spring and early summer – the period during which grain ships arrived in Egypt (after the winter lull in the sailing season) and merchants exchanged their foreign coin for Egyptian *tetradrachms* in order to purchase grain stored over the winter. This schedule allowed ships to load their cargoes and finish the trip to Rome, which took two to three months (because of contrary winds and a long route along the northern coastline), before the end of the sailing season in September or October.[84] The metal supplies of the Alexandrian mint were firmly hitched to the grain harvest; in fact, more specifically, new supplies of bullion depended upon the presence of surplus grain for private sales after the imperial and local authorities had taken their cut in taxes and tribute. In bad years, such as 184/5, when a tax account records a nearly 75 percent shortfall against the expected grain tribute from the meris of Herakleides (an administrative division of the Arsinoite nome), it seems as though there may have been little or no grain left over for private purchases.[85]

Until very recently there was no reliable way to assess the health of Egyptian grain harvests. Recent studies – many of them using paleo-climatological proxies – have now shown, however, that a rash of local problems afflicted Egypt beginning as early as the AD 150s. Some of these were simple acts of God: volcanoes, Pacific Ocean cooling and Ethiopian droughts produced bad harvests and perhaps some related outbreaks of disease, malnutrition and depopulation.[86] Although these natural factors certainly represent a deviation from norms over the previous few centuries, they were neither catastrophic nor necessarily insurmountable. The inflexibility of state grain prices, the practice of *adaeratio* in Egypt and the

[84] Greene (1990), 28–9; Erdkamp (2005), 191–2.

[85] *P. Oxy* 66.4527. Commentary in Bagnall (2000); van Minnen (2001).

[86] Elliott (2016).

Roman state's regulation of grain shipments, however, magnified the damage caused by nature.[87] Violence too, in the form of the *Boukoloi* revolt, disrupted the Nile Delta.[88] In summary, the 160s through 190s witnessed difficult conditions for grain production and, hence, for the importation of precious metals into Egypt. The reduced quality of *tetradrachms* seemingly reflects these conditions. Consequently, the mint reduced the quality of *tetradrachms* to the point that their appearance suffered in ways that were apparent to coin-users. So now we must ask: did individual coin-users value coins of lower quality differently than coins of higher quality?

Coin Quality and Value

Above, I argue that the *tetradrachm* debasement of the mid-to-late second century – a debasement which reduced the silver content of the denomination by more than half and which also correlated with a doubling of wheat prices (and perhaps other prices) – was obvious to coin-users. I stopped just short of saying that coin-users valued coins in correlation to their quality. Naïve metallism assumes that such a relationship is automatic when, in fact, it is a question of meaning and understanding. The presence of certain 'external' conditions (i.e. the mere fact that coin debasements were obvious) is insufficient to prove the presence of an 'internal' cognitive process. The value preferences of coin-users are a matter of *Verstehen*. After Weber, therefore, I think of this relationship as an ideal-typical 'metallist mode': a disposition among coin-users in which a significant part of the value they place upon coins is correlated to the value they place upon the materials which make up (or which they believe make up) the physical coins they use in exchange.[89] As an ideal type, this metallist mode would be shared by many (but not necessarily all) coin-users. I will compare this ideal type to the purposeful actions taken by coin-users – not to confirm or falsify the ideal type against experience, but to better understand coin-users' preferences and the embedding contexts which governed their actions. Some guiding questions are useful for identifying the purposeful actions of Roman coin-users. Is there evidence that coin-users discerned

[87] Elliott (forthcoming). [88] Alston (1999); Blouin (2010).

[89] The term 'metallist mentality' appears in Butcher and Ponting (2009), 567. It denotes a tendency among emperors (specifically) to uses as much silver in *denarii* as possible because they were "concerned about the nobility of their coinage." I have expanded this concept to include coin-users as well as coin-producers.

between coins of different quality? If coin-users evaluated coin quality and showed preferences, how prevalent was such discernment?

The evidence is sparse, but there is enough of it to gain some perspective on the sorts of views held by some segments of the coin-using population in certain geographic areas and certain social contexts of the Roman world. A few literary sources from the second century AD make points about rhetoric or philosophy by drawing upon the practice of coin discrimination, such as a letter of AD 163 from Marcus Fronto to his former student (and then emperor) Marcus Aurelius. Fronto advises Marcus to stick to older-style rhetoric in the same way that he (Fronto) picks out older higher-fineness *denarii* instead of the more recently minted *denarii* of "lead and debased metal."[90] The practice of discerning between coins also shows up in Arrian's *Discourses of Epictetus.* The text speaks of judging "the marks in [a man's] mind with which he came into the world, such as we seek also on coins, and if we find them, we approve of the coins, and if we do not find the marks, we reject them."[91] Trajan's coins, according to the philosopher, should be kept while Nero's should be thrown away. In order to clarify their arguments about non-economic matters, both Fronto and Arrian use coin discernment as though it were a common practice.[92]

As for Nero's silver *denarii*, surface enrichment hid the coin's debased substance.[93] Often, however, the Roman mint was hesitant to push the limits of public trust by sudden or severe changes to currency standards over the first two centuries of the Principate. Minot officials certainly acted as if a metallist disposition was not only present among coin-users, but dominated coin-users' value preferences. Why, after all, would the state mint costly precious-metal coins, as well as invest large amounts of time and technology to give coins the appearance of precious-metal content, if coin quality was irrelevant? Also, inhabitants of the Roman world could and perhaps did exchange gold and silver bullion for coins, and they certainly used bullion as a store of value.[94]

It may also be possible to use hoard evidence to understand coin-users' mentalities, but there are some obstacles. Even the experts struggle to understand and systematically categorize the intentions behind specific hoards.[95] Numismatists have been aware for some time, for example, that

90 Fronto, *de Orationibus* 17.10–18.6. 91 Arr. *Epict. diss.* 4.5.
92 As did Aristophanes, see Ar. *Frogs* 719–735.
93 Butcher and Ponting (2009), 567; Butcher and Ponting (2015b), 23; Elliott (2014).
94 Verboven (2002), 80. Contra Harris (2006). 95 Christiansen (2004), 15–6.

the hoard evidence from the first two centuries of the Principate shows at best a mixture of motives; some hoarders appear to have preferred finer coins over debased ones, but others did not.[96] Third-century AD coin-hoarders, on the other hand, seem to have been more selective about the coins they held back.[97] Although more precise metallurgical analyses of third-century coins are still yet to come, the pace and severity of debasements during this period increased markedly from that shown in the first two centuries AD. Only a little evidence hints at whether coin-users noticed and cared about these more pronounced debasements.

Scheidel, rightly I believe, assumes as a "null hypothesis" that precious-metal content was central to coin-users' valuation and acceptance of Roman money – even in the third century AD.[98] Many scholars, however, following Jean-Pierre Callu, think of the third-century as "une période de fiduciarité."[99] The debased billon *antoninianus* has been called an "effective ... token coinage," and a seminal article on the Aurelianic currency reform declares that "trust in the currency, although in decline due to the steep debasement, was by no means lost."[100] Statements such as these are bolstered by the seeming stability of the aforementioned Egyptian prices during a period of punctuated coinage debasement – although, in addition to Scheidel's logical argument, there is, as I discussed in the previous section, some empirical evidence which complements his case against a chartalist view of Roman money. Ultimately, this evidence only offers limited hints at coin-users' motives.

One piece of evidence – a well-known and much-debated papyrus dated to early AD 260s Oxyrhynchus – provides a tentative basis for arguing that coin-users may have discerned between coins of different quality. The papyrus reveals that professional banks in the city refused official currency for exchange and many banks had in fact ceased to operate:

> the public officials have assembled and have accused the bankers of the exchange banks of having closed them because of their unwillingness to accept the divine coin of the emperors, it has become necessary to issue an order to all the owners of the banks to open them and to accept and exchange all coin except the absolutely spurious and counterfeit – and not alone to them but to those who engage in business transactions of any kind whatever – knowing full well that if they disobey this order they

96 Bolin (1958), 78–86; Duncan-Jones (1994), 102; Butcher and Ponting (2015a), 449–56.

97 Bland (1996), 76–7; Verboven (2007), 249–51. Others have wondered whether third-century AD hoards show state-led recall and reminting; see Duncan-Jones (1994), 102.

98 Scheidel (2010b), 97. 99 Callu (1969), 186.

100 Ando (2008), 45; Haklai-Rotenberg (2011), 9.

> will experience the penalties which the magnificence of the prefect has imposed upon them even before this.[101]

By "closed," the document may mean that banks either went out of business or even moved into the unofficialdom of shadow banking. Some scholars surmise that the closures were a temporary measure during the political crisis perpetuated by the Persian capture of Valerian and the usurpations of Macrianus and Quietus.[102] A political cause for this specific law seems possible, but is by no means certain. The new *tetradrachms* of the Macriani were a full gram heavier (at 11.01 grams) than the average of those issued under Valerian just before his coinage ceased to be struck (10.01 grams).[103] Money-changers who rejected the coins of the Macriani would be getting a bad deal. At the same time, the average weight standard of the new coins is about a quarter-gram below Valerian's final full issue (11.28 g), which presumably had greater representation in the circulation pool.[104] Therefore, the specific cause behind banks' rejection of coins is likely to remain unclear to scholars. What the document does show – and this cannot be questioned – is that currency specialists could and did refuse to accept official coinage, and this in spite of the decree's stated penalties as well as the pre-existing penalties also referenced in the papyrus.

Around the same time money-changers closed their shops in the city of Oxyrhynchus, private contracts from this city and others in Egypt show some perplexing behavior by currency-users. In the mid-third century, individuals distinguished 'Ptolemaic' or 'old Ptolemaic' coinage from 'new', 'new silver' or coins 'of the Augusti'.[105] There is no consensus as to what these terms mean, nor are there any obvious causes behind the change in terminology – but the distinctions persist in documents until the AD 290s.[106] The distinctions may not have meant much in practice, as a late papyrus (AD 289) specifies that a loan of 1,000 "Ptolemaic silver *drachms*" was paid with an installment of 1,000 "new silver *drachms*."[107] This single papyrus, however, does not necessarily indicate that all such coin terms were synonyms. Scholars have put forward several competing scenarios to explain the behavior. Was coinage difficult to obtain at this time, prompting those who had access to privately hoarded older coins to put them into circulation? Do the terms simply show coin-users' fear of future revaluations or even "general chaos"?[108] It is difficult not to see

[101] *P. Oxy.* 12.1411.
[102] Legutko (2002); Christiansen (2004), 116; Harl (2006), 143; Callu (1969), 186–8.
[103] Bowman (1986), 92. [104] Legutko (2002), 136–7. [105] Callu (1969), 186–93.
[106] Christiansen (1984). [107] *P. Oxy.* 2587. [108] After Rathbone (1996a), 336–8.

parallels in the mendacious *Historia Augusta*'s discerning valuations of various third-century AD coins, mostly *aurei*, based upon the emperor who issued them – an echo of earlier and more reliable sentiments of Fronto and Arrian.[109] Another explanation for conventional names for mid-third century coins is that they served to indicate change in standards – whether in terms of coin weight, fineness, face value or some combination thereof – within the same denomination.[110]

Finally, roughly contemporary with all the evidence already discussed, imperial coins from the mid-third century begin to show mintmarks.[111] This phenomenon may suggest that coin quality was important to coin-users (or at least was perceived to be) even in the case of billon coins. Mint marks indicated the physical locations where coins were minted and even in some cases the particular *officina* (workshop) within a given mint, presenting (although not necessarily providing) some sense of accountability for coinage quality. As the use of mintmarks and the number of imperial mints and *officinae* rose in the third century, the production of provincial coinages declined; some denominations vanish entirely, never to be revived.[112] The wish that Cassius Dio placed in the mouths of Agrippa and Maecenas – that "none of the cities should be allowed to have its own separate coinage or system of weights and measures; they should all be required to use ours" – was realized within a couple generations after Dio wrote.[113] While the specific meanings of individual mintmarks were undoubtedly lost on payees, including soldiers, the functions of the mintmarks was in no small part performative, impressing upon coin-users a sense that the authorities were taking concrete steps to ensure coin quality and centralize the monetary system. A revival of *aequitas* imagery, complete with scales, upon the reverse of many third-century *antoniniani* communicated as much even to coin-users who were illiterate. For those who could understand the mintmarks, the image of *aequitas* reinforced the mint's sacred duty to provide accurate weights and measures.[114] Still, such performative claims do not automatically indicate a working fiduciary monetary system that enjoyed unquestioning public trust. It is no coincidence that images and marks of quality control appear on coins at roughly the same time as laws against 'unofficial' money-changing, laws

[109] SHA *Claud.* 14.3, 17.7; *Aurel.* 9.7, 12.1; *Prob.* 4.5; *Firm.* 15.8. See Harl (1996), 133.
[110] See Chapter 6, pp. 151–5. [111] Abdy (2012), 501. [112] Callu (1969), 147–287.
[113] Words which Dio placed in the mouths of Agrippa and Maecenas. See Dio Cass. 52.30.9.
[114] Manders (2012), 161.

commanding acceptance of imperial coin, rapid changes in coinage standards and evidence of currency confusion in marketplaces.[115]

Ultimately, the limits of the evidence make it difficult to know exactly *how* coin-users factored coin quality into their overall valuation of coinage, but that they *did* seems a reasonable conclusion. Some coin-users clearly not only noticed differences in coins, but, at times, they acted upon those differences. Nevertheless, a metallist mode was unlikely to have been ubiquitous among coin-users in the Roman world – this is why it carries ideal-typical rather than *a priori* status. At the same time, precious metal seems to have affected patterns of coin use among some users; certainly, the perception of such discernment seems to have influenced the monetary decisions of minting authorities. What remains unclear is how these contextual elements, which bounded the means–ends rationality of coin-users, influenced their purposeful actions. It is probably not the case, for example, that minor changes in coin quality triggered automatic and proportional hoarding/spending behaviors. Clearly, however, neither did coin-users altogether ignore coin quality. So while it is possible to construct an ideal-typical metallist mode from limited empirical evidence and even to then apply it back onto the evidence, it is also possible, using many of this same evidence, to undermine the ideal type. In the next chapter, I use the monetary theory known as Gresham's law to overcome this impasse.

Conclusions

The assumptions built into the quantity theory of money severely limit its usefulness for studying the Roman monetary system if not all pre-industrial monetary systems. Quantity theory may help historians theorize about the relationships between certain macroeconomic elements of a monetary system, but the theory fails to account for the complexity and disaggregated nature of the Roman monetary economy. Neither the Fisher equation nor the Cambridge equation provides historians with sufficient material for understanding purposeful actions of coin-users.

An approach that disaggregates the workings of the monetary system by considering the spatial and temporal properties of money, both money quantity and quality and, finally, money's value as a product of the subjective preferences of individuals may be of more use to historians. The anti-historical construct of money neutrality certainly cannot be

[115] See Chapter 6, pp. 166–70.

assumed. Instead, Roman economic historians can and should examine the specific social, economic and political channels through which money entered the Roman economy. Depending upon the location of these channels, both socially and geographically, as well as the volume of money distributed through them, it may be possible to understand the human responses to money supply changes in the Roman world as well as the wider systemic effects of these changes – effects which not only include price movements and the shifts in the structure of production but also realignments in social hierarchies.

There are many ways historians might seek to understand the value preferences of Roman coin-users, but in this chapter I propose that an ideal-typical metallist mode may help historians perform a more generalized analysis. At this point, I have merely defined the scope of the ideal type and suggested, from limited evidence, its relevance to Roman money-users. To explain the actions of money-users, monetary historians typically rely upon Gresham's law.[116] In the book's final chapter, I refine this metallist mode further in light of a version of Gresham's law that accounts for purposeful action and draws upon counterfactual comparisons in order to understand both the Roman monetary system as well as the values of those who participated in it.

[116] Temin (2012b), 3.

CHAPTER 6

Understanding Money Use and Value

> A coin was a coin. More than that, who could say? – looking at some botched, anomalous, trashy bit of metal in the hand, the work of an emperor, it might be, or of a pretender, or of a counterfeiter. How much was it worth, apparently anyone could declare, or try to declare, by putting a mark on it. That was one lesson learned by everyone. But would the tariff be observed in daily buying and selling? Apparently not. That was a second lesson even more thoroughly driven home. Before the economy could ultimately regain its health, economic man would require a long-drawn-out reeducation.
>
> Ramsay MacMullen[1]

In order to understand the behavior of coin-users, historians of Roman money typically look to numismatic evidence – hoards and stray coin finds – as well as to the few inscriptions and literary passages which give impressions of how Romans thought about and valued the money they used. To make better sense of the evidence, monetary historians sometimes deploy the economic proposition known as Gresham's law. While Gresham's law is routinely summarized as 'bad money drives out good', some crucial *a posteriori* conditions must be assumed for the 'law' to work.[2] There must be 'bad' money. 'Bad' money is *overvalued* money: money for which the fiduciary value is higher than the value of its constituent materials (usually precious metal) in marketplace transactions. Overvalued money is typically a creature of the state – most commonly when the state guarantees the value of money by accepting it for tax payments or by enforcement of legal tender laws in transactions. Gresham's law, therefore, ultimately describes money-users' collective response to the state's price controls on money.[3] When two or more circulating currencies are given the same legal value by the state but their precious-metal values are

[1] MacMullen (1976), 113. [2] Duncan-Jones (1994), 102.

[3] Selgin (1996). Selgin reasserts and amplifies a point made earlier by Hayek (1990), 41–3. For the Roman world see Verboven (2007), 251. Contra Collingwood (1926), 182.

unequal, the currency with the lower precious-metal value (the overvalued 'bad' money) will, over time, 'drive out' the currency with the higher (the undervalued 'good' money).[4] Thus, the operation of Gresham's law assumes both a heterogeneous money supply as well as some form of effective legal tender laws.

Gresham's law is often used to explain coin-users' behavior in bimetallic monetary systems, but the main principles of Gresham's law are easily illustrated using a single denomination such as the Roman silver *denarius*.[5] If coin-users have access to a heterogeneous stock of circulating *denarii* at different fineness standards – say one standard at roughly 68percent silver (the standard under Commodus) and another of, say, 45 percent silver (the standard under Septimius from AD 194 onward) – but the state declares that Septimius' *denarii* are equal in value to Commodus' *denarii*, then some coin-users may purposefully use Septimius' *denarii* for purchases and hold back the legally undervalued *denarii* of Commodus. Whereas both coins are equally able to buy one *denarius* worth of goods or services, they are unequal in terms of their commodity value, despite their legal equality. If this difference in commodity value is enough to make Commodus' *denarii* or the material of which they are made more useful for some purpose other than monetary exchange (e.g. as savings, as bullion, as jewelry etc.) at the legal value of one *denarius*, some coin-users may effectively 'demonetize' their undervalued *denarii* – trading exchange-value for use-value. Over time, the cumulative effect of such actions is that overvalued coins will come to dominate the coin supply whereas undervalued coins will disappear from it.

The simple scenario above hints at the subsidiary assumptions Gresham's law makes about both 'internal' rationality as well as 'external' market conditions – assumptions which historians must not import into their narratives unexamined. The observation that gold *aurei* were hoarded during the mid-third century AD, for example, does not automatically prove that *aurei* were 'good' money or even that Gresham's law operated at all. Connecting empirical observations to the logic of Gresham's law requires historians to first investigate the law's constituent assumptions. The counterfactual logic of Gresham's law itself tells historians what to look for. Mises, for example, argued that if the expected results of Gresham's law do not appear in a historical instance, it is because the

4 See also the excellent summary of Aubert (2003), 260.

5 A concise illustration of the operation of Gresham's law under bimetallism is found in Temin (2012b), 2–3. See also Selgin (in press).

conditions that trigger the behavior summarized in Gresham's law were not present:

> If the conditions that Gresham's law assumes are not given, then action such as the law describes does not take place. If the actor does not know the market value differing from the legally controlled value, or if he does not know that he may make his payments in money that is valued lower by the market, or if he has another reason for giving the creditor more than is due him – for example, because he wants to give him a present, or because he fears violent acts on the part of the creditor – then the assumptions of the law do not apply. Experience teaches that for the mass of debtor–creditor relationships these assumptions do apply. But even if experience were to show that the assumed conditions are not given in the majority of cases, this could in no way weaken the chain of reasoning that has led to the construction of the law or deprive the law of the importance that is its due.[6]

Gresham's law's *a posteriori* conditions must never be imposed upon Roman monetary history; rather, Gresham's law should be used heuristically and counterfactually to frame the questions asked in historical investigations. What if strictly enforced legal tender laws were/were not in place in parts of the Roman Empire? Were inequalities between the legal value of coins and the bullion value of coins noticeable and significant? Did coin-users value the difference in content in the first place?[7] This chapter explores ways in which an ideal-typical version of Gresham's law – one which accounts for purposefulness – can be used to help identify and explore such questions. With such modifications, Gresham's law provides insights into both the thought processes of those who used Roman coins and the institutional structure of the Roman monetary system.

Gresham's Rationality: Some Methodological Implications

Unfortunately, economists and even historians rarely scrutinize the core 'internal' assumption of Gresham's law: that coin-users are always and everywhere economically rational.[8] In his dissection of Gresham's law, Weber did economists and historians a great service by identifying the form of rationality embedded in Gresham's law as well as its *a posteriori* epistemological status:

> the generalization called Gresham's law is a rationally clear interpretation of human action under *certain conditions* and under the assumption that it will

6 Mises (1933), 94.
7 An issue which has been debated for some time. See Temin (2001), 174; Crawford (1975), 46.
8 An important exception is Crawford (1983a), 198.

> follow a *purely rational course*. How far any actual course of action corresponds to this can be verified only by the available statistical evidence for the actual disappearance of under-valued monetary units from circulation.[9]

Weber distinguished between 'external' and 'internal' conditions, while also observing that *all* the conditions of Gresham's law are *a posteriori*, including a particular flavor of rationality. Gresham's law, therefore, is not really a 'law', but an ideal type in which the 'choices' of coin-users follow a preprogrammed 'purely rational course'. In Gresham's law, actors 'choose' between coins via an automated and unshakable desire to trade away 'bad' coins and hold back 'good' ones as a form of profit maximization. There is seemingly no freely choosing purposeful action here; instead Gresham's law appears premised upon a form of 'perfect rationality' which, interestingly, operates similarly to instinct, and therefore antonymic to choice.[10] Our hypothetical coin-user cannot help but maximize profit; there exists *no choice* in the matter.

This assumed rationality should bother economic historians much more than it typically has. Perhaps one reason for historians' lack of ire is that Gresham's law has an impressive track record in monetary history. When silver was removed from United States' coinage in the mid-1960s, for example, Gresham's law both describes with near perfection what occurred and also accurately portrays conditions in the monetary system at the time (legal tender laws, low transaction costs, widespread knowledge of the change, coin-users' preference for the older silver coins). Indeed, Roman historians routinely use Gresham's law as an explanatory hypothesis for numismatic evidence, especially coin hoards. If hoards show a mix of 'good' and 'bad' coins, or if stray find evidence (which better represents circulating coin) suggests that coins of different fineness circulated side by side, then Gresham's law is falsified. If Gresham's law's final (predicted) results appear in the hoards – i.e. hoards are full of 'good' money – then the operation of the other parts of the law, including its rationality, are usually assumed.[11] Roman historians thus sometimes find themselves in the Popperian trap: using the same evidence to support opposing conclusions. Pre-reform *denarii* of Septimius, for example, appear in many early third-century *denarius* hoards in high numbers.[12] Gold *aurei*, however,

[9] Weber (1968), 10. Emphasis added.

[10] Mises claimed that there was a purposeful rationality in Gresham's law – a point he never explains. See Mises (1933), 94–6. Mises and Weber, in fact, appear to agree, but Mises may be drawing a contrast because "in his mind, he is still fighting the *Methodenstreit*"; Friedman (1996), 23–4 n. 4.

[11] Temin (2013), 81. [12] Duncan-Jones (2001), 81–2.

rarely appear in hoards from between AD 220 and 275, and of the *aurei* that do appear, many are pierced – presumably because they were mounted in jewelry.[13] Does the evidence confirm that coin-users pulled *aurei* out of circulation because they had higher non-monetary value as objects of prestige?[14] Or is the relative dearth in hoarded gold coins a sign that *aurei* circulated as a better money compared to *denarii*? One way proponents of the latter position might account for the mounted coins which have been found is to claim that these represent only the very best (older, finer, heavier) *aurei.*[15] Historians generally favor the first interpretation, but do they have an inherently *logical* reason to do so? Coin-users and hoarders both inside and outside of the Roman Empire did not always behave as expected. Sture Bolin in the late 1950s, for example, was puzzled: if Gresham's law always and everywhere applied, why did coin finds at Pompeii seem to indicate that coin-users used *denarii* of various weight and fineness standards simultaneously?[16] Duncan-Jones, summarizing the numismatic evidence he surveyed, observes that

> In classical economic theory, Gresham's law, that bad money drives out good, should be triggered by quite small differences in quality. In practice during the first two centuries of the Empire, coins with differing metallic content seem to have gone on circulating on more or less equal terms, unless there was a state initiative to remove the better coin.[17]

What Duncan-Jones intuited was taken further by Butcher and Ponting: nuances in transaction costs and available information may have led Gresham's law to apply in certain situations and geographic regions and not in others.[18] Indeed, a Gresham's law which lacks *a priori* elements – especially purposeful action – would be a poor arbiter of historical interpretations on epistemological grounds, even if it has, to quote Friedman, "survived many opportunities for contradiction."[19]

In the *a posteriori* logic of Gresham's law, *everything* must be assumed; therefore, when it comes to supposed historical operations of Gresham's law, *nothing* should be assumed. Not all the *a posteriori* assumptions in

13 Bland (2013), 266, 274.
14 Estiot (2012), 543–4; Bland (1996), 65; Drinkwater (1987), 157 n. 45. Connecting this directly to Gresham's law is Katsari (2011), 92.
15 Verboven (2007), 249. 16 Bolin (1958), 78–86. 17 Duncan-Jones (1994), 102.
18 One refreshing example is Butcher and Ponting (2015a), 48–52, 447–56.
19 Friedman (1953), 8–9.

Gresham's law, however, are equal. Weber's observations above hint at a difference between 'internal' and 'external' conditions – categories which recall Collingwood's use of methodological dualism. The value-judgments of the coin-user, which would normally be predicated upon choice, can be thought of as 'internal' because they take place inside the mind of the actor – an actor disposed toward the kind of ideal-typical metallist mode described in the previous chapter. Conversely, the 'external' elements are the market conditions, legal tender regimes and so on which create 'good' and 'bad' money in the first place – the ecological stimuli which trigger the 'internal' response in actors. Should historians accept the 'internal' conditions of Gresham's law as given and direct their investigation toward finding empirical evidence that confirms that the necessary 'external' conditions were present? How might historians harness the power of Gresham's Law without begging the most interesting historical question: what did money-users value and why?

Gresham's law places strong restraints upon human choice, but there is still room for purposefulness in the theory as it applies to history. The law's operation in monetary history in fact accommodates a diversity of means–ends values among coin-users. Unlike economic theories that assume a mapped rationality in which *all* actors are required to pursue profit relentlessly, Gresham's law is different: it ultimately describes the *systemic consequences* when *some* users hold and act upon what I described in the previous chapter as an ideal-typical 'metallist mode'. In the case of coin-users in the Roman world, for example: perhaps only a fraction of the coin-using population was sensitive to the precious-metal content of coins. The size and influence of this group, however, would merely affect the speed at which bad money presumably drove out good money. As long as some users acted roughly consistent with the metallist mode whenever the 'external' conditions of Gresham's law were also present, then the composition of the money supply would have changed eventually. Under the logic of Gresham's law, Roman monetary historians, therefore, are not required to assume that *all* coin-users perfectly followed a mapped rationality; they need merely investigate, as was done in the previous chapter, whether *enough* coin-users over the course of innumerable monetized transactions showed preferences for the 'good' money and spent the 'bad' money.

Only modest changes, therefore, are needed to make the 'internal' conditions of Gresham's law unmapped. Gresham's Law can indeed help monetary historians investigate intersections between coin-user's 'internal' values and changes in 'external' elements of the monetary system such as the heterogeneity of money (e.g. coins of different metals or fineness), and the homogeneity of currency values (e.g. laws, rules or customs which effectively require coin-users to accept all coins at face value). Such an investigation is complex, so in this chapter I draw upon several case studies in a roughly chronological order. First, focusing mostly on the first two centuries of the Roman monetary system, I examine the issue of homogenous currency values (i.e. nominal values or legal tender laws). Part of this investigation involves asking to what extent legal coin values were effective during this period. It also involves observing some of the purposeful actions of coin-users to better understand their conception of state declarations of coin value. The section that follows introduces the element of monetary heterogeneity to help account for changes in the effectiveness of legal value, especially by the late second century AD. Were differences between circulating and newly debased coins noticeable or measurable? Did debasements draw out metallist impulses in some coin-users?[20] How did coin-users react to changing transaction costs and information asymmetries? A final section explores reactions on both the part of coin-users and of reform-minded state officials to an apparently unstable monetary system. These historical questions arise directly from counterfactual comparisons using the bounded logic of Gresham's law. They offer historians useful scaffolding for understanding the Roman monetary system and the choices of coin-users within the system and its embedding contexts.

Assessing the Strength of Legal Value

Economist George Selgin articulates that bad money drives out good "whenever legal-tender laws are used to enforce a 'fixed exchange rate' between two economically distinct monies."[21] There is no doubt that the Roman state declared what coin and bullion values were meant to be at several points in time – what Scheidel pithily calls "a strong belief in – or at least a desperate hope for – nominal acquiescence."[22] It is another argument altogether, however – one which requires a great deal of additional speculation and a direct assault upon Occam's razor – to say that the Roman state successfully brought into being the monetary world it appears to have proclaimed. Weber observed that only the modern "rational state" has the kind of monopolistic power over money required to regulate the

[20] Temin (2001), 174; Crawford (1975), 46.
[21] Selgin (1996), 640.
[22] Scheidel (2010b), 97.

value of money.[23] It is a modernistic anachronism to grant the Roman state the same fiat power to declare and enforce legal monetary value as that of modern states. In fact, even in the modern world, legal tender laws do not automatically *prevent* coin-users from discounting 'bad' coins or placing premiums on 'good' coins. It is more accurate to say that such laws make it *costly* (economically, legally, socially) for coin-users to openly assign different values to coins of different quality.[24] In other words, legal tender laws do not dictate the choices of coin-users; instead, such laws present coin-users with costs which may be sufficient to alter their choices compared to those they might take in a counterfactual world in which legal tender laws were absent. By the same reasoning, where legal coin values are redundant, absent, unenforced or at least irregularly enforced, Gresham's law will not operate or will not operate consistently. In fact, the *enforcement* of legal tender laws most influences the purposeful action of coin-users. The mere fiat declarations of the state will have comparably limited influence.

One way to explore the effectiveness of legal monetary values in the Roman Principate is to engage with the scholarship on the behavior and characteristics of officials in the Roman world. Legal texts from the fourth century AD show emperors delegating enforcement of monetary laws to high-level officials.[25] In turn, practical supervision of markets was passed down to local *aediles* or *agoranomoi* – officials who carried out their duties according their personalities, whims and individual interests.[26] In rare cases, communities policed themselves, such as Jews in fourth-century AD Palestine, who were allowed to appoint their own market officials to set and enforce price regulations.[27] Von Reden observes that the main function of such officials, however, was "law and order rather than fair prices."[28] In fact, Roman officials and emperors often show an intense fear – some might even say paranoia – toward unofficial gatherings and private associations, especially in provincial cities.[29] Trajan's own words to Pliny belie the emperor's anxiety that the establishment of a fire brigade in Nicomedia could lead to political insurrection.[30] At the same time, when the Bithynian governor asked to have a guard of imperial soldiers sent to Juliopolis to protect the city from abuses from troops passing through, Trajan rejected the request, indicating that even the *optimus princeps*

23 Weber (1968), 178; Swedberg (2005), 133–4. 24 Selgin (in press).
25 *Cod. Theod.* 9.21.1–23.2. 26 MacMullen (1970). 27 *Cod. Theod.* 16.8.10
28 Von Reden (2010), 135. See also the summary in Andreau (2010), 206–7.
29 Shaw (1981), 47. 30 Plin. *Tra.* 43

tolerated a certain amount of official abuse.[31] The overall impression from the specialists on Roman officialdom is that gaps in enforcement were routine rather than exceptional. A papyrus letter from the early second century AD mentions in passing that the Alexandrian procurator Lucius had been removed from office without a ready replacement.[32] Even when the old procurator was in office, the coin exchange rates mentioned in the letter diverge from the nominal rates (see below). Historians cannot take the mere presence of officials, laws and policies as proof of enforcement or compliance. Similarly, declarations of 'official' values of commodities or currencies do not automatically indicate that such values were always and everywhere in effect.

Studies of officialdom in the Principate reveal "endemic and institutionalized" predation, fraud and abuse of power at all levels of government, including among officials in charge of prices, weights and measures.[33] So long as law and order were preserved, officials otherwise had broad leeway to intentionally abuse their authority for personal gain. An often-cited second-century AD edict from Egypt provides an illustration: "the customs officials have employed fraudulent and cunning tricks against those who are passing through the country . . . demanding what is not owed to them and [they are] detaining those who are in urgent haste, in order that some might pay for a speedier release."[34] In another case from Pergamum, it took special action by Hadrian himself to stop long-standing collusion between an *agoranomos* and the city's money-changers.[35] The official punished groups of clever customers who made bulk purchases with *denarii* to avoid bankers' change fee (*agio*) on bronze to silver exchanges. Hadrian's rescript provided customers with some relief from high change fees, but the emperor also banned the bulk purchases in *denarii* – thus, in essence, affirming and upholding the corrupt actions of the *agoranomos* and his banker partners. Modern readers might categorize such institutionalized predation as exploitative, but even the highest level of Roman governance accepted that collusion and corruption were natural features of the marketplace.[36]

31 Plin. *Tra.* 78.
32 *P. Bad.* 37 (= *P. Sarap.* 90). A date of AD 108 is preferred by Maresch (1996), 179.
33 Bang (2012), 216 n. 59. 34 *P. Princ.* 2.20.
35 *OGIS* 484 (= *IGR* 4.352). The argument that the perpetrators, who are not explicitly named in the inscription, were the monopoly bank is made in Macro (1976). See also Katsari, Lightfoot and Ozme (2012), 29.
36 Bang (2008), 240.

As long as marketplaces were not associated with outright rioting and rebellion, local officials appear to have pursued their duties with dispassionate negligence, avaricious corruption or something in between. Did coin-users in such an environment abide by legally declared coin values? Enough evidence survives to suggest that, yes, they could and did, but perhaps not in all instances. In the late Republic, bronze (and perhaps silver) coins of erratic weights seem to have caused confusion about their value until the *popularis* praetor Gratidianus imposed regulations (their specific nature remains unknown) in 85 BC.[37] Coins may have been discounted and given premiums but both Cicero and Pliny are unclear on this matter.[38] The earliest explicit evidence that Roman coin-users applied premiums to higher-quality precious-metal coins is perhaps found in the aforementioned early second-century letter (*P. Baden* 37). The Alexandrian Heliodorus sent his brother Eutychides a note which records that the exchange rate between "a gold coin" (χρυσοῦς) and "*drachms*" (δραχμῶν) has changed from "fifteen" to "eleven" due to the fact that the prefect Sulpicius had not replaced the outgoing procurator.[39] What is sometimes translated as "gold" (χρυσος) here is in fact "gold/golden coin" (χρυσοῦς) – a likely reference to the Roman *aureus*.[40] Scholars also contest the meaning of "*drachms*" in the papyrus. Some readers wonder whether Heliodorus meant *one hundred* and fifteen and *one hundred* and eleven *drachms*, but "one hundred" is absent for the sake of convention or brevity.[41] If this is true, exchanges between *drachms* and *aurei*, which would have been carried out in billon *tetradrachms* at an official rate of 25:1, must have been supplemented by a surcharge (*agio*) of fifteen *drachms* (which fell to eleven *drachms* in the procurator's absence).[42] Another possibility is that δραχμῶν is shorthand for *tetradrachms* – an abnormal convention which does, however, occasionally appear in other papyri.[43] Such a translation, however, stipulates *tetradrachm* to *aureus* exchange rates of 15:1 and 11:1 – a premium on silver coins which deviates

[37] Hollander (2007), 28–9. [38] Cic. *Off.* 3.80; Plin. *HN* 33.132.

[39] *P. Bad.* 37 (= *P. Sarap.* 90).

[40] The idea that the passage speaks of a purely theoretical *aureus* because "Es war nicht notwendig, für derartige Zahlungen Aurei zu kaufen, zumal diese in Ägypten offensichtlich nicht im Umlauf waren" seems, to me at least, to be problematic in light of the hoard evidence. For this view, see Strobel (2002), 89–92. Convincing and underappreciated (probably because it appeared in Polish) arguments for a circulating *aureus* are found especially in Kunisz (1983). See also Rathbone (1996a), 326; Christiansen (1994), 480; Duncan-Jones (1994), 91; West and Johnson (1944), 70.

[41] Strobel (2002), 91; West and Johnson (1944), 90.

[42] Verboven (2007), 254; Strobel (2002), 89–91; Geissen (2012), 563.

[43] Maresch and Packman (1990), 132; Verboven (2009), 102. Advocates of this view include Schwartz (1961) and Lo Cascio (1981), 78 n. 14.

markedly from the well-attested official ratio of 25:1. Despite the lack of consensus over the exact meaning of "*drachms*," the letter shows flexibility in the value of the *aureus* in Egypt – a hypothesis which, despite a small sample of corroborating evidence, makes sense of this otherwise perplexing document.[44]

Hoard evidence and coin metrology also provide indications that legal values were not ubiquitous in the Roman Empire. New metallurgical studies of Roman gold and silver coinage have provided monetary historians with a reliable, often annualized record of changes in Roman coin standards over time.[45] Ongoing efforts to compare changes in coin standards with patterns in the hoard evidence are yielding preliminary observations about the strength of legal coin values. Such comparisons show, for example, that Nero's substantial reduction in the fineness of the *denarius* prompted some coin-users to treat pre-reform and post-reform coins differently, perhaps valuing the former at a premium.[46] Such discernment seems to be present, as expected, in hoards at the geographic fringes of Roman influence such as in Britain and India. Some hoards found inside the *limes*, however, also give the impression that hoarders preferred pre-reform silver coins – especially those minted in Lugdunum, which produced finer *denarii* than those of other mints, especially at Rome.[47] Pre-reform coins nevertheless continued to circulate, suggesting to Butcher and Ponting the existence of ad hoc premiums on older coins of higher fineness.[48]

One benefit of standardized precious-metal money is its convenience – that coins can be counted rather than weighed. Flexible coin values, therefore, required coherent conventions to ensure that currencies with premiums retained exchange-value. Coin-users might, for example, use the emperor's image on a coin's obverse as a convenient way to assign (perhaps even negotiate?) coin value. If the notoriously problematic *Historia Augusta* can be believed on this matter, third-century AD coin-users compensated for erratic *aureus* standards by naming coins after the emperor on the obverse (e.g. *philippei* or *valeriani* – names which appear side-by-side in

44 Howgego (1995), 142 n. 2; Howgego (1992), 11. A variation of this argument where currency floats via variable exchange commissions is in Verboven (2007), 254.

45 The literature is growing and so I mention only a few examples: Howgego, Butcher and Ponting (forthcoming); Butcher and Ponting (2015a); Butcher and Ponting (2012); Butcher and Ponting (2009); Rodrigues et al. (2011); Woytek (2008); Woytek et al. (2007); Butcher, Ponting and Chandler (1997).

46 Butcher and Ponting (2009), 561. The reform also included many of the provincial coinages as well; see Burnett (2005a), 272–5.

47 Turner (2016), 33–4, 42; Hunter (2007).

48 Butcher and Ponting (2015a), 26–7, 37, 49–50, 449–50, 692–3.

the text instead of *aurei*) and exchanged them at separate rates.[49] Surviving mid-third-century inscriptions that give higher values for gold *aurei* than the official ratio of one *aureus* to twenty-five Alexandrian *tetradrachmae* suggest that the *Historia Augusta* may accurately represent coin-user's behavior.[50] It is true that these inscriptions originate in Nubia, and hence come from just outside the often porous Roman borders.[51] Due to the presence of well-used trade routes, however, some Nubian urban centers were well-connected to the Roman Empire, even more so than many rural zones within the Roman *limes*. In the previous chapter, I referenced some of the evidence for variable values for precious-metal currency.[52] Arrian used the imperial portrait to determine which coins were to be kept and which were to be "thrown away."[53] The aforementioned letter of Fronto references similar conventions, and it is worth quoting the relevant passage in full here:

> Cleave to the old coinage. Coins of lead and debased metal of all sorts are more common in our recent issues than in the archaic ones which are stamped with the names of Perperna or Trebanius. What then? Am I not to prefer for myself a coin of Antoninus or Verus or Pius? Those old words are stained and contaminated and discoloured and spotted, aye, more spotted than a nurse's apron. There is need, therefore, of all your pains to render your language, if possible, current coin; be ever on the look-out for some word, not one coined by you, for that, indeed, is an absurdity, but used by you more elegantly or more aptly or more happily than by others.[54]

This passage has much to offer Roman historians, but for my purposes here, it shows that Fronto summarizes coin quality by referring to the mark of the issuing authority, whether the emperor's name/head or the republican moneyer's name/mark.[55] Fronto tells the emperor that he should prefer established rhetoric in the same way that Fronto prefers Republican *denarii* to those 'debased' coins minted in the past couple of decades (including under Marcus himself!).

It is difficult to imagine that coin-users kept a running list of coin values based upon issuing emperors and republican moneyers. If standards had

49 SHA *Aurel.* 9.7, 12.1, *Prob.* 4.5, *Clod.* 14.3, 17.7 and *Firm* et al. 15.8.

50 *CIG* 5008, 5010. The exact numbers are unclear. Some have suggested 125 and 175 *drachmae*: Harl (1996), 133–4. Forty-four *tetradrachms* is another interpretation: Lo Cascio (1984), 157. Unsure is Howgego (1995), 142 n. 2. I reproduce the most cautious interpretation (we cannot say) and hence use 'higher' after Rathbone (1996a), 324 n. 12. See additional discussion in Scheidel (2010b), 104–5; Ehling (2008), 853.

51 Whittaker (1994), 201.

52 See also the evidence discussed in Wolters (1999), 371–4.

53 Arr. *Epict. diss.* 4.5.

54 Fronto, *de Orationibus* 17.10–18.6.

55 Additional thoughts on this passage in Duncan-Jones (2005), 464; Yarrow (2012), 452.

changed only after a long period of stability, it might have been easier to refer merely to 'old' and 'new' coins in some fashion. There is evidence of such conventions in Egyptian papyri from two periods: between Roman annexation and the reign of Nero as well as the mid-to-late third century AD.[56] Hoard evidence from the earlier period suggests that Ptolemaic *tetradrachms* and the first Roman *tetradrachms* (issued by Tiberius from AD 20) circulated side-by-side, despite different weights of silver.[57] Other references to such conventions, such as the one made by the caravan chief who set up a statue in Palmyra at a cost of 300 "old" *aurei* (χρυσᾶ παλαιὰ δηνάρια) in AD 193, may or may not refer to such behavior.[58]

Even if coin-users sometimes used premiums and had conventions to do so, could such defiance of legal values take place openly and regularly? The problem, of course, is that functioning black or gray markets by nature leave few traces of their existence. Duncan-Jones suspects that "black market currency dealing is clearly implied," for example, in an imperial decree which reinforces the currency exchange monopoly in Mylasa in AD 210.[59] An even later source – an invective penned by the emperor Julian against the city of Antioch – tells of how even the physical presence of the emperor did not dissuade "rich men" from subverting Julian's price controls and "secretly selling wheat in the country for an exaggerated price."[60] Rural transactions were only supervised on officially permitted "market days" (*nundinae*), if at all.[61] Whether or not the countryside was under-monetized and under-marketized, it was under-regulated. The combination of predation, corruption and/or indifference among supervisory officials, along with the general lack of bureaucracy, allowed seasoned merchants and customers plenty of leeway to use and value coins as they wished.

Another explanation for limited evidence of coin premiums is that coins only floated in value under limited circumstances, such as when the coinage stock was in transition from one standard to another (and thus we see yet another way temporality disaggregates money supply). The regularity of stable currency standards, especially during the first two centuries of the Principate, encouraged coin-users to treat the stock of precious-metal coinage as homogenous. Nero's debasement, for example,

[56] Christiansen (1984); Callu (1969), 186–93. [57] Christiansen (1984), 296. [58] *CIS* 3948.

[59] Duncan-Jones (1994), 219. An argument which has been expanded; see Katsari (2011), 147–51; Elliott (2014).

[60] Julian *Mis.* 368a–370d. See also Amm. Marc. 22.12–14 and other sources mentioned in Wiemer (1995), 269ff.

[61] MacMullen (1970).

may have been a temporary shock to the system, but after some variation in *denarius* weight and fineness over the following decades, minters from near the beginning of Trajan's reign through the 150s produced coins at or near enough to Nero's *denarius* weight and fineness.[62] Even as *denarius* fineness trended downwards in the late second and early third centuries, minters often returned to the Neronian-Trajanic standard for overall coin weight.[63] Historians should not doubt Harris' claim that "in the high Empire Romans counted out coins, they did not weigh them out."[64] Arrian's aforementioned advice that Trajan's coins be kept while Nero's be thrown away also includes the caveat that a money-changer or merchant "is not allowed to reject Caesar's coin . . . whether he chooses or not, he must give up what is sold for the coin."[65] Still, the presence of premiums – even if infrequently used – suggests that coin-users could and occasionally did subvert legal coin values. The existence of laws or rules requiring coin-users to accept certain coins did not prevent coin-users from developing informal, practical conventions for valuing some precious-metal coins above the legal baseline of legal value.

Under the aegis of Gresham's law, the limited presence of floating coin values in the Roman Empire undermines the notion of uniformly effective legal coin values. Official predation and indifference may be partly responsible for such gaps. It seems that only vast differences in legal value and bullion value may have been sufficient to tempt coin-users to subvert the law. In the next section, I explore these differences, which we should think of as transaction costs. Were coin premiums rare because legal coin values were redundant due to a homogenous coin supply? Did coin-users adjust their uses for currency when the coinage supply became increasingly more heterogeneous?

Money Homogeneity, Heterogeneity and Transaction Costs

Crawford posited that "when Commodus was murdered during the evening of 31st December 192, the monetary system established by Augustus was for the most part still as Augustus had left it. The *aureus* was still worth twenty-five *denarii*."[66] In other words, the most important denominational relationship in Rome's tri-metallic monetary system – the

62 Butcher and Ponting (2012), 73–4. 63 Elliott (2014).
64 Harris (2006), 20. See also Scheidel (2010b), 97; Wolters (1999), 358–9.
65 Arr. *Epict. diss.* 3.3. 66 Crawford (1975), 560.See also Duncan-Jones (1994), 218.

25:1 exchange rate between silver *denarii* and gold *aurei* – was stable.[67] The price of silver and gold, however, also affected the value of *aurei* and *denarii*. Rathbone declares that "from Augustus to Diocletian there was a standard official [12:1] weight ratio between the two."[68] Both Crawford and Rathbone would no doubt admit, however, that the assumption of centuries of stable legal coin values and bullion prices hangs on very little evidence.

It is true that the roughly three centuries of the Principate are bookended with clear evidence for a 12:1 ratio between silver and gold bullion. Historians can calculate the figure for the rate under Augustus due to the purity of his gold and silver coinage. At the other end of the time range, Diocletian's *Price Edict* imposes a silver to gold ratio of 12:1. What exactly happened in between these two boundaries is anyone's guess, but did each imperial regime in succession for three hundred years hold to a continuous bureaucratic standard for gold and silver prices? In order to work around such problems, historians can and have used the next best evidence: the physical bullion present in coins, which can be compared to official exchange rates between coins to calculate 'real' silver to gold bullion ratios over time.[69] This approach counterfactually assumes that legal coin values held perfectly – a purely heuristic choice that allows the use of legal exchange rates as a consistent measure of value over time. Studies using this approach tend to show a steadily decline in the value of gold bullion relative to silver between Augustus and Severus Alexander. It is impossible, however, to know whether exchange rates or bullion rates held at particular times and places. Declarations such as those found in the *Price Edict* merely confirm the fiat wishes of the authorities, not the real conditions in marketplaces.[70] Therefore, historians should treat the numbers generated by such an approach as qualitative rather than quantitative, and as ideal-typical rather than hypothetical. What historians gain from the exercise, however, is a set of boundaries – 'limits of the possible' – for bullion ratios and coin exchange rates at particular times. For my purposes in this chapter, such limits illuminate a set of counterfactual and ideal-typical 'external' conditions which suggest comparisons with the historically bounded choices of coin-users.

67 A caveat: "it is true that the gradual debasement of the denarius during the second century AD must have placed this relationship increasing strain," Bland (1996), 63.

68 Rathbone (2009), 302. See also Corbier (2005), 352.

69 Duncan-Jones (1994), 217.

70 Diocletian's government, for example, may have attempted to push the price of gold and silver downward to support requisitions of precious metals. See Lo Cascio (2005), 177; Bransbourg (2011), 116–7.

Before engaging in a similar exercise, however, I should note that during the Principate (and for much of the middle and late republic), Roman coins were struck *al marco* (so many coins to a weight of metal) rather than *al pezzo* (so much metal to each individual coin).[71] This process gave individual coins, even those minted in the same batch, slight variances in silver fineness. Bernhard Woytek guesses that the silver weight of individual *denarii* produced between Nero and Trajan, for example, varied by up to a gram.[72] For the *denarii* of Septimius, Gitler and Ponting's calculations show disparities near one quarter of a gram for issues from between AD 193 and 198.[73] Thus, in order to compensate for quality control, wear or other issues which might have influenced coin metallurgy, numismatists use a 'theoretical weight' or 'target weight' when discussing coins produced *al marco*. Such a convention is not as anachronistic as it may sound; Roman mints themselves used weight and fineness targets for coin issues, although they were expressed as so many coins to the pound (*libra*). Numismatists, however, usually measure their theoretical standards in modern units (grams) so that results are comparable and comprehensible across studies.[74]

So, we now return to the issue at hand: although some coin users in certain situations may have used conventional values for coins, legal coin values presumably held over much of the first two centuries of the Principate. Was this stability due to the enforcement of legal tender laws? Metrological figures from select issues during the first through mid-second century AD are revealing. Fig. 6.1 shows selected coin data for which there were chemical composition analyses available and which reflect meaningful changes in either weight or fineness. I should caution that the final two columns represent counterfactual *boundaries*. Still, for the first century and a half of the Principate, the nominal and bullion value of *denarii* and *aurei* show little potential for separation. The overvaluation of the *denarius* against the *aureus* could have at most reached five *denarii* per *aureus* (assuming a 12:1 silver to gold bullion ratio). The difference is small enough that even minor fluctuations in bullion values – a temporary rise in the value of silver or decline in the value of gold, for instance – could easily push the *denarius* to *aureus* exchange rate back toward the official 25:1 rate. Even in the most extreme coin exchange ratio above, for example – the 32:1 rate for most of the second century AD – a decrease in the bullion ratio from 12:1 down to 10:1 makes the exchange rate between *denarii* and *aurei* fall back down to 27:1.

71 Howgego, Butcher and Ponting (forthcoming), 27. 72 Woytek et al. (2007), 154.
73 Gitler and Ponting (2003), 50. 74 Rathbone (2009), 301; Duncan-Jones (1994), 213–5.

Date range of issue(s) (AD)	Theoretical *denarius* weight	Theoretical *denarius* silver weight	Theoretical *denarius* fineness	Theoretical *aureus* weight	'Real' silver to gold bullion ratio (if coin exchange rate is 25:1)	'Real' *denarius* to *aureus* exchange rate (if bullion ratio is 12:1)
15–51	3.75 grams	3.75 grams	100%	7.78 grams	12:1	25:1
54–64	3.65 grams	3.65 grams	100%	7.70 grams	12:1	25:1
64–66	3.45 grams	2.83 grams	80%	7.35 grams	10:1	31:1
85–96	3.45 grams	3.19 grams	90%	7.63 grams	10:1	29:1
99–117, 128–156	3.41 grams	2.73 grams	80%	7.27 grams	9:1	32:1

Fig. 6.1 Selected metrological data for *aurei* and *denarii*, AD 15–156
All fineness figures are taken from chemical composition analyses. Most figures for the first century AD are summarized in Butcher and Ponting (2015a), 434–60. Second-century figures come from Butcher and Ponting (2012); Woytek et al. (2007); Woytek (2008). See also Duncan-Jones (1994), 215–32. Ratios are expressed to the nearest whole number.

What do these figures mean? The near parity between coin values and bullion ratios in the first century and a half of the Principate suggests that historians and numismatists should see most debasements during the period as cautious or perhaps even accidental adjustments in standards. Even the most metallist-minded coin-users may not have shown much proclivity to hold back 'good' coins during this period. During the first two centuries of the Principate, with only a few exceptions, the legal value and precious-metal content of coins were roughly synchronous.[75] Under such conditions of relative money supply homogeneity, legal coin values would have been redundant. Coin-users may have complied with legal exchange rates despite state power, not because of it. Melting coin into bullion made little financial sense for coin-users during much of the first century and a half of the Principate.[76] It is also unclear how individuals would have coined hoarded bullion, as most scholars dispute if not reject entirely the existence of 'free minting' – the unrestricted ability of individuals to sell or otherwise convert bullion into coinage at mints – in the

[75] Bransbourg (2013), 187. Echoing Crawford (1985), 260. [76] Rathbone (1996b), 319.

Roman world.[77] Even if free minting was available to individuals, it was probably uncommon because such re-coinages would have incurred additional fees, adding to transaction costs. Even the simple act of hoarding during this period was likely done temporarily – perhaps as a form of short-term hedging behavior. Wealthy Romans were far more likely to 'invest' their cash or money-like assets in gifts and loans to friends – social capital which offered more attractive returns than the financial autonomy (assuming such autonomy was even desirable to elite Romans) offered by hoarding cash or bullion.[78] 'Savings hoards' have certainly been identified in the first century and a half of the Principate, but most hoards are categorized by specialists – in so far as such categorization is possible – as 'emergency hoards' or accidental losses.[79] When combined with the homogeneity of the coinage supply, these cultural and economic factors alone would have kept denominational exchange rates more stable in the first and second centuries AD than they might have otherwise been on a counterfactual 'frictionless' market in which there were no costs to melting, hoarding or exchanging currency. Few if any metallist-minded coin-users would have held back coins, ensuring that the monetary system's legal framework was practically synchronous with other value-forming aspects.[80]

By the late second century AD, it may have been more difficult for officials to hold concurrently the constants of a 12:1 gold to silver bullion ratio and a 25:1 *denarius* to *aureus* exchange rate. Recent analyses of the metallurgical content of coins from the period provide high-resolution data on annual changes in coin standards. These data show, for example, a punctuated debasement of the silver *denarius* in AD 194, the last decade of the second century AD. Analyses of gold *aurei* issued during this same period provide similarly reliable figures, enabling historians to calculate a reliable silver to gold ratio as well as to reasonably assume that contemporary coin-users themselves thought of gold coins as reliably standardized.[81] In AD 193, when *denarii* were minted with a theoretical 1.92 grams of silver and *aurei* contained 7.25 grams of gold, then the 'real' exchange rate between *denarii* and *aurei*, if the gold/silver bullion ratio of 12:1 applied, was 45:1 (rather than the legal 25:1 rate).[82] By contrast, assuming the 25:1

77 Foraboschi (2003); Butcher and Ponting (2015a), 29–30; Bolin (1958), 108–17.

78 Verboven (2002), 81, 148–62.

79 Christiansen (2004), 15–6, 35; Duncan-Jones (1994), 67.

80 On transaction costs see especially now Kehoe, Ratzan and Yiftach (2015a), 4–8. On 'clean' neoclassical models, see Morris (2002).

81 Bland (1996), 83.

82 The 'real' exchange rate is calculated by multiplying the official bullion ratio by the bullion content of the *aureus* (in grams) and dividing by the bullion content of the *denarius* (also in grams).

Date range of issue(s) (AD)	Theoretical *denarius* weight	Theoretical *denarius* silver weight	Theoretical *denarius* fineness	Theoretical *aureus* weight	'Real' silver to gold bullion ratio (if coin exchange rate is 25:1)	'Real' *denarius* to *aureus* exchange rate (if bullion ratio is 12:1)
187–92	2.83 grams	1.92 grams	68%	7.25 grams	7:1	45:1
193/4	3.16 grams	1.90 grams	60%	7.25 grams	7:1	45:1
194–8	3.16 grams	1.45 grams	46%	7.25 grams	5:1	60:1

Fig. 6.2 Metrological data for *aurei* and *denarii*, AD 187–198
All fineness figures are taken from chemical composition analyses. *Denarii* of AD 187–92 are Butcher and Ponting (2012), 75–7. *Denarii* of AD 193/4 are Gitler and Ponting (2003), 50, 55–7. *Denarii* of 194–8 are Butcher, Ponting and Chandler (1997), 25–30. Target weights are taken from Duncan-Jones (1994), 215–32. Ratios are expressed to the nearest whole number.

denomination exchange rate held and that the bullion ratio was flexible, then the 'real' ratio between the silver and gold bullion in the coins was just under 7:1 (rather than 12:1).[83] Again, these figures offer heuristic benefits only; they represent the boundaries of what was historically possible. Their purpose is to aid in understanding the thinking of coin-users, not to predict historical circumstances.

After the AD 194 debasement, when the silver in the *denarius* dropped to 1.45 grams, the gaps in values widen. Against an assumed bullion ratio of 12:1, the 'real' exchange rate between *denarii* and *aurei* depreciates to exactly 60:1. Contrastingly, against an assumed official 25:1 *denarius* to *aureus* exchange rate, the post-debasement bullion ratio between the coins is exactly 5:1.[84] I summarize these boundaries below (Fig. 6.2) and include the numbers for Commodus' coins of 187–92 to provide a sense of the likely quality of the circulating stock of coinage.

These figures, even the so-called 'real' values, are for counterfactual comparative purposes only; historians do not know how flexible coin values were. Nevertheless, the numbers perform two useful functions: (1) they provide non-arbitrary boundaries within which historical coin and

[83] Similarly, the 'real' bullion ratio is calculated by multiplying the bullion content of the *denarius* (in grams) by twenty-five (the number of *denarii* officially required to exchange for one *aureus*) and dividing by the bullion content of the *aureus* (in grams). Something similar is done by Hobbs (2006), 18–9.

[84] Figure derived from target weight of 3.36 grams and a silver fineness of 46 percent after Butcher, Ponting and Chandler (1997).

bullion values fell, and (2) they show the potential for vast differences between legal and 'real' values. Clearly even the 'bounded' figures, however, skew toward extremities. Unless silver bullion was commanding a 5:1 ratio with gold bullion, for example, the post-debasement *denarius* was substantially overvalued against both pre-debasement *denarii* and gold *aurei*. If the bullion ratio was the often-assumed 12:1, post-debasement *denarii* were overvalued by more than 33 percent against the most recently issued pre-debasement *denarii* and by double their bullion value against *aurei*.

Comparisons with broader historical trends help illuminate the significance of these bounding figures. Historical ratios between silver and gold in pre-industrial Mediterranean and European societies rarely fell outside the boundaries of 8:1 on the low end and 15:1 on the upper end.[85] There are also a few pieces of evidence which indicate that the ratio between silver and gold bullion within the expansive and diverse territory of the Roman Empire varied from place to place and was influenced by regional changes in precious metal supply and demand. Julius Caesar evidently plundered so much gold from Gaul, for example, that he offered it to inhabitants of Italy "and the provinces" at a rate of 3,000 sesterces per pound, or, in terms of silver, at a 9:1 ratio.[86] Likewise, the historian Josephus may not have been exaggerating when he noted that the abundance of gold taken and sold after the sack of Jerusalem in AD 70 caused the value of gold to fall by half in the area.[87] Historians agree that wars and conquests directly influenced gold and silver values; it is much riskier to argue that a generalized 'free market' in bullion was available to inhabitants of the Roman world. An early second-century papyrus declares that the prices of silver in Coptos "change from day to day."[88] Coptos was, however, a transition point for traders who sold wares in Indian and African markets – local merchants likely had little use for debased Egyptian *tetradrachms* and imperial *denarii*, at least at full value; hence, there was a vibrant local trade in precious metals.[89] Whether dynamic bullion markets existed elsewhere may be an open question, but historians have noted broader trends which may have contributed to large-scale shifts in bullion values.

Judging from their *terminus post quem*, precious-metal hoards (especially of silver) outside of the Roman Empire peak under Commodus and

85 Bransbourg (2011), 117.
86 Suet. *Jul.* 54.2. See Harris (2008a), 10–1.
87 Joseph. *BJ* 5.13.4; 6.6.1.
88 *P. Giss.* 1.47.
89 Tomber (2018); Young (2001), 45; Gibbs (2012), 48; Howgego (1992), 10; West and Johnson (1944), 94.

Septimius; many (but not all) scholars interpret this to mean that the AD 194 debasement encouraged an outflow of older and purer coins.[90] There is also now firm evidence that gold and silver mines (including the silver mines at Alburnus Maior and Rio Tinto) were under-producing and may even have become exhausted during or just before the Severan era.[91] The gold-producing province of Dacia, however, seems to have been at peace and even prosperous under Septimius. The emperor's consolidation of Dacia may have allowed increased exploitation of local gold mines to offset the hoarding behavior of coin-users, although how far a surplus of Dacian gold would have affected bullion prices in a wider geographic radius is unknown.[92] Regardless, these conditions were short-lived. Not long after the Severan era, Dacia soon again became a disputed province (along with several other resource-rich areas) and gold mines which were not abandoned in the Marcomannic Wars of the mid-second century AD may have been unavailable for exploitation in the mid-third century.[93]

Such general impressions can do little more than hint at the idea that bullion mattered to Roman coin-users as well as suggest that bullion prices were at least partially formed apart from state fiat. It is unclear, for instance, whether bullion values in fact moved toward the extremities of the 'boundaries' provided in Figs. 6.1 and 6.2. It may be possible, however, to give these 'frictionless' numbers – which do not account for transaction costs associated with melting or hoarding coins – more substance. Under Weber's dissected version of Gresham's law, such transaction costs are 'external' elements – elements which include formal or informal incentives and disincentives (e.g. laws, market rules or social taboos) which either made it easier or more difficult to discount coins or trade them at premium. The counterfactual logic of Gresham's law can help historians understand the interaction between transaction costs and the choices of coin-users despite not being able to describe or quantify these elements with precision. A historically bounded Gresham's law, for instance, identifies three broad outcomes (and these are the *only* possible outcomes): (1) *denarii* were overvalued against *aurei*, (2) *aurei* were overvalued against *denarii* or (3) the two denominations were valued at par or near enough to par to ensure that the transaction costs associated with storage or melting nullified Gresham's law. The first scenario is by far the

90 Arguments summarized neatly by Howgego (1995), 104–5. See also Duncan-Jones (1994), 92–4. Contra Bursche (1996), 88–90, 123–5.

91 Bowman and Wilson (2009), 64–5; von Reden (2010), 138–9; Jones (1980), 161–3; Wilson (2007), 113; Howgego (1992), 6.

92 Phang (2008), 165.

93 Howgego (1992), 7; Gazdac (2002).

most likely one in response to the AD 194 debasement, but exploring each of these scenarios as counterfactual choices helps historians understand the historical context which framed such choices.

Let us begin with the most likely scenario based upon comparative evidence: *denarii* were overvalued against *aurei*, presumably because the official coin exchange rate of 25:1 was commonly held in transactions and the 'real' silver/gold bullion ratio was at or higher than 5:1 post-debasement. The AD 194 debasement would have made it more advantageous for metallist-minded coin-users to use *denarii* for purchases. At the same time, hoarding *aurei* and possibly melting *aurei* into bullion (if the associated transaction costs were not too high) or converting the coins into stored wealth in some form (e.g. by mounting *aurei* in jewelry) was also more advantageous. We cannot quantify the transaction costs of melting and/or mounting – but the 'frictionless' 'real' value, on the one hand, and the official value, on the other hand, represent the limits between which such costs *must* have fallen.[94] Based upon a counterfactual official bullion ratio of 12:1, for example, *aurei*-holders could have obtained as many as sixty post-debasement *denarii* in exchange for the bullion obtained from a single *aureus* – a net profit of thirty-five *denarii* per 7.25 grams of gold bullion! Even if silver bullion was particularly dear in certain geographic regions in the latter half of the 190s – say at a 'real' silver to gold ratio at a historically low 8:1 (as it apparently was during the Second Punic War) – one could still obtain forty *denarii* from each *aureus*-worth of gold.[95] These counterfactual numbers illustrate the significance of the AD 194 debasement, which clearly put tremendous pressure on the legal *denarius/aureus* exchange rate of 25:1, especially if most coin-users still used this rate even in the midst of such disparities.

It is difficult to imagine that transaction costs in this scenario were greater than the difference between official and real rates, thus creating incentives to 'demonetize' *aurei* in some fashion, either temporarily through storage or on a more permanent basis by conversion to jewelry or bullion. There is also evidence that the social importance and performative function of gold created social and cultural incentives which, in this case, further minimized transaction costs. Apart from serving as a reliable long-term savings instrument, gold, when finished into jewelry and other objects for display, obtained ornamentation value, allowing owners to

[94] In many respects, after the approach used to discuss the monetary reform of Aurelian by Haklai-Rotenberg (2011).

[95] Crawford (1985), 59; Harl (1996), 33.

redirect their money into displays of wealth and status, enhancing their social capital.[96] In Roman Egypt, if not elsewhere in the Roman Empire, for example, gold jewelry was manufactured and valued in standardized units (the *mnaieion* and the *tetarte* or 'quarter' in social contracts). In dowries and other forms of social contracts, it was useful for the value of jewelry to be easily reckoned in liquid currency.[97] Such conventions reduced transaction costs. The informal conventions developed by inhabitants of the Roman Empire to facilitate non-market interactions could still in fact lower transaction costs – in this case, through the conversion of *aurei* into alternative forms of wealth or media of exchange. Simultaneously, the use of widespread accounting units protected those who made such conversions and enabled their bullion objects to have an account value in currency. All of this suggests that in the years following the Septimian debasement there were lowered barriers for *aurei*-holders who wished to store and/or melt their coins.

A second possible outcome of Septimius' debasement is that *aurei* were overvalued against *denarii*. If functioning as a deductive hypothesis, Gresham's law would *predict* that 'bad' gold *aurei* will be used on markets and that silver *denarii* might now have their turn in the melting pot. Any historian familiar with the evidence knows that this scenario is unlikely to align with the empirical record, but the point of the counterfactual comparison is better understanding of choice and the historical context rather than falsifying hypotheses. Because I use Gresham's law to think about the purposeful action of coin-users, it is not enough to know that a historical scenario is implausible, it is also important to know *why* it is implausible, because such an examination helps historians better understand the thinking of coin-users. So historians should ask: what external conditions needed to have existed in late AD 190s currency and bullion markets to achieve an overvalued *aureus*? Silver would have needed to be so dear as to pull the silver to gold ratio down to below 5:1. At an implausibly low 5:1 ratio, an *aureus*, in a counterfactual 'frictionless' exchange, could have fetched twenty-three or perhaps twenty-four post-debasement *denarii*. This exercise shows that the incentives to hoard or melt silver *denarii* would have been comparably meager compared to the first scenario because of the sheer numbers of *denarii* needed for overcoming the transaction costs associated with converting them to silver bullion. In the first scenario, in which the *denarius* was overvalued, transaction costs would have had to be

[96] Bland (2013), 274. [97] Ogden (1996), 191–2; Maresch (1996), 108; Cuvigny (2002).

implausibly high to prevent any metallist-minded coin-users from withdrawing *denarii*. In the second scenario, however, in which an implausibly low 5:1 bullion ratio only overvalued the *aureus* by a mere one or two *denarii* per exchange, even very low transaction costs would have disincentivized such exchanges except in cases of bulk transactions in thousands or perhaps tens of thousands of *denarii*. For the vast majority of coin-users, therefore, hoarding *denarii* offered no gain. An informal examination of the evidence has already revealed that an overvalued *aureus* was unlikely after (and before, frankly) AD 194, but counterfactual comparisons show exactly *why* this second scenario is so problematic and – unless good evidence for the existence of a 5:1 silver to gold ratio emerges – unrealistic.

Finally, for the same reason that transaction costs problematize the second scenario, they also problematize the third and final scenario, in which there was parity between *aurei* and *denarii* – that is, the exchange rate and bullion ratio were synchronous and neither denomination is overvalued. At parity, coin-users would have encountered no economic disincentives to using official currency exchange rates. Some historians have in fact wondered whether the Roman state purposefully aimed at achieving parity among precious-metal denominations.[98] The most likely mechanism for achieving such stability would have been to adjust the precious-metal content of coins as the bullion ratio changed. If silver became dear, for instance, then the silver currency could have been debased to avoid undervaluing the *denarius*. Butcher and Ponting have now shown the extent to which the mint hid *denarius* debasements from the coin-using public (as well as modern scholars!), mostly through surface enrichment. Arguments that the Roman state openly "wished to adjust the relationship between the intrinsic values of the coins to a new ratio between gold and silver" may need to be re-evaluated in light of Butcher and Ponting's studies.[99]

Gresham's law, through a robust set of causal relationships, provides historians with concrete (although qualitative) comparative counterfactual ideal types. Rather than set up these *a posteriori* conditions and cliometric hypotheses to be confirmed or falsified, a counterfactual ideal-typical approach instead helps historians establish the boundaries of 'external' market conditions and the 'internal' choices of coin-users. These counterfactual ideal types also provide historians with useful comparisons for

98 Lo Cascio (1981). Also: "From Nero's day onwards the influence of the rising silver price was compensated for by reducing the silver content of the denarius," Wassink (1991), 475.

99 Lo Cascio (1981), 80.

histories written using other approaches. Because the degree of heterogeneity of the money supply matters in the logic of Gresham's law, historians can know to examine the discrepancies between bullion values and legal coin exchange rates. A modified Gresham's law also helps historians understand the meaning of such information; in this case, differences between bullion ratios and coin exchange rates illuminate the strength of enforcement required to preserve official values of bullion or the legal values of coins. This chapter's remaining section offers some final examples of how Gresham's law helps historians understand how the real, purposefully acting inhabitants of the Roman world interpreted and responded to such conditions, as well as the extent to which coin-users' and coin-producers' reactions contributed to monetary stability.

Understanding Coin-Users' Responses to Changing Monetary Standards

The analysis in the previous section showed that by the late second century AD there existed a sizeable gap between the legal value and bullion value of *denarii*. Septimius' mint may have restored the Neronian-Trajanic standard for total *denarius* weight as a superficial attempt to convince coin-users that mint had restored the Neronian-Trajanic standard for *denarius* fineness.[100] Around AD 215, Septimius' son Caracalla introduced the silver *antoninianus*. This 'double' *denarius*, however, only contained about one and a half *denarii* worth of silver by weight. The coin, therefore, was yet another punctuated reduction of the monetary system's silver standard. In the same year, the mint reduced Caracalla's *aurei* in weight by some 10 percent to around 6.46 grams or fifty to the pound.[101] The complaints in contemporary literary sources, although they are wrong in detail, expose the new half-copper *antoninianus* as a coin of dubious quality.[102] Why, then, does money use appear to continue and perhaps even expand in the third century AD? Was it the case that coin-users were what Scheidel calls "socially caged"; that is, trust or "inertia" made coin-users "more likely to accept [state-issued currency] at face value than they would have done in more fragmented currency systems where diverse issues were free to compete on intrinsic quality"?[103]

[100] Elliott (2014); Duncan-Jones (1994), 102. [101] Duncan-Jones (1994), 216–18.
[102] Dio Cass. 78.14.3–4, 15.1, for example. See also Bland (1996), 74–5.
[103] Scheidel (2010b), 95.

MacMullen argues that monetary events in the third century AD taught money-users two lessons: that anyone could attempt to declare coin value, but that such declarations did not need to be obeyed.[104] Future metallurgical analyses will allow scholars to more precisely pinpoint key changes in third-century AD monetary standards – especially changes which overcame transaction costs associated with coin hoarding or converting coin into other forms of wealth. The data that do exist – imperfect as they are – suggest that debasements of *denarii* and subsequently *antoniniani* continued into the third century. The mint abandoned the *denarius* in the early AD 240s and the *antoninianus*' silver content declined to a thin wash by the 260s.[105] Did the monetary system shift to some kind of 'gold standard' in which fiduciary billon coins could be redeemed for *aurei*?[106] *Aurei*, however, had also been debased and, more crucially, reduced in weight – and it is difficult to understand how a denomination which became minted at such obviously erratic standards could underpin an already damaged monetary system. Despite these problems, marketplaces – at least officially – seem to have doggedly held to the use of imperial coinage. Coin-users, whether they purchased or sold goods, probably complied with legal coin values to avoid the ire of the increasingly vigilant authorities. In certain situations, traders, bankers, suppliers and payees were forced to take losses and accept or use the state's debased currency. To refuse the state was costly – perhaps even deadly – but were there situations and spaces where these costs and risks could be reduced? If the financial losses that came from using debased coinage were high enough, some coin-users may have gone to great lengths to avoid dealing with the state and its contracted financial institutions wherever possible. Such avoidance may be partly behind the closed banks in Oxyrhynchus in the early 260s.[107] Because of the regularity of civil and foreign wars during this period, however, state officials perhaps were themselves more willing to collect and, in the case of soldiers at least, distribute commodities rather than coin – behavior which may have relaxed pressures to use the imperial currency at legal values.

Another explanation for the endurance of money prices in the midst of ever-increasing reductions in coin standards is the fact that coin-based units still served as units of account. Economists Arthur Rolnick and Warren Weber show the importance of money's unit of account function to the operation (or non-operation) of Gresham's law:

104 MacMullen (1976), 113. 105 Estiot (2012), 542. 106 Howgego (1995), 125.
107 *P. Oxy.* 12.1411; see Chapter 3, pp. 137–8.

> If both the undervalued and the overvalued currency must be accepted for all payments at their par values, however, agents will set their price in the overvalued currency and be more than willing to accept the undervalued at par. A legal tender law can thus be viewed as placing transaction costs on undervalued money when it is used as the unit of account, thereby breaking the indeterminacy implied by general equilibrium theory in favour of the overvalued money . . .[108]

Units of account in the Roman world vary both over time and in different contexts, but the most common unit was the base-metal *sestertius*.[109] As a small-denomination token coin, and one which was chronically under-produced, the coin made for a natural unit of account (or 'ghost currency' – a term for account monies which lack a readily available physical medium).[110] By the end of the third century, the *sestertius* still performed this function – yet mints had not produced physical *sestertii* for decades. Curiously, however, a new unit of account also came into use sometime in the third-century: the *denarius communis*, a unit based upon either a non-existent coin or perhaps the rarely produced copper *denarius*.[111] Either way, the main accounting units used from the third century onward were undervalued base-metal units, not the overvalued gold *aureus* or billon *antoniniani*. Because overvalued money served as accounting units, debased *antoniniani*, which were unlikely to have been undervalued, could continue to work as functioning media of exchange for the reasons described by Rolnick and Weber. Coin-users now likely held back substantially undervalued currency (e.g. gold *aurei* and older *denarii*), except where suitable premiums for these coins could be offered. In fact, it may even by the case that some (older) heavier bronze and copper coins were overvalued enough to be removed from circulation, creating a dearth of small change in addition to the dearth of higher-quality coins.

With no clear commodity anchor, the 'silver' currency was merely a token of obligation in state-enforced exchange. The full-value silver *denarius* had long ceased to function as a unit of account. The logic of Gresham's law suggests that under such conditions the areas where legal values were most enforced would have also been the areas with the greatest

108 Rolnick and Weber (1986).

109 Lo Cascio (2008), 173; Lo Cascio (2007), 628; Temin and Kessler (2008), 138; Burnett (2005b), 176; Rathbone (1996b), 317.

110 Bransbourg (2013), 221–2; Hollander (2007), 85–6.

111 Sutherland (1961). It is true that a scarcely produced bronze 'denarius' with a mark of 'VSV' (VSV [alis]?) appears under Aurelian (*RIC* 71). Perhaps this coin represents a new or reformed small-change unit in the larger Aurelianic monetary reform? See the interesting thoughts in Woods (2013).

shortages of 'good' money. Severely debased *antoniniani*, by contrast, would have enjoyed widespread use, but perhaps only for low-value transactions.[112] High-value transactions, with the credit system unreliable at best, probably took place in bullion, whether coined or uncoined, assuming bullion could even be obtained. Specialists in currency exchanges and assay (*argentarii* and *nummularii*) are not mentioned in any third-century AD sources.[113] Local surplus commodities may have taken on an increased role as media of exchange in some areas. Large hoards of billon *antoniniani* found in Britain and elsewhere, such as the famous Frome hoard, could be seen as attempts to use billon coins for high-value transactions, but most scholars believe the deposits were made either for religious purposes or, due to the currency reform under Aurelian, for repurposing or recycling.[114] In any event, reduced availability of high-value media of exchange would have severely increased transaction costs for monetized transactions, disconnecting markets and perhaps leading to the increasing use of localized special-purpose monies.

There was an attempt in the latter half of the third century to return the Roman monetary system to a quasi-precious-metal standard. The erratic *aureus* standard meant that the gold coin could not anchor the system. The effects of Gresham's law, diminishing mining output and decades of debasement had led to a dearth of precious metals. Zosimus, in his early sixth century AD *Historia Nova*, speaks of monetary "confusion" (συγχύσεως) preceding the reform under Aurelian. The chosen solution was what Zosimus calls a "new silver" (ἀργύριον νέον) coin: "[Aurelian] distributed to the public 'new silver' (ἀργύριον νέον), after providing that the people give up the 'adulterated' (χίβδηλον) coin; thus, he removed confusion from contracts."[115] Aurelian's coin – which numismatists often call an *aurelianus* to distinguish it from the pre-reform *antoninianus* – was only fractionally silver, but the coin was, nevertheless, as its value-mark (XX.I) declares, minted to a consistent standard of twenty parts copper to one part silver.[116] It is telling that even two centuries after the reform, the enduring memory as recorded by Zosimus was that the emperor replaced adulterated coin with 'silver.' The new coin was, however, unmistakably a billon coin, probably because silver availability was so low that it was impossible to issue a pure silver coin in significant numbers. Rather, an essentially fiduciary coin was introduced which nonetheless carried upon it an honest mark indicating its small but consistent silver content of

112 Harl (1996), 135. 113 Andreau (1999), 33; Andreau (1994), 201; Silver (2011).
114 Walton and Moorhead (2016), 843. 115 Zos. 1.61.3. 116 Haklai-Rotenberg (2011).

5 percent. Other markers of quality – a consistent flan, a finely etched inscription – accompanied the transition from the *antoninianus* to the *aurelianus*.[117] Where Aurelian's coinage took hold, increased prices in terms of *denarii communes* or other units show that he successfully created a new standard. The sudden price rises from AD 274/5 onward may indicate that coin-users chose to trust and use Aurelian's reformed coinage. The *aurelianus* was, for a brief time, a reliable commodity-based coin. The tenfold price increases represent price-clearing after decades of the process being held back by monetary incoherence. Perhaps the impressive survival of *antoninianus* hoards indicate that Gresham's law began operating in reverse due to changing 'external' conditions; 'good' money drove out 'bad' money because the commodity value in billon coins once again matched their legal value.

Whatever their aims and consequences, several factors ultimately undid the Aurelianic reforms. For one, the premature death of the emperor probably had an effect, as did the fact that coin standards under subsequent rulers appear to have changed. The effects of Gresham's law seem to have had a profound impact upon both the conditions before the reform and the reform itself, as more than a century of outbound state payments, export of precious metals and hoarding or melting of higher-quality silver coins drained both privately held and state stocks of precious metals. Estimates of coin output show a severe decline under Aurelian.[118] Worked-out or shut-down mines compounded difficulties. Aurelian had little gold and only enough silver to raise his 'silver' standard to a fractional silver coinage instead of something more robustly metallist. Although the mints openly disclosed the fractional nature of the new standard with a mark of value, the reform inherited a great deal of public mistrust due to the preceding decades of monetary deception and manipulation.

By the 270s, coin-users were probably relying at least in part on commodities for high-value transactions and using billon *antoniniani* and copper coinage for day-to-day exchange. A system with so many special-purpose monies, after decades of use, had likely embedded certain habits in the population; there was indeed some 'social caging'. Only a total systematic reform, such as the one which was completed over much of the early fourth century, seems to have successfully enticed money-users to once again use imperial coinage as general-purpose money.

[117] Callu (1969), 324. [118] Estiot (1996).

Conclusions

A Gresham's law in which 'bad money drives out good' always and everywhere cannot be used reliably by historians. It is better to deploy Gresham's law as a complex and interconnected set of conditions and premises involving 'external' elements (legal tender laws, differing coinage standards, transaction costs, etc.) and an 'internal' sensitivity among (some!) coin-users to the precious-metal content of coins. This Weberian form of Gresham's law better guides historical investigations of monetary systems and the construction of historical narratives more broadly.

As for the Roman monetary system, the 'external' conditions of Gresham's law seem to have been inconsistently present at best. A study of the bounded counterfactual limits of *denarius* metal content and the silver to gold bullion ratio, shows legal coin values and precious-metal values were more or less redundant during first century and a half of the Principate. State fiat, even if present, was of secondary importance at best. Legal values and metal values were close enough that the transaction costs associated with melting and hoarding money discouraged coin-users from putting any metallist preferences they may have held into action. As the bedrock of the system, the silver *denarius* was not perfectly homogenous during this period – the metallurgical analyses of Butcher and Ponting have revealed attempts to standardize the system under both Nero and Trajan. Coin-users treated *denarii* as though they were homogenous, making imperial currency an attractive and reliable general-purpose money. The near-universal acceptability of the coinage no doubt drew users into the monetary system, contributing to expanding monetization across the empire and voluntary acquiescence to the system's practical rules, including legal values.

A growing dissonance between legal value and metal value, however, emerged by the late second century AD, putting pressure on coin-users' monetary habits. The debasement of the silver currency augmented the problem, and state officials reacted not by decreasing their needs for expenditure or ceasing to debase, but apparently by stepping up the enforcement of legal coin values in several ways. Privileged money-changers were protected from competitors.[119] Banks were forced to remain open and accept all official coinage.[120] Informers were given incentives to collaborate with officials. The sum total of these actions, and perhaps others, is that Roman coin-users were forced to "treat moneys they

[119] *OGIS* 515. [120] *P. Oxy* 12.1411.

consider unequal equally."[121] Historians cannot assume that coin-users were uniformly metallist-minded, only that enough of them had such preferences and acted upon them to bring about a gradual withdrawal of high-fineness coins from the money pool.

This narrative, which would be impossible to write without the aid of a modified Gresham's law, is a little different from the narrative in which the strictly enforced legal coin values of the early Principate were abandoned in the third century, causing crisis. Instead, officials seem to have *increased* the enforcement of legal value (making the coinage nominally homogenous) while, at the same time, adjusting *denarius*, *aureus* and eventually *antoninianus* standards rapidly and drastically (making the coinage practically heterogeneous). Using Gresham's law's counterfactual and ideal-typical properties to think about the purposeful action of coin-users suggests that the actions of Roman authorities encouraged any metallist-minded coin-users to avoid the now relative high costs of monetary exchange at legal values and instead adopt special-purpose uses for money. The counterfactual logic of Gresham's law, therefore, offers historians, through comparison, both improved understanding of Roman coin-users' thinking as well as broader insights into the workings of the Roman monetary economy – especially insights on the strength of legal value beyond the fiat desires of officials as well as a better understanding of the behavior of coin-users.

[121] Selgin (in press), 25.

Conclusion

Roman monetary history, like all history, is history of mind. Economic models, methods and agendas, therefore, which ignore or assume away the mind are of only limited use for historians. Deductive economics has undoubtedly made positive contributions to Roman economic history. Some specific concepts from the new institutional framework – especially bounded rationality and transaction costs – are useful to historians so long as they are divorced from any teleology that privileges the unique and often dubious economic mentalities of modern capitalism. Historians should avoid methodological monism – the idea that economic phenomena behave according to incontrovertible, quasi-naturalistic 'laws'. It is equally problematic, however to dismiss many if not most economic principles on the unsustainable suspicion that all economic principles are in fact contingent and therefore anachronistic products of modern culture. Historians are uniquely equipped to negotiate these methodological complexities on a case-by-case basis. Historians' main ally in this laborious task is *understanding*.

In this book, I argue that no historical argument – whether or not it relies upon economic theory – should beg questions of understanding. The historian's humanistic agenda best serves economic history when deployed patiently with the aim of redeeming from economic theories whatever may aid historians' understanding of historical minds, even in cases where there is little available to redeem. Polanyi's substantivism, ironically, resulted from a redemptive approach to economics in which he sought to "chop the value-theoretical branch from the neoclassical trunk and to graft it onto a historicist stem."[1] While it is true that such radical methodological reconfigurations sometimes create monsters, Polanyi's exceptional efforts imbued life into the primitivist resistance to the modernist orthodoxy that dominated in his day. Ironically, Polanyi's substantivism could not have

[1] Dale (2010), 103.

been conceived without Polanyi's willingness to engage critically and patiently with economics, rather than dismiss it whole cloth. Historians can and should use the *Verstehen* approaches of Weber, Mises and Collingwood (and others) to imbue economic theory with a phenomenological and humanistic agenda.

I did not, however, write this book to glorify the methodologies of the past, but to propose some forward-looking possibilities. Progression, however, requires that ancient historians back out of the ditch that has been dug by almost a century of reactionary back-and-forth movement between narrow and overly stereotyped dichotomies. There are probably many productive ways ancient historians might escape the rut; my own suggestion is to embrace a dualistic approach to economic theory which studies the 'internal' motivations and value-judgments of actors and the 'external' events of the actors' world differently. Internal motivations are grasped through an *a priori* purposefulness – a fundamental form of rationality shared by all acting human beings (including observers), and which comes prior to external action. Unlike formal economic rationality, purposefulness is not synonymous with acquisitive behavior or wealth maximization, nor does it distinguish between 'economic' and 'non-economic' action or 'embedded' rationality and 'capitalistic' rationality.[2] Purposefulness may be ubiquitous but its articulations and practical results are anything but. The unique ways in which purposeful action is articulated in human history (let me again emphasize that profit-seeking is merely *one* of many forms purposefulness might take) – the unpredictable and unmappable means and ends chosen by real human beings who are inescapably influenced and even channeled by embedded social, cultural, emotional, habitual and other contexts – are specific and unique rather than universal. These choices require analysis by the methods of history, anthropology, sociology and other humanistic disciplines.[3] Any parts of an economic theory which are not apodictically true, however, must be understood as conditional rather than as predictive or universal. *A priori* logic *must* happen; ideal-typical action *usually* or *conditionally* happens. Purposeful action is apodictic, but the meanings of action and the larger social, cultural and institutional environment in which purposeful action occurred in the historical Roman world, cannot be and in fact *must not be* mapped or dictated by any model – economic or otherwise.

[2] Selgin (1988), 17. [3] Koppl (2002), 28.

Purposeful action, as a product of the human mind, creates history. If there is no purposeful action, to borrow from Collingwood, "there can be no history."[4] Purposefulness, moreover, is common to both observers and their subjects, as Mises articulated:

> There is for history nothing beyond people's ideas and the ends they were aiming at motivated by these ideas. If the historian refers to the meaning of a fact, he always refers either to the interpretation acting men gave to the situation in which they had to live and to act, and to the outcome of their ensuing actions, or to the interpretation which other people gave to the result of these actions. The final causes to which history refers are always the ends individuals and groups of individuals are aiming at. History does not recognize in the course of events any other meaning and sense than those attributed to them by acting men, judging from the point of view of their own human concerns.[5]

Collingwood proposed that shared purposefulness be used for "re-enactment" of historical thoughts. Economic theories which accommodate purposefulness offer historians formal theoretical frameworks for engaging in such re-enactments. These theories present ideal-typical counterfactuals based upon both the *a posteriori* conditions of the theory's alternative reality and the unrealized actions which were subordinated to the action ultimately chosen by historical individuals. These actions, both realized and unrealized, can be compared. Moreover, economic theory – albeit theory which is bounded by substantive embedding contexts and which is used comparatively rather than predictively – is a helpful tool for understanding both the actions taken by historical human beings and the embedding contexts which shaped those actions. In the hands of the historian, therefore, economic theory becomes a phenomenological tool which helps historians identify variables of value, society, culture and other influences on the thinking of money-users in the historical past. My uses of quantity theory and Gresham's law in this book – both of which are theories which lack an *a priori* core in typical neoclassical applications – show that even neoclassical economics can still be of help to historians who wish to understand the motivations and actions of money-users in the Roman world.

The approach in this book is hardly the only way of rethinking and redeploying economic theory, and I certainly would not presume to say it is the best approach. Indeed, there is much work to be done, so I publish this book in the hope that other scholars – especially those outside my own

[4] Collingwood (1994), 310. [5] Mises (1957), 161.

discipline – will offer refinements, alternatives and necessary criticisms. I expect that new evidence will also stimulate revisions to the approach. Like many Roman historians, for example, I eagerly await future metallurgical studies of Roman coins – especially from the third and fourth centuries AD. These studies, combined with continued improvements in the organization and accessibility of existing hoard evidence and information about the locations of armies and emperors in the third century AD, will reveal more about the influence of physical and social geography on the value of money. Furthermore, environmental proxies – especially those which are related to mining, smelting and perhaps coin production – will shape historians' understanding of money production and value in the ancient Mediterranean.[6]

Finally, while the approach advocated in this book prioritizes understanding the 'internal' meanings of economic action in the Roman world, it nevertheless produces descriptive information about the 'external' attributes of the Roman monetary system. I expect that scholars will ask critical and constructive questions about my characterizations of key monetary episodes in Roman history such as the post-Actium monetary injection, the credit crisis of AD 33, the debasement of AD 194 and the mid-third-century AD changes in monetary standards. I hope, however, that the methodological approach and historical analyses in this book will be of value and perhaps even practical usefulness, both to formalist and substantivist historians, as well as to the majority of scholars who find themselves somewhere in the middle.

[6] McConnell et al. (2018).

Bibliography

Aarts, J. (2005). Coins, Money and Exchange in the Roman World: A Cultural-Economic Perspective. *Archaeological Dialogues* 12 (1): 1–28.

Abdy, R. (2012). Tetrarchy and the House of Constantine. In W. E. Metcalf (Ed.), *The Oxford Handbook of Greek and Roman Coinage*, pp. 584–600. Oxford: Oxford University Press.

Addleson, M. (1995). *Equilibrium Versus Understanding: Towards the Restoration of Economics as Social Theory*. London: Routledge.

Alston, R. (1999). The Revolt of the Boukoloi: Geography, History and Myth. In K. Hopwood (Ed.), *Organised Crime in the Ancient World*, pp. 129–53. London: Duckworth.

Ando, C. (2008). Decline, Fall, and Transformation. *Journal of Late Antiquity* 1 (1): 31–60.

Andreau, J. (2010). *L'Économie du monde romain*. Paris: Ellipses.

(2002). Twenty Years after Moses I. Finley's *The Ancient Economy*. In S. von Reden and W. Scheidel (Eds.), *The Ancient Economy*, pp. 33–52. London: Routledge.

(1999). *Banking and Business in the Roman World*. Trans. K. Lloyd. Cambridge: Cambridge University Press.

(1994). L'Italie impériale et les provinces: déséquilibre des échanges et flux monétaires. *Publications de l'École Française de Rome* 198(1): 175–203.

Andreau, J. and J. Maucourant. (1999). A propos de la "rationalité économique" dans l'antiquité gréco-romaine. *Topoi* 9 (1): 47–102.

Ankersmit, F. R. (2005). *Sublime Historical Experience*. Stanford: Stanford University Press.

(2001). *Historical Representation: F. R. Ankersmit*. Stanford: Stanford University Press.

Aubert, J.-J. (2014). For Swap or Sale? The Roman Law of Barter. In C. Apicella, M.-L. Haack and Fr. Lerouxel (Eds.), *Les affaires de Monsieur Andreau: Économie et société du monde romain*, pp. 109–21. Bordeaux: Ausonius.

(2003). Monetary Policy and Gresham's Law in the Late Third Century AD. In E. Lo Cascio (Ed.), *Credito e moneta nel mondo romano. Atti degli Incontri capresi di storia dell'economia antica (Capri 12–14 ottobre 2000)*, pp. 245–63. Bari: Edipuglia.

Bagnall, R. S. (2000). P. Oxy 4527 and the Antonine Plague in Egypt: Death or Flight? *Journal of Roman Archaeology* 13: 288–92.

(1995). *Reading Papyri, Writing Ancient History*. London: Routledge.

(1993). *Egypt in Late Antiquity*. Princeton: Princeton University Press.

Bang, P. F. (2012). Predation. In W. Scheidel (Ed.), *The Cambridge Companion to the Roman Economy*, pp. 197–217. Cambridge: Cambridge University Press.

(2009). The Ancient Economy and New Institutional Economics. *Journal of Roman Studies* 99: 194–206.

(2008). *The Roman Bazaar: A Comparative Study of Trade and Markets in a Tributary Empire*. Cambridge: Cambridge University Press.

(2007). Trade and Empire: In Search of Organizing Concepts for the Roman Economy. *Past & Present* 195 (1): 3–54.

(1998). Antiquity between 'Primitivism' and 'Modernism'. Working paper. Centre for Cultural Research, University of Aarhus.

Bang, P. F., M. Ikeguchi and H. G. Ziche (2006). Introduction. In P. F. Bang, M. Ikeguchi and H. G. Ziche (Eds.), *Ancient Economies, Modern Methodologies: Archaeology, Comparative History, Models and Institutions*, pp. 7–24. Bari: Edipuglia.

Bannon, C. (2009). *Gardens and Neighbors: Private Water Rights in Roman Italy*. Ann Arbor: University of Michigan Press.

Barbieri, F. (2013). Complexity and the Austrians. *Filosofía de la Economía* 1(1): 47–69.

Baronian, L. (2013). *Marx and Living Labour*. London: Routledge.

Bauman, Z. (2010). *Hermeneutics and Social Science: Approaches to Understanding*. London: Routledge.

Beck, L., S. Bosonnet, S. Reveillon, D. Eliot and F. Pilon. (2004). Silver Surface Enrichment of Silver-Copper Alloys: A Limitation for the Analysis of Ancient Silver Coins by Surface Techniques. *Nuclear Instruments and Methods in Physics Research. Section B, Beam Interactions with Materials and Atoms* 226 (1–2): 153–62.

Bedford, P. R. (2007). The Persian Near East. In W. Scheidel, I. Morris and R. P. Saller (Eds.), *The Cambridge Economic History of the Greco-Roman World*, pp. 302–32. Cambridge: Cambridge University Press.

Bernard, S. (2018). The Social History of Early Roman Coinage. *Journal of Roman Studies* 108: 1–26.

Bland, R. (2013). What Happened to Gold Coinage in the 3rd c. AD? *Journal of Roman Archaeology* 26: 263–80.

(1996). The Development of Gold and Silver Coin Denominations, AD 193–253. In C. E. King and D. G. Wigg (Eds.), *Coin Finds and Coin Use in the Roman World*, pp. 64–100. Berlin: Gebrüder Mann Verlag.

Blaug, M. (1997). *Economic Theory in Retrospect*. Cambridge: Cambridge University Press.

(1980). *Methodology of Economics*. Cambridge: Cambridge University Press.

Block, W. (2003). Realism: Austrian vs. Neoclassical Economics, Reply to Caplan. *Quarterly Journal of Austrian Economics* 6 (3): 63–76.

Blouin, K. (2010). La révolte des Boukoloi (delta du Nil, Égypte, ~166–172 de notre ère): regard socio-environnemental sur la violence. *Phoenix* 64 (3–4): 386–422.

Boldizzoni, F. (2011). *The Poverty of Clio: Resurrecting Economic History*. Princeton: Princeton University Press.

Bolin, S. (1958). *State and Currency in the Roman Empire to 300 AD*. Stockholm: Almqvist & Wiksell.

Bowman, A. (2009). Quantifying Egyptian Agriculture. In A. Bowman and A. Wilson (Eds.), *Quantifying the Roman Economy: Methods and Problems*, pp. 177–204. Oxford: Oxford University Press.

(1986). *Egypt After the Pharaohs 332 BC–AD 642: From Alexander to the Arab Conquest*. Berkeley: University of California Press.

Bowman, A. and J. D. Thomas. (1983). *Vindolanda: The Latin Writing Tablets*. London: Society for the Promotion of Roman Studies.

Bowman, A. and A. Wilson. (2018). Introduction: Trade, Commerce, and the State. In A. Bowman and A. Wilson (Eds.), *Trade, Commerce, and the State in the Roman World*, pp. 1–24. Oxford: Oxford University Press.

(2009). Quantifying the Roman Economy: Integration, Growth, Decline? In A. Bowman and A. Wilson (Eds.), *Quantifying the Roman Economy: Methods and Problems*, pp. 3–84. Oxford: Oxford University Press.

Bransbourg, G. (2014). Les taux d'intérêt flottants des Sulpicii. In C. Apicella, M.-L. Haack and Fr. Lerouxel (Eds.), *Les affaires de Monsieur Andreau. Économie et société du monde romain*, pp. 123–35. Bordeaux: Ausonius.

(2013). Fides et pecunia numerata, Part II: The Currencies of the Roman Republic. *American Journal of Numismatics* 25: 179–242.

(2011). Fides et pecunia numerata. Chartalism and Metallism in the Roman World, Part I: The Republic. *American Journal of Numismatics* 23: 87–152.

Bresson, A. (2015). *The Making of the Ancient Greek Economy: Institutions, Markets, and Growth in the City-States*. Princeton: Princeton University Press.

Browning, G. (2004). *Rethinking R. G. Collingwood: Philosophy, Politics and the Unity of Theory and Practice*. Basingstoke: Palgrave Macmillan.

Bücher, K. (1917). *Die Entstehung der Volkswirtschaft*. Tübingen: Laupp.

Burnett, A. (2012). Early Roman Coinage and Its Italian Context. In W. E. Metcalf (Ed.), *The Oxford Handbook of Greek and Roman Coinage*, pp. 297–314. Oxford: Oxford University Press.

(2005a). The Imperial Coinage of Egypt in the First Century AD. In F. Duyat and O. Picard (Eds.), *L'exception égyptienne? Production et échanges monétaires en Égypte hellénistique et romaine: Actes du Colloque d'Alexandrie, 13–15 Avril 2002*, pp. 261–77. Cairo: Institut Français d'Archéologie Orientale.

(2005b). The Roman West and the Roman East. In C. Howgego, V. Heuchert and A. Burnett (Eds.), *Coinage and Identity in the Roman Provinces*, pp. 171–80. Oxford: Oxford University Press.

(1987). *Coinage in the Roman World*. London: Spink.

Bursche, A. (1996). *Later Roman–Barbarian Contacts in Central Europe: Numismatic Evidence*. Berlin: Gebr. Mann Verlag.

Butcher, K. and M. Ponting. (2015a). *The Metallurgy of Roman Silver Coinage: From the Reform of Nero to the Reform of Trajan*. Cambridge: Cambridge University Press.

(2015b). The Reforms of Trajan and the End of the Pre-Neronian Denarius. *Annali Dell'Istituto Italiano Di Numismatica* 61: 21–43.

(2012). The Beginning of the End? The Denarius in the Second Century. *Numismatic Chronicle* 172: 63–83.

(2009). The Denarius in the First Century. In N. Holmes (Ed.), *Proceedings of the XIV International Numismatic Congress, Glasgow 2009*, pp. 557–68. Glasgow: International Numismatic Council.

Butcher, K., M. Ponting and G. Chandler. (1997). A Study of the Chemical Composition of Roman Silver Coinage, AD 196-197. *American Journal of Numismatics* 9: 17–36.

Callu, J. P. (1969). *La politique monétaire des empereurs romains, de 238 à 311*. Paris: Editions de Boccard.

Camic, C., P. Gorski and D. Trubek, Eds. (2005). *Max Weber's Economy and Society: A Critical Companion*. Stanford: Stanford University Press.

Cartledge, P. (1998). Cambridge Classics for the Third Millennium. In S. J. Ormrod (Ed.), *Cambridge Contributions*, pp. 103–21. Cambridge: Cambridge University Press.

Christiansen, E. (2004). *Coinage in Roman Egypt: The Hoard Evidence*. Aarhus: Aarhus University Press.

(1994). The Roman Coins of Alexandria: State of Affairs. In A. Bülow-Jacobsen (Ed.), *Proceedings of the 20th International Congress of Papyrologists, Copenhagen, 23–29 August, 1992*, pp. 478–83. Copenhagen: Museum Tusculanum Press.

(1988). *The Roman Coins of Alexandria*. Vol. 1. Aarhus: Aarhus University Press.

(1984). On Denarii and Other Coin-Terms in the Papyri. *Zeitschrift für Papyrologie und Epigraphik* 54: 271–99.

Coffee, N. (2017). *Gift and Gain: How Money Transformed Ancient Rome*. Oxford: Oxford University Press.

Cohen, E. E. (2002). Introduction. In P. Cartledge, E. E. Cohen and L. Foxhall (Eds.), *Money, Labour and Land; Approaches to the Economies of Ancient Greece*, pp. 1–7. London: Routledge.

(1992). *Athenian Economy and Society: A Banking Perspective*. Princeton: Princeton University Press.

Collingwood, R. G. (1999). *The Principles of History: And Other Writings in Philosophy of History*. Ed. W. H. Dray and W. J. van der Dussen. Oxford: Oxford University Press.

(1995). *Essays in Political Philosophy*. Ed. D. Boucher. Oxford: Clarendon Press.

(1994). *The Idea of History*. Revised Edn. Oxford: Oxford University Press.
(1926). Economics as a Philosophical Science. *International Journal of Ethics* 36 (2): 162–85.
Cooley, A. E. (2009). *Res Gestae Divi Augusti*. Cambridge: Cambridge University Press.
Corbier, M. (2005). Coinage and Taxation: The State's Point of View, AD 193–337. In A. K. Bowman, A. Cameron and P. Garnsey (Eds.), *The Cambridge Ancient History*, Second Edn., pp. 327–92. Cambridge: Cambridge University Press.
Crawford, M. H. (1985). *Coinage and Money Under the Roman Republic: Italy and the Mediterranean Economy*. Berkeley: University of California Press.
(1983a). Numismatics. In M. H. Crawford (Ed.), *Sources for Ancient History*, pp. 185–234. Cambridge: Cambridge University Press.
(1983b). Roman Imperial Coin Types and the Formation of Public Opinion. In C. N. L. Brooke, B. H. I. Stewart, J. G. Pollard and T. R. Volk (Eds.), *Studies in Numismatic Method: Presented to Philip Grierson*, pp. 47–64. Cambridge: Cambridge University Press.
(1975). Finance, Coinage and Money from the Severans to Constantine. *Aufstieg und Niedergang der römischen Welt* 2: 560–93.
(1974). *Roman Republican Coinage*. Cambridge: Cambridge University Press.
(1970). Money and Exchange in the Roman World. *Journal of Roman Studies* 60: 40–8.
(1964). War and Finance. *Journal of Roman Studies* 54: 29–32.
Cuvigny, H. (2002). Les avatars du chrysous dans l'Égypte ptolémaïque et romain. *Bulletin de l'Institut Français d'archéologie Orientale* 103: 111–30.
Dale, G. (2010). *Karl Polanyi: The Limits of the Market*. Cambridge: Polity.
Damon, C. (2013). *Tacitus: Annals*. London: Penguin Classics.
Davidson, P. (2012). Is Economics a Science? Should Economics Be Rigorous? *Real World Economics Review* 59: 58–66.
Davies, J. K. (2007). Linear and Nonlinear Flow Models for Ancient Economies. In J. G. Manning and I. Morris (Eds.), *The Ancient Economy: Evidence and Models*, pp. 127–56. Stanford: Stanford University Press.
(2006). Hellenistic Economies in the Post-Finley Era. In Z. H. Archibald, J. Davies, V. Gabrielsen and G. J. Oliver (Eds.), *Hellenistic Economies*, pp. 7–44. London: Routledge.
(1998). Ancient Economies: Models and Muddles. In H. Parkins and C. Smith (Eds.), *Trade, Traders and the Ancient City*, pp. 221–52. London: Taylor & Francis.
De Cecco, M. (2000). Conclusioni. In E. Lo Cascio (Ed.), *Mercati permanenti e mercati periodici nel mondo romano. Atti degli Incontri Capresi di Storia dell'Economia Antica (Capri 13–15 Ottobre 1997). Pragmateiai 2*, pp. 269–73. Bari: Edipuglia.
(1985). Monetary Theory and Roman History. *Journal of Economic History* 45 (4): 809–22.

Dillon, J. N. (2007). Octavian's Finances after Actium, before Egypt: The CAESAR DIVI F / IMP CAESAR Coinage and Antony's Legionary Issue. *Chiron* 37: 35–48.

Dilthey, W. (1976a). Ideas about a Descriptive and Analytical Psychology. In H. P. Rickman (Ed.), *W. Dilthey: Selected Writings*, pp. 87–97. Cambridge: Cambridge University Press.

(1976b). The Development of Hermeneutics. In H. P. Rickman (Ed.), *W. Dilthey: Selected Writings*, pp. 246–63. Cambridge: Cambridge University Press.

(1910). *The Formation of the Historical World in the Human Sciences*. 2002 Edn. Princeton: Princeton University Press.

D'Oro, G. (2002). *Collingwood and the Metaphysics of Experience: Reinterpretation*. London: Routledge.

Drinkwater, J. F. (2007). The Principate: Lifebelt, or Millstone around the Neck of the Empire? In O. Hekster, G. de Kleijn and D. Slootjes (Eds.), *Crises and the Roman Empire*, pp. 67–74. Leiden: Brill.

(1987). *The Gallic Empire: Separatism and Continuity in the North-Western Provinces of the Roman Empire, AD 260–274*. Stuttgart: Franz Steiner Verlag Wiesbaden.

Duncan-Jones, R. (2006). Economic Change and the Transition to Late Antiquity. In S. Swain and M. Edwards (Eds.), *Approaching Late Antiquity: The Transformation from Early to Late Empire*, pp. 20–52. Oxford: Oxford University Press.

(2005). Implications of Roman Coinage: Debates and Differences. *Klio* 87 (2): 459–87.

(2001). The Denarii of Septimius Severus and the Mobility of Roman Coin. *Numismatic Chronicle* 161: 75–89.

(1996). The Impact of the Antonine Plague. *Journal of Roman Archaeology* 9: 108–36.

(1994). *Money and Government in the Roman Empire*. Cambridge: Cambridge University Press.

(1990). *Structure and Scale in the Roman Economy*. Cambridge: Cambridge University Press.

(1982). *Economy of the Roman Empire*. Cambridge: Cambridge University Press.

Dusek, T. (2008). Methodological Monism in Economics. *The Journal of Philosophical Economics* 1 (2): 26–50.

Easterly, W. and S. Fischer. (2001). Inflation and the Poor. *Journal of Money, Credit and Banking* 33 (2): 160–78.

Edwards, C. (1993). *The Politics of Immorality in Ancient Rome*. Cambridge: Cambridge University Press.

Ehling, K. (2008). Das Münzwesen. In K.-P. Johne (Ed.), *Die Zeit der Soldatenkaiser: Krise und Transformation des Römischen Reiches im 3. Jahrhundert n. Chr. (235–284), Vol. II*, pp. 843–60. Berlin: Oldenbourg Akademieverlag.

Elliott, C. P. (2016). Climate Change, Plague and Local Violence in Roman Egypt. *Past & Present* 230 (2): 3–31.

(2015). The Crisis of AD 33: Past and Present. *Journal of Ancient History* 3 (2): 267–81.

(2014). The Acceptance and Value of Roman Silver Coinage in the Second and Third Centuries AD. *Numismatic Chronicle* 174: 129–52.

(forthcoming). Disease, Grain Supply and State Inflexibility in the Late Second Century AD. In R. Arnott and R. Breitwieser (Eds.), *Disease in the Ancient World*. Oxford: Oxbow.

(forthcoming). Disease Proxies and the Diagnosis of the Late Antonine Economy. In K. Verboven (Ed.), *Complexity Economics: Building a New Approach to Ancient Economic History*. Palgrave Macmillan.

(forthcoming). Coin Debasement, Climate and Contagion in Second-Century Egypt: Some Intersections. In K. Butcher (Ed.), *Debasement: Manipulation of Coin Standards in Pre-Modern Monetary Systems*. Oxford: Oxbow.

Elster, J. (1989). *Nuts and Bolts for the Social Sciences*. Cambridge: Cambridge University Press.

Erdkamp, P. (2014). How Modern Was the Market Economy of the Roman World? *Œconomia: History, Methodology, Philosophy* 4 (2): 225–35.

(2005). *The Grain Market in the Roman Empire: A Social, Political and Economic Study*. Cambridge: Cambridge University Press.

Estiot, S. (2012). The Later Third Century. In W. E. Metcalf (Ed.), *The Oxford Handbook of Greek and Roman Coinage*, pp. 538–60. Oxford: Oxford University Press.

(1996). Le troisième siècle et la monnaie: crises et mutations. In J.-L. Fiches (Ed.), *Le IIIe siècle en Gaule Narbonnaise: données régionale sur la crise de l'Empire*, pp. 33–70. Sophia Antipolis: Editions APDCA.

Evans, R. J. (1997). The Augustan "Purge" of the Senate and the Census of 86 bc. *Acta Classica* 40: 77–86.

Fine, B. (2002). 'Economic Imperialism': A View from the Periphery. *Review of Radical Political Economics* 34 (2): 187–201.

(1999). A Question of Economics: Is It Colonizing the Social Sciences? *Economy and Society* 28 (3): 403–25.

Finley, M. I. (1985a). *Ancient History: Evidence and Models*. New York: Viking.

(1985b). *The Ancient Economy*. Second Edn. Berkeley: University of California Press.

Fiorini, L. and M. Torelli. (2007). La fusione, Afrodite e l'emporion. *Facta* 1: 75–106.

Fisher, I. (1913). A Compensated Dollar. *The Quarterly Journal of Economics* 27 (2): 213–35.

(1911). *The Purchasing Power of Money: Its Determination and Relation to Credit, Interest and Crises*. 1922 Revised Edn. New York: Macmillan.

Fogel, R. W. (1966). The New Economic History, I: Its Findings and Methods. *The Economic History Review* 19 (3): 642–56.

Foraboschi, D. (2003). Free Coinage e scarsezza di moneta. In E. Lo Cascio (Ed.), *Credito e moneta nel mondo romano*, pp. 231–44. Bari: Edipuglia.

Forsythe, G. (2006). *A Critical History of Early Rome: From Prehistory to the First Punic War*. Berkeley: University of California Press.

Foucault, M. (2008). *The Birth of Biopolitics*. Ed. M. Senellart. Palgrave Macmillan.

Friedman, J. (1996). Introduction: Economic Approaches to Politics. In J. Friedman (Ed.), *The Rational Choice Controversy: Economic Models of Politics Reconsidered*. New Haven: Yale University Press.

Friedman, M. (1969). *The Optimum Quantity of Money*. London: Macmillan.

(1953). *Essays in Positive Economics*. Chicago: University of Chicago Press.

Frier, B. W. and D. P. Kehoe. (2007). Law and Economic Institutions. In W. Scheidel, I. Morris and R. P. Saller (Eds.), *The Cambridge Economic History of the Greco-Roman World*, pp. 113–43. Cambridge: Cambridge University Press.

Friesen, J. P., T. H. Campbell and A. C. Kay (2015). The Psychological Advantage of Unfalsifiability: The Appeal of Untestable Religious and Political Ideologies. *Journal of Personality and Social Psychology* 108 (3): 515–29.

Gallagher, R. L. (2018). *Aristotle's Critique of Political Economy: With a Contemporary Application*. London: Routledge.

Gane, N. (2014). Sociology and Neoliberalism: A Missing History. *Sociology* 48 (6): 1092–106.

(2013). The Emergence of Neoliberalism: Thinking Through and Beyond Michel Foucault's Lectures on Biopolitics: *Theory, Culture & Society* 31(4): 3–27.

Garnsey, P. and R. P. Saller. (2014). *The Roman Empire: Economy, Society, and Culture*. Second Edn. London: Bloomsbury.

(1987). *The Roman Empire: Economy, Society, and Culture*. Berkeley: University of California Press.

Gazdac, C. (2002). Monetary Circulation and the Abandonment of the Auxiliary Forts in Roman Dacia. In P. Freeman, J. Bennett, Z. T. Fiema and B. Hoffmann (Eds.), *Limes XVIII. Proceedings of the XVIIIth International Congress of Roman Frontier Studies Held in Amman, Jordan (September 2000)*, pp. 737–55. Oxford: British Archaeological Reports.

Geertz, C. (1973). *The Interpretation of Cultures*. New York: Basic Books.

Geissen, A. (2012). The Coinage of Roman Egypt. In W. E. Metcalf (Ed.), *The Oxford Handbook of Greek and Roman Coinage*, pp. 561–83. Oxford: Oxford University Press.

Gibbs, M. (2012). Manufacture, Trade, and the Economy. In C. Riggs (Ed.), *The Oxford Handbook of Roman Egypt*, pp. 38–55. Oxford: Oxford University Press.

Giovannini, A. (1975). Athenian Currency in the Late Fifth and Early Fourth Century BC. *Greek, Roman, and Byzantine Studies* 16: 185–95.
Gitler, H. and M. Ponting (2003). *The Silver Coinage of Septimius Severus and His Family, 193–211 AD: A Study of the Chemical Composition of the Roman and Eastern Issues*. Milan: Ed. Ennerre.
Goldsmith, R. W. (1987). *Premodern Financial Systems: A Historical Comparative Study*. Cambridge: Cambridge University Press.
(1984). An Estimate of the Size and Structure of the National Product of the Early Roman Empire. *Review of Income and Wealth* 30 (3): 263–88.
Goodhart, C. A. E. (1998). The Two Concepts of Money: Implications for the Analysis of Optimal Currency Areas. *European Journal of Political Economy* 14 (3): 407–32.
Graeber, D. (2011). *Debt: The First 5,000 Years*. New York: Melville House.
Granovetter, M. (2007). Comment on Liverani and Bedford. In J. G. Manning and I. Morris (Eds.), *The Ancient Economy: Evidence and Models*, pp. 84–8. Stanford: Stanford University Press.
(1985). Economic Action and Social Structure: The Problem of Embeddedness. *American Journal of Sociology* 91 (3): 481–510.
Grantham, G. (2015). A Search-Equilibrium Approach to the Roman Economy. In P. Erdkamp and K. Verboven (Eds.), *Structure and Performance in the Roman Economy. Models, Methods and Case Studies*, pp. 59–96. Brussels: Latomus & Leuven Peeters.
Greene, K. (1990). *The Archaeology of the Roman Economy*. Berkeley: University of California Press.
Greenfield, R. L. and J. T. Salerno. (1983). Another Defense of Methodological Apriorism. *Eastern Economic Journal* 9 (1): 45–56.
Gurval, R. A. (1998). *Actium and Augustus: The Politics and Emotions of Civil War*. Ann Arbor: University of Michigan Press.
Hahn, U. and A. J. L. Harris. (2014). What Does It Mean to Be Biased: Motivated Reasoning and Rationality. *Psychology of Learning and Motivation* 61: 41–102.
Haklai-Rotenberg, M. (2011). Aurelian's Monetary Reform: Between Debasement and Public Trust. *Chiron* 41: 1–39.
Haley, E. W. (2003). *Baetica Felix: People and Prosperity in Southern Spain from Caesar to Septimius Severus*. Austin: University of Texas Press.
Harl, K. W. (2006). A Hoard of Roman Antoniniani from the Bath at Metropolis, Ionia. *American Journal of Numismatics (1989–)* 18: 75–111.
(1996). *Coinage in the Roman Economy, 300 BC to AD 700*. Baltimore: Johns Hopkins University Press.
Harper, K. (2017). *The Fate of Rome: Climate, Disease, and the End of an Empire*. Princeton: Princeton University Press.
(2016a). Database of Prices, Wages, and Rents for Roman Egypt from the First through Seventh Centuries AD. DARMC Scholarly Data Series 2016-5, Center for Geographic Analysis, Harvard University.

(2016b). People, Plagues, and Prices in the Roman World: The Evidence from Egypt. *Journal of Economic History* 76 (3): 803–39.

Harris, W. V. (2008a). Introduction. In W. V. Harris (Ed.), *The Monetary Systems of the Greeks and Romans*, pp. 1–11. Oxford: Oxford University Press.

(2008b). The Nature of Roman Money. In W. V. Harris (Ed.), *The Monetary Systems of the Greeks and Romans*, pp. 174–207. Oxford: Oxford University Press.

(2007). The Late Republic. In W. Scheidel, I. Morris and R. P. Saller (Eds.), *The Cambridge Economic History of the Greco-Roman World*, pp. 511–39. Cambridge: Cambridge University Press.

(2006). A Revisionist View of Roman Money. *Journal of Roman Studies* 96: 1–24.

(1993). Between Archaic and Modern: Some Current Problems in the Economic History of the High Roman Empire. In W. V. Harris (Ed.), *The Inscribed Economy: Production and Distribution in the Roman Empire in the Light of Instrumentum Domesticum*, pp. 11–29. Ann Arbor: University of Michigan Press.

(1988). On the Applicability of the Concept of Class in Roman History. In T. Yuge and M. Doi (Eds.), *Forms of Control and Subordination in Antiquity*, pp. 598–610. Leiden: Brill.

Hart, K. (2012). Money: One Anthropologist's View. In J. G. Carrier (Ed.), *A Handbook of Economic Anthropology*, pp. 160–75. Second Edn. London: Edward Elgar Publishing.

(1986). Heads or Tails? Two Sides of the Coin. *Man* 21 (4): 637–56.

Haselgrove, C. and S. Krmnicek. (2012). The Archaeology of Money. *Annual Review of Anthropology* 41 (1): 235–50.

Hasler, K. (1980). *Studien zu Wesen und Wert des Geldes in der römischen Kaiserzeit von Augustus bis Severus Alexander*. Bochum: Brockmeyer.

Häuser, K. (1988). Historical School and *Methodenstreit*. Journal of Institutional and Theoretical Economics (JITE)/Zeitschrift für die gesamte Staatswissenschaft 144 (3): 532–42.

Hawkins, C. (2017). Artisans, Retailers, and Credit Transactions in the Roman World. *Journal of Ancient History* 5 (1): 66–92.

Hawthorn, G. (1993). *Plausible Worlds: Possibility and Understanding in History and the Social Sciences*. Cambridge: Cambridge University Press.

Hayek, F. A. (1990). *Denationalisation of Money: The Argument Refined*. Third Edn. London: Institute of Economic Affairs.

(1967). *Prices and Production*. Second Edn. New York: Augustus M. Kelley.

(1952). *The Sensory Order: An Inquiry into the Foundations of Theoretical Psychology*. Chicago: University of Chicago Press.

(1942). Scientism and the Study of Society, Part I. *Economica* 9 (35): 267–91.

Hill, L. E. (1968). A Critique of Positive Economics. *The American Journal of Economics and Sociology* 27 (3): 259–66.

Hirsch, P., S. Michaels and R. Friedman. (1987). 'Dirty Hands' versus 'Clean Models': Is Sociology in Danger of Being Seduced by Economics? *Theory and Society* 16 (3): 317–36.
Hitchner, B. (2007). 'The Advantages of Wealth and Luxury': The Case for Economic Growth in the Roman Empire. In J. G. Manning and I. Morris (Eds.), *The Ancient Economy: Evidence and Models*, pp. 207–22. Stanford: Stanford University Press.
(2002). Olive Production and the Roman Economy: The Case for Intensive Growth in the Roman Empire. In W. Scheidel and S. von Reden (Eds.), *The Ancient Economy*, pp. 71–83. London: Routledge.
Hobbs, R. (2006). *Late Roman Precious Metal Deposits c. AD 200–700: Changes over Time and Space*. Oxford: British Archaeological Reports.
Hodgson, G. M. (2002). *How Economics Forgot History: The Problem of Historical Specificity in Social Science*. London: Routledge.
Hollander, D. B. (2007). *Money in the Late Roman Republic*. Leiden: Brill.
Holleran, C. (2012). *Shopping in Ancient Rome: The Retail Trade in the Late Republic and the Principate*. Oxford: Oxford University Press.
Hollis, M. (1996). The Social Destruction of Reality. In *Reason in Action: Essays in the Philosophy of Social Science*, pp. 221–41. Cambridge: Cambridge University Press.
(1977). *Models of Man: Philosophical Thoughts on Social Action*. Cambridge: Cambridge University Press.
Hollis, M. and E. J. Nell. (1975). *Rational Economic Man*. Cambridge: Cambridge University Press.
Hong, H. (2000). Marx and Menger on Value: As Many Similarities as Differences. *Cambridge Journal of Economics* 24 (1): 87–105.
Hopkins, K. (2018). *Sociological Studies in Roman History*. Ed. C. Kelly. Cambridge: Cambridge University Press.
(2009). The Political Economy of the Roman Empire. In I. Morris and W. Scheidel (Eds.), *The Dynamics of Ancient Empires: State Power from Assyria to Byzantium*, pp. 178–204. Oxford: Oxford University Press.
(2002). Rome, Taxes, Rents and Trade. In W. Scheidel and S. von Reden (Eds.), *The Ancient Economy*, pp. 190–232. London: Routledge.
(1980). Taxes and Trade in the Roman Empire (200 BC–AD 400). *Journal of Roman Studies* 70: 101–25.
(1978). *Conquerors and Slaves*. Cambridge: Cambridge University Press.
Horwitz, S. (1996). Capital Theory, Inflation and Deflation: The Austrians and Monetary Disequilibrium Theory Compared. *Journal of the History of Economic Thought* 18 (2): 287–308.
Howells, P. G. A. (1997). The Demand for Endogenous Money: A Rejoinder. *Journal of Post Keynesian Economics* 19 (3): 429–35.
(1995). The Demand for Endogenous Money. *Journal of Post Keynesian Economics* 18 (1): 89–106.
Howgego, C. (1995). *Ancient History from Coins*. London: Routledge.

(1994). Coin Circulation and the Integration of the Roman Economy. *Journal of Roman Archaeology* 7: 5–21.

(1992). The Supply and Use of Money in the Roman World 200 BC to AD 300. *Journal of Roman Studies* 82: 1–31.

Howgego, C., K. Butcher and M. Ponting. (forthcoming). Coinage and the Roman Economy in the Antonine Period: The View from Egypt. In A. K. Bowman and A. Wilson (Eds.), *Mining, Metal Supply and Coinage in the Roman Empire*. Oxford: Oxford University Press.

Hoyer, D. (2018). *Money, Culture, and Well-Being in Rome's Economic Development, 0–275 CE*. Leiden: Brill.

Hunter, F. (2007). Silver for the Barbarians: Interpreting Denarii Hoards in North Britain and Beyond. In R. Hingley and S. Willis (Eds.), *Roman Finds in Context: Theory and Practice*, pp. 214–24. Oxford: Oxbow.

Ingham, G. (2012). Revisiting the Credit Theory of Money and Trust. In J. Pixley (Ed.), *New Perspectives on Emotions in Finance: The Sociology of Confidence, Fear and Betrayal*, pp. 121–39. London: Routledge.

(2004a). *The Nature of Money*. Cambridge: Polity Press.

(2004b). The Emergence of Capitalist Credit Money. In L. R. Wray (Ed.), *Credit and State Theories of Money*, pp. 173–222. Edward Elgar Publishing.

(1996). Money Is a Social Relation. *Review of Social Economy* 54 (4): 507–29.

Innes, A. M. (1914). The Credit Theory of Money. *The Banking Law Journal* 31: 151–68.

(1913). What Is Money? *The Banking Law Journal* 30: 377–408.

Jacob, J., M. Brinkerhoff, E. Jovic and G. Wheatley. (2004). The Social and Cultural Capital of Community Currency: An Ithaca HOURS Case Study Survey. *International Journal of Community Currency Research* 8: 42–56.

Jersey, P. de and C. Haselgrove, Eds. (2006). Early Potin Coinage in Britain: An Update. *Celtic Coinage: New Discoveries, New Discussion*, pp. 17–28. Oxford: Archaeopress.

Johnson, O. A. (1960). Denial of the Synthetic "A Priori." *Philosophy* 35 (134): 255–64.

Jones, D. W. (2014). *Economic Theory and the Ancient Mediterranean*. Oxford: Wiley-Blackwell.

Jones, G. D. B. (1980). The Roman Mines at Riotinto. *Journal of Roman Studies* 70: 146–65.

Jongman, W. M. (2014a). The New Economic History of the Roman Empire. In F. de Callataÿ (Ed.), *Quantifying the Greco-Roman Economy and Beyond*, pp. 169–88. Bari: Edipuglia.

(2014b). Why Modern Economic Theory Applies, Even to the Distant Roman Past. In H. Platts, J. Pearce, C. Barron, J. Lundock and J. Yoo (Eds.), *Proceedings of the Twenty-Third Annual Theoretical Roman Archaeology Conference, Kings College London 2013*, pp. 27–36. Oxford: Oxbow.

(2003). A Golden Age: Death, Money Supply and Social Succession in the Roman Empire. In E. Lo Cascio (Ed.), *Credito e Moneta Nel Mondo Romano*, pp. 181–96. Bari: Edipuglia.

Jördens, A. (2009). *Statthalterliche Verwaltung in der Römischen Kaiserzeit: Studien zum praefectus Aegypti*. Stuttgart: Franz Steiner Verlag.

Kahan, D. M. (2013). Ideology, Motivated Reasoning, and Cognitive Reflection: An Experimental Study. *Judgment and Decision Making* 8: 407–24.

Kalberg, S. (1980). Max Weber's Types of Rationality: Cornerstones for the Analysis of Rationalization Processes in History. *American Journal of Sociology* 85 (5): 1145–79.

Kaldor, N. (1986). *The Scourge of Monetarism*. Second Edn. Oxford: Oxford University Press.

Kaplan, J. T., S. I. Gimbel and S. Harris. (2016). Neural Correlates of Maintaining One's Political Beliefs in the Face of Counterevidence. *Scientific Reports* 6: 39589.

Karwiese, S. (1991). The Artemisium Coin Hoard and the First Coins of Ephesus. *Revue Belge de Numismatique* 137: 1–28.

Katsari, C. (2011). *The Roman Monetary System: The Eastern Provinces from the First to the Third Century* AD. Cambridge: Cambridge University Press.

Katsari, C., C. S. Lightfoot and A. Ozme. (2012). *The Amorium Mint and the Coin Finds: Amorium Reports 4*. Berlin: Walter de Gruyter.

Kay, P. (2018). Financial Institutions and Structures in the Last Century of the Roman Republic. In A. K. Bowman and A. Wilson (Eds.), *Trade, Commerce, and the State in the Roman World*, pp. 133–74. Oxford: Oxford University Press.

(2014). *Rome's Economic Revolution*. Oxford: Oxford University Press.

Kehoe, D. P. (2012). Contract Labor. In W. Scheidel (Ed.), *The Cambridge Companion to the Roman Economy*, pp. 114–30. Cambridge: Cambridge University Press.

(2007). *Law and the Rural Economy in the Roman Empire*. Ann Arbor: University of Michigan Press.

(1997). *Investment, Profit, and Tenancy: The Jurists and the Roman Agrarian Economy*. Ann Arbor: University of Michigan Press.

Kehoe, D. P., D. Ratzan and U. Yiftach (2015a). Introduction: Transaction Costs, Ancient History, and the Law. In D. P. Kehoe, D. Ratzan and U. Yiftach (Eds.), *Law and Transaction Costs in the Ancient Economy*, pp. 1–35. Ann Arbor: University of Michigan Press.

Kehoe, D. P., D. Ratzan and U. Yiftach, Eds. (2015b). *Law and Transaction Costs in the Ancient Economy*. Ann Arbor: University of Michigan Press.

Kennedy, D. (2005). The Disenchantment of Logically Formal Legal Rationality or Max Weber's Sociology in the Genealogy of the Contemporary Mode of Western Legal Thought. In C. Camic, P. Gorski and D. Trubek (Eds.), *Max Weber's Economy and Society: A Critical Companion*, pp. 322–65. Stanford: Stanford University Press.

Keppie, L. J. F. (1983). *Colonisation and Veteran Settlement in Italy: 47–14 BC* London: British School at Rome.
Kessler, D. and P. Temin. (2007). The Organization of the Grain Trade in the Early Roman Empire. *The Economic History Review* 60 (2): 313–32.
Keynes, J. M. (1936). *The General Theory of Employment, Interest and Money*. New York: Harcourt, Brace and Co.
Kim, K. and T. Berard. (2009). Typification in Society and Social Science: The Continuing Relevance of Schutz's Social Phenomenology. *Human Studies* 32 (3): 263–89.
Knapp, G. F. (1924). *The State Theory of Money*. London: Macmillan.
Knight, F. H. (1921). *Risk, Uncertainty and Profit*. Boston: Hart, Schaffner & Marx.
Koedijk, M. (forthcoming). Does Wealth Beget Wealth? The Case of Cicero. In N. Morley (Ed.), *Capital in Classical Antiquity*.
Koops, E. (2016). Price Setting and Other Attempts to Control the Economy. In P. J. du Plessis, C. Ando and K. Tuori (Eds.), *The Oxford Handbook of Roman Law and Society*, pp. 609–20. Oxford: Oxford University Press.
Koppl, R. (2002). *Big Players and the Economic Theory of Expectations*. New York: Palgrave Macmillan.
Kripke, S. A. (1980). *Naming and Necessity*. Cambridge: Harvard University Press.
Kroll, J. H. (2008). The Monetary Use of Weighed Bullion in Archaic Greece. In W. V. Harris (Ed.), *The Monetary Systems of the Greeks and Romans*, pp. 12–37. Oxford: Oxford University Press.
Kunda, Z. (1990). The Case for Motivated Reasoning. *Psychological Bulletin* 108 (3): 480–98.
Kunisz, A. (1983). Udzial Zlotego Pienadza w Cyrkulacji Na Terytorium Egiptu w I–III w n.e. *Wiadomisci Numizmatyczne* 27: 121–65.
Kurke, L. (1999). *Coins, Bodies, Games, and Gold: The Politics of Meaning in Archaic Greece*. Princeton: Princeton University Press.
(1995). Herodotus and the Language of Metals. *Helios* 22 (1): 36–64.
Lankenau, S. E. (2001). Smoke 'Em If You Got 'Em: Cigarette Black Markets in US Prisons and Jails. *The Prison Journal* 81 (2): 142–61.
Lavan, M. (2013). *Slaves to Rome: Paradigms of Empire in Roman Culture*. Cambridge: Cambridge University Press.
(forthcoming). *Making Citizens*. Cambridge: Cambridge University Press.
Lazear, E. P. (1991). *Prices and Wages in Transition Economies*. Stanford: Hoover Press.
Legutko, P. A. (2002). The Revolt of Macrianus and Quietus and Its Effect on Alexandrian Coinage, ad 260–263. *Numismatic Chronicle (1966–)* 162: 135–68.
Levine, D. N. (2005). The Continuing Challenge of Weber's Theory of Rational Action. In C. Camic, P. Gorski and D. Trubek (Eds.), *Max Weber's Economy and Society: A Critical Companion*, pp. 101–26. Stanford: Stanford University Press.

Lintott, A. (2009). *The Romans in the Age of Augustus*. London: John Wiley & Sons.
(1999). *The Constitution of the Roman Republic*. Oxford: Oxford University Press.
Lo Cascio, E. (2018). Market Regulation and Transaction Costs in the Roman Empire. In A. Bowman and A. Wilson (Eds.), *Trade, Commerce, and the State in the Roman World*, pp. 117–32. Oxford: Oxford University Press.
(2008). The Function of Gold Coinage in the Monetary Economy of the Roman Empire. In W. V. Harris (Ed.), *The Monetary Systems of the Greeks and Romans*, pp. 160–73. Oxford: Oxford University Press.
(2007). The Early Roman Empire: The State and the Economy. In W. Scheidel, I. Morris and R. P. Saller (Eds.), *The Cambridge Economic History of the Greco-Roman World*, pp. 619–47. Cambridge: Cambridge University Press.
(2006). The Role of the State in the Roman Economy: Making Use of the New Institutional Economics. In P. F. Bang, M. Ikeguchi and H. G. Ziche (Eds.), *Ancient Economies, Modern Methodologies: Archaeology, Comparative History, Models and Institutions*, pp. 215–34. Bari: Edipuglia.
(2005). The New State of Diocletian and Constantine: From the Tetrarchy to the Reunification of the Empire. In A. K. Bowman, A. Cameron and P. Garnsey (Eds.), *The Cambridge Ancient History, 2nd Edn.*, pp. 170–83. Cambridge: Cambridge University Press.
(2000). The Roman Principate: The Impact of the Organisation of the Empire on Production. In E. Lo Cascio and D. W. Rathbone (Eds.), *Production and Public Powers in Classical Antiquity*, pp. 77–85. Cambridge: Cambridge Philosophical Society.
(1996). How Did the Romans View Their Coinage and Its Function? In C. E. King and D. G. Wigg (Eds.), *Coin Finds and Coin Use in the Roman World*, pp. 273–87. Berlin: Gebrüder Mann Verlag.
(1984). Dall'antoninianus al 'laureato grande': L'evoluzione monetaria del III secolo alla luce della nuova documentazione di età dioclezianea. *Opus* 3: 133–201.
(1981). State and Coinage in the Late Republic and Early Empire. *Journal of Roman Studies* 71: 76–86.
Long, R. T. (2009). R. G. Collingwood: Historicist or Praxeologist? Working Paper, Auburn University.
Lorber, C. C. (2012). The Coinage of the Ptolemies. In W. E. Metcalf (Ed.), *The Oxford Handbook of Greek and Roman Coinage*, pp. 211–34. Oxford: Oxford University Press.
Love, J. R. (1991). *Antiquity and Capitalism: Max Weber and the Sociological Foundations of Roman Civilization*. London: Routledge.
Luhmann, N. (1982). *The Differentiation of Society*. New York: Columbia University Press.
Lyttkens, C. H. (2012). *Economic Analysis of Institutional Change in Ancient Greece*. London: Routledge.

MacMullen, R. (1988). *Corruption and the Decline of Rome*. New Haven: Yale University Press.

(1976). *Roman Government's Response to Crisis, AD 235–337*. New Haven, CT: Yale University Press.

(1970). Market-Days in the Roman Empire. *Phoenix* 24 (4): 333–41.

Macro, A. D. (1976). Imperial Provisions for Pergamum: OGIS 484. *Greek, Roman, and Byzantine Studies* 17: 169–79.

Madra, Y. M. (2017). *Late Neoclassical Economics: The Restoration of Theoretical Humanism in Contemporary Economic Theory*. London: Routledge.

Manders, E. (2012). *Coining Images of Power: Patterns in the Representation of Roman Emperors on Imperial Coinage, AD 193–284*. Leiden: Brill.

(2007). Mapping the Representation of Roman Imperial Power in Times of Crisis. In O. Hekster, G. de Kleijn and D. Slootjes (Eds.), *Crises and the Roman Empire*, pp. 275–90. Leiden: Brill.

Manning, J. G. (2011). Networks, Hierarchies, and Markets in the Ptolemaic Economy. In Z. Archibald, J. Davies and V. Gabrielsen (Eds.), *The Economies of Hellenistic Societies, Third to First Centuries BC*, pp. 296–323. Oxford: Oxford University Press.

Manning, J. G. and I. Morris. (2007). *The Ancient Economy: Evidence and Models*. Stanford: Stanford University Press.

Maresch, K. (1996). *Bronze und Silber: Papyrologische Beiträge zur Geschichte der Währung im ptolemäischen und römischen Ägypten bis zum 2. Jahrhundert n. Chr.* Opladen: VS Verlag für Sozialwissenschaften.

Maresch, K. and Z. Packman. (1990). *Papyri from the Washington University Collection St. Louis, Missouri: Part II (P. Wash. Univ. II)*. Opladen: Springer.

Martin, M. (2000). *Verstehen: The Uses of Understanding in the Social Sciences*. London: Routledge.

Martin, R. (2001). *Tacitus Annals V & VI*. Warminster: Aris & Phillips.

Marx, K. (1887). *Capital: Volume 1: A Critique of Political Economy*. Trans. B. Fowkes. 1976 Edn. London: Penguin Classics.

(1847). *The Poverty of Philosophy*. Ed. K. Marx and F. Engels. 1976 Edn. London: Lawrence and Wishart.

Marzano, A. (2007). *Roman Villas in Central Italy: A Social and Economic History*. Leiden: Brill.

Maucourant, J. (2012). New Institutional Economics and History. *Journal of Economic Issues* 46 (1): 193–208.

(1995). The Substantive Economy of Money: Karl Polanyi in the Tradition of 'Old Institutionalism'. Working Paper, Centre Walras, N177.

(1991). La question de la monnaie en Égypte ancienne. *La Revue du Mauss* 13: 155–64.

Maurer, B., T. C. Nelms and L. Swartz. (2013). "When Perhaps the Real Problem Is Money Itself!": The Practical Materiality of Bitcoin. *Social Semiotics* 23(2): 261–77.

McConnell, J. R., A. I. Wilson, A. Stohl, M. M. Arienzo, N. J. Chellman, S. Eckhardt, E. M. Thompson, A. M. Pollard and J. P. Steffensen (2018). Lead

Pollution Recorded in Greenland Ice Indicates European Emissions Tracked Plagues, Wars, and Imperial Expansion during Antiquity. *Proceedings of the National Academy of Sciences* 115 (22): 5726–31.

McCormick, M. (2013). What Climate Science, Ausonius, Nile Floods, Rye, and Thatch Tell Us about the Environmental History of the Roman Empire. In W. V. Harris (Ed.), *The Ancient Mediterranean Environment between Science and History*, pp. 61–88. Leiden: Brill.

McCormick, M., U. Büntgen, M. A. Cane, E. R. Cook, K. Harper, P. Huybers, T. Litt et al. (2012). Climate Change during and after the Roman Empire: Reconstructing the Past from Scientific and Historical Evidence. *Journal of Interdisciplinary History* 43 (2): 169–220.

McGinn, T. A. J. (2012). *Obligations in Roman Law: Past, Present, and Future.* Ann Arbor: University of Michigan Press.

Meikle, S. (2002). Modernism, Economics and the Ancient Economy. In W. Scheidel and S. von Reden (Eds.), *The Ancient Economy*, pp. 233–50. London: Routledge.

Menger, C. (2007). *Principles of Economics.* Trans. J. Dingwall and B. F. Hoselitz. Auburn: Ludwig von Mises Institute.

(1985). *Investigations into the Method of the Social Sciences.* Ed. L. Schneider. Trans. F. J. Nock. New York: New York University Press.

Metcalf, W. E. (1980). *The Cistophori of Hadrian.* Cambridge: American Numismatic Society.

Metcalfe, J. S. (2010). Complexity and Emergence in Economics: The Road from Smith to Hayek (via Marshall and Schumpeter). *History of Economic Ideas* 18 (2): 45–75.

Meyer, E. (1924). Die wirtschaftliche Entwicklung des Altertums. In E. Meyer (Ed.), *Kleine Schriften*, pp. 81–168. Halle: M. Niemeyer.

Meyer, E. A. (2004). *Legitimacy and Law in the Roman World: Tabulae in Roman Belief and Practice.* Cambridge: Cambridge University Press.

Milne, J. G. (1971). *Catalogue of Alexandrian Coins.* Oxford: Spink.

Mirowski, P. (2002). *Machine Dreams: Economics Becomes a Cyborg Science.* Cambridge: Cambridge University Press.

Mises, L. von (2009). *Memoirs.* Auburn: Ludwig von Mises Institute.

(2000). The Main Issues in Present-Day Monetary Controversies. In R. M. Eveling (Ed.), *Selected Writings of Ludwig von Mises: The Political Economy of International Reform & Reconstruction, Volume 3*, pp. 119–32. Indianapolis: Liberty Fund.

(1957). *Theory and History: An Interpretation of Social and Economic Evaluation.* New Haven: Yale University Press.

(1953). *The Theory of Money and Credit.* Trans. H. E. Batson. New Haven: Yale University Press.

(1949). *Human Action: A Treatise on Economics.* New Haven: Yale University Press.

(1933). *Epistemological Problems of Economics.* Trans. G. Reisman. 2003 Edn. Auburn: Ludwig Von Mises Inst.

(1920). Die Wirtschaftsrechnung im sozialistischen Gemeinwesen. *Archiv für Sozialwissenschaften und Sozialpolitik* 47 (1): 86–121.

Moore, B. J. (1988). The Endogenous Money Supply. *Journal of Post Keynesian Economics* 10 (3): 372–85.

Morley, N. (2014). Orders of Magnitude, Margins of Error. In F. de Callataÿ (Ed.), *Quantifying the Greco-Roman Economy and Beyond*, pp. 29–42. Bari: Edipuglia.

(2010). *The Roman Empire: Roots of Imperialism*. London: Pluto Press.

(2007). *Trade in Classical Antiquity*. Cambridge: Cambridge University Press.

(2006a). Narrative Economy. In P. F. Bang, M. Ikeguchi and H. G. Ziche (Eds.), *Ancient Economies, Modern Methodologies: Archaeology, Comparative History, Models and Institutions*, pp. 27–50. Bari: Edipuglia.

(2006b). Social Structure and Demography. In N. Rosenstein and R. Morstein-Marx (Eds.), *A Companion to the Roman Republic*, pp. 299–323. Oxford: John Wiley & Sons.

(2004). *Theories, Models and Concepts in Ancient History*. London: Routledge.

(2000a). Markets, Marketing and the Roman Elite. In E. Lo Cascio (Ed.), *Mercati permanenti e mercati periodici nel mondo romano. Atti degli Incontri Capresi di Storia dell'economia Antica (Capri 13–15 Ottobre 1997). Pragmateiai 2*, pp. 211–21. Bari: Edipuglia.

(2000b). Trajan's Engines. *Greece & Rome* 47 (2): 197–210.

(1999). *Writing Ancient History*. Ithaca: Cornell University Press.

Morris, I. (2002). Hard Surfaces. In P. Cartledge, E. E. Cohen and L. Foxhall (Eds.), *Money, Labour and Land; Approaches to the Economies of Ancient Greece*, pp. 8–43. London: Routledge.

Mueller, G. H. (1979). The Notion of Rationality in the Work of Max Weber. *European Journal of Sociology* 20 (1): 149–71.

Munslow, A. (2000). *The Routledge Companion to Historical Studies*. London: Routledge.

Nafissi, M. (2005). *Ancient Athens and Modern Ideology. Value, Theory and Evidence in Historical Sciences: Max Weber, Karl Polanyi and Moses Finley*. London: Institute of Classical Studies.

Nee, V. (1994). The New Institutionalisms in Economics and Sociology. In N. J. Smelser and R. Swedberg (Eds.), *The Handbook of Economic Sociology*, pp. 49–74. Princeton: Princeton University Press.

North, D. C. (1996). Epilogue: Economic Performance Through Time. In L. J. Alston, T. Eggertsson and D. C. North (Eds.), *Empirical Studies in Institutional Change*, pp. 342–56. Cambridge: Cambridge University Press.

(1990). *Institutions, Institutional Change and Economic Performance*. Cambridge: Cambridge University Press.

(1981). *Structure and Change in Economic History*. New York: W. W. Norton & Company.

(1977). Markets and Other Allocation Systems in History: The Challenge of Karl Polanyi. *Journal of European Economic History* 6 (3): 703–16.

(1973). *Growth and Welfare in the American Past: A New Economic History*. Second Edn. Englewood Cliffs: Prentice Hall.

North, D. C., J. J. Wallis and B. R. Weingast. (2009). *Violence and Social Orders: A Conceptual Framework for Interpreting Recorded Human History*. Cambridge: Cambridge University Press.

North, J. A. (2009). Ancient History Today. In A. Erskine (Ed.), *A Companion to Ancient History*, pp. 89–98. Chichester: Wiley-Blackwell.

O'Connor, J. (2002). *The Fiscal Crisis of the State*. Piscataway: Transaction Publishers.

Ogden, J. (1996). Weight Units of Romano-Egyptian Gold Jewellery. In D. M. Bailey (Ed.), *Archaeological Research in Roman Egypt*, pp. 191–6. Ann Arbor: Journal of Roman Archaeology.

Panagopoulou, K. (2007). Between Necessity and Extravagance: Silver as a Commodity in the Hellenistic Period. *Annual of the British School at Athens* 102: 315–43.

Parry, J. and M. Bloch, Eds. (1989). *Money and the Morality of Exchange*. Cambridge: Cambridge University Press.

Phang, S. E. (2008). *Roman Military Service: Ideologies of Discipline in the Late Republic and Early Principate*. Cambridge: Cambridge University Press.

Poblome, J. (2015). The Economy of the Roman World as a Complex Adaptive System. Testing the Case in Second to Fifth Century CE Sagalassos. In P. Erdkamp and K. Verboven (Eds.), *Structure and Performance in the Roman Economy. Models, Methods and Case Studies*, pp. 97–140. Brussels: Latomus & Leuven Peeters.

Polanyi, K. (1968). The Semantics of Money-Uses. In G. Dalton (Ed.), *Primitive, Archaic, and Modern Economies: Essays of Karly Polanyi*, pp. 175–203. Boston: Beacon Press.

(1957). The Economy as Instituted Process. In K. Polanyi, C. M. Arensberg and H. W. Pearson (Eds.), *Trade and Market in the Early Empires: Economies in History and Theory*, pp. 243–70. New York: The Free Press.

(1944). *The Great Transformation: The Political and Economic Origins of Our Time*. Boston: Beacon Press.

Popper, K. R. (1963). *Conjectures and Refutations: The Growth of Scientific Knowledge*. 2004 Reprint. London: Routledge.

(1957). *The Poverty of Historicism*. 2004 Reprint. London: Routledge.

Potter, D. S. (2014). *The Roman Empire at Bay, AD 180–395*. Second Edn. London: Routledge.

Potts, C. (forthcoming). Made in Etruria. Recontextualizing the Ramo Secco. *American Journal of Numismatics* 31.

Radford, R. A. (1945). The Economic Organisation of a POW Camp. *Economica* 12(48): 189–201.

Rathbone, D. (2009). Earnings and Costs: Living Standards and the Roman Economy. In A. K. Bowman and A. Wilson (Eds.), *Quantifying the Roman Economy: Methods and Problems*, pp. 299–326. Oxford: Oxford University Press.

(2007). Roman Egypt. In W. Scheidel, I. Morris and R. P. Saller (Eds.), *The Cambridge Economic History of the Greco-Roman World*, pp. 698–719. Cambridge: Cambridge University Press.
(2005). Economic Rationalism and the Heroninos Archive. *Topoi* 12 (1): 261–9.
(2002). The Ancient Economy and Graeco-Roman Egypt. In W. Scheidel and S. von Reden (Eds.), *The Ancient Economy*, pp. 155–72. London: Routledge.
(1997). Prices and Price Formation in Roman Egypt. In J. Andreau, P. Briant and R. Descat (Eds.), *Économie antique. Prix et formation des prix dans les économies antiques*, pp. 183–244. Saint-Bertrand-de-Comminges: Musée Archéologique.
(1996a). Monetisation, Not Price Inflation, in Third Century AD Egypt? In C. E. King and D. G. Wigg (Eds.), *Coin Finds and Coin Use in the Roman World*, pp. 321–39. Berlin: Gebrüder Mann Verlag.
(1996b). The Imperial Finances. In A. K. Bowman, E. Champlin and A. Lintott (Eds.), *The Cambridge Ancient History*, pp. 309–23. Cambridge: Cambridge University Press.
(1991). *Economic Rationalism and Rural Society in Third-Century AD Egypt: The Heroninos Archive and the Appianus Estate*. Cambridge: Cambridge University Press.
Rathbone, D. and S. von Reden. (2015). Mediterranean Grain Prices in Classical Antiquity. In R. J. Van der Spek, J. L. van Zanden and B. van Leeuwen (Eds.), *A History of Market Performance: From Ancient Babylonia to the Modern World*, pp. 149–235. London: Routledge.
Reece, R. (1981). The Third Century: Crisis or Change. In A. King and M. Henig (Eds.), *The Roman West in the Third Century: Contributions from Archaeology and History*, pp. 27–38. Oxford: British Archaeological Reports.
Reibig, A. (2001). The Bücher–Meyer Controversy: The Nature of the Ancient Economy in Modern Ideology. Unpublished Ph.D. thesis, University of Glasgow.
Rizzo, M. J. (2015). The Problem of Rationality: Austrian Economics between Classical Behaviorism and Behavioral Economics. In C. J. Coyne and P. J. Boettke (Eds.), *The Oxford Handbook of Austrian Economics*, pp. 364–92. Oxford: Oxford University Press.
Robbins, L. (1934). *The Great Depression*. New York: Books for Libraries.
(1932). *An Essay on the Nature and Significance of Economic Science*. London: Macmillan.
Rodewald, C. (1976). *Money in the Age of Tiberius*. Manchester: Manchester University Press.
Rodrigues, M., F. Cappa, M. Schreiner, P. Ferloni, M. Radtke, U. Reinholz, B. Woytek and M. Alram (2011). Further Metallurgical Analyses on Silver Coins of Trajan (AD 98–117). *Journal of Analytical Atomic Spectrometry* 26 (5): 984–91.
Rolnick, A. J. and W. E. Weber. (1986). Gresham's Law or Gresham's Fallacy? *Journal of Political Economy* 94 (1): 185–99.

Roselaar, S. T. (2010). *Public Land in the Roman Republic: A Social and Economic History of Ager Publicus in Italy, 396–89 BC*. London: Oxford University Press.

Rostovtzeff, M. I. (1936). The Hellenistic World and Its Economic Development. *The American Historical Review* 41 (2): 231–52.

(1933). Review of J. Hasebrock, Griechische Wirtschaftsund Handelsgeschichte. *Zeitschrift für die gesamte Staatswirtschaft* 92: 333–9.

Rowan, C. (2014). The Value of Coinage in the Second Punic War and After. In A. Bokern and C. Rowan (Eds.), *Embodying Value? The Transformation of Objects in and from the Ancient World*, pp. 77–88. Oxford: British Archaeological Reports.

Rowlandson, J. (2001). Money Use among the Peasantry of Ptolemaic and Roman Egypt. In A. Meadows and K. Shipton (Eds.), *Money and Its Uses in the Ancient Greek World*, pp. 145–55. Oxford: Oxford University Press.

(1998). *Women and Society in Greek and Roman Egypt: A Sourcebook*. Cambridge: Cambridge University Press.

Roymans, N. and J. Aarts. (2009). Coin Use in the Dynamic Frontier Region: Late Iron Age Coinages in the Lower Rhine Area. *Journal of Archaeology in the Low Countries* 1: 5–26.

Sahlins, M. D. (2000). *Culture in Practice: Selected Essays*. New York: Zone Books.

(1974). *Stone Age Economics*. New York: Aldine.

Saller, R. P. (2002). Framing the Debate over Growth in the Ancient Economy. In S. von Reden and W. Scheidel (Eds.), *The Ancient Economy*, pp. 251–69. London: Routledge.

(1982). *Personal Patronage Under the Early Empire*. Cambridge: Cambridge University Press.

Samson, R. (1989). Rural Slavery, Inscriptions, Archaeology and Marx: A Response to Ramsay MacMullen's "Late Roman Slavery." *Historia: Zeitschrift Für Alte Geschichte* 38 (1): 99–110.

Schaps, D. (2003). *The Invention of Coinage and the Monetization of Ancient Greece*. Ann Arbor: University of Michigan Press.

Scheid, J. (2007). *Res gestae divi Augusti: hauts faits du divin Auguste*. Paris: Les Belles Lettres.

Scheidel, W. (2017). *The Great Leveler: Violence and the History of Inequality from the Stone Age to the Twenty-First Century*. Princeton: Princeton University Press.

(2014). Roman Real Wages in Context. In F. de Callataÿ (Ed.), *Quantifying the Greco-Roman Economy and Beyond*, pp. 209–18. Bari: Edipuglia.

(2012). Slavery. In W. Scheidel (Ed.), *The Cambridge Companion to the Roman Economy*, pp. 89–113. Cambridge: Cambridge University Press.

(2010a). Real Wages in Early Economies: Evidence for Living Standards from 1800 BCE to 1300 CE. *Journal of the Economic and Social History of the Orient* 53 (3): 425–62.

(2010b). Coin Quality, Coin Quantity, and Coin Value in Early China and the Roman World. *American Journal of Numismatics* 22: 93–118.

(2009). In Search of Roman Economic Growth. *Journal of Roman Archaeology* 22 (1): 46–70.
(2005). From Monetization to Culture Change. *Archaeological Dialogues* 12(1): 35–7.
(1996). Finances, Figures and Fiction. *The Classical Quarterly* 46 (1): 222–38.
Scheidel, W., I. Morris and R. P. Saller. (2007). Introduction. In W. Scheidel, I. Morris and R. P. Saller (Eds.), *The Cambridge Economic History of the Greco-Roman World*, pp. 1–12. Cambridge: Cambridge University Press.
Schiavone, A. (2000). *The End of the Past: Ancient Rome and the Modern West*. Cambridge: Harvard University Press.
Schmoller, G. von. (1896). *The Mercantile System and Its Historical Significance*. New York: Macmillan.
Schumpeter, J. A. (1954). *History of Economic Analysis*. New York: Oxford University Press.
(1909). On the Concept of Social Value. *The Quarterly Journal of Economics* 23: 213–22.
(1908). *Das Wesen und der Hauptinhalt der theoretischen Nationalökonomie*. Leipzig: Duncker & Humblot.
Schütz, A. (1970). *Alfred Schutz on Phenomenology and Social Relations*. Ed. H. R. Wagner. Chicago: University of Chicago Press.
(1967). *The Phenomenology of the Social World*. Chicago: Northwestern University Press.
Schwartz, J. (1961). *Les Archives de Sarapion et de ses fils. Une exploitation agricole aux environs d'Hermoupolis Magna*. Cairo: Institut français d'archéologie orientale.
Scott, D. A. (2011). *Ancient Metals: Microstructure and Metallurgy*. Los Angeles: Conservation Science Press.
Seaford, R. (2004). *Money and the Early Greek Mind: Homer, Philosophy, Tragedy*. Cambridge: Cambridge University Press.
Selgin, G. (1996). Salvaging Gresham's Law: The Good, the Bad, and the Illegal. *Journal of Money, Credit and Banking* 28 (4): 637–49.
(1988). Praxeology and Understanding: An Analysis of the Controversy in Austrian Economics. *The Review of Austrian Economics* 2: 19–58.
(in press). Gresham's Law. In S. Battilossi, Y. Cassis and K. Yago (Eds.), *Handbook of the History of Money and Currency*. Heidelberg: Springer.
Shaw, B. D. (1981). Rural markets in North Africa and the Political Economy of the Roman Empire. *Antiquités Africaines* 17 (1): 37–83.
Silver, M. (2011). Finding the Roman Empire's Disappeared Bankers. *Historia: Zeitschrift für Alte Geschichte* 60: 1–27.
Simon, H. A. (1983). *Reason in Human Affairs*. Stanford: Stanford University Press.
(1957). *Models of Man: Social and Rational- Mathematical Essays on Rational Human Behavior in a Social Setting*. London: Wiley.
(1955). A Behavioral Model of Rational Choice. *The Quarterly Journal of Economics* 69 (1): 99–118.

Snooks, G. D. (1996). *The Dynamic Society: Exploring the Sources of Global Change*. London: Routledge.

Southern, P. (2001). *The Roman Empire from Severus to Constantine*. London: Routledge.

Spengler, J. J. (1954a). Richard Cantillon: First of the Moderns, I. *Journal of Political Economy* 62 (4): 281–95.

(1954b). Richard Cantillon: First of the Moderns, II. *Journal of Political Economy* 62 (5): 406–24.

Strobel, K. (2002). Geldwesen und Währungsgeschichte des Imperium Romanum im Spiegel der Entwicklung des 3. Jahrhunderts n. Chr.: Wirtschaftsgeschichte im Widerstreit von Metallismus und Nominalismus. In K. Strobel (Ed.), *Die Ökonomie des Imperium Romanum: Strukturen, Modelle und Wertungen im Spannungsfeld von Modernismus und Neoprimitivismus*, pp. 86–168. Gutenberg: Scripta Mercaturae Verlag.

(1993). *Das Imperium Romanum im '3. Jahrhundert': Modell einer historischen Krise? Zur Frage mentaler Strukturen breiterer Bevölkerungsschichten in der Zeit von Marc Aurel bis zum Ausgang des 3. Jh.n.Chr.* Stuttgart: Franz Steiner Verlag.

Sutherland, C. H. V. (1961). Denarius and Sestertius in Diocletian's Coinage Reform. *Journal of Roman Studies* 51: 94–7.

Swartz, L. (2017). Blockchain Dreams: Imagining Techno-Economic Alternatives After Bitcoin. In M. Castells (Ed.), *Another Economy Is Possible: Culture and Economy in a Time of Crisis*, pp. 82–105. Cambridge: Polity Press.

Swedberg, R. (2005). Max Weber's Economic Sociology: The Centerpiece of Economy and Society? In C. Camic, P. Gorski and D. Trubek (Eds.), *Max Weber's Economy and Society: A Critical Companion*, pp. 127–42. Stanford: Stanford University Press.

(1998). *Max Weber and the Idea of Economic Sociology*. Princeton: Princeton University Press.

Tchernia, A. (2016). *The Romans and Trade*. Oxford: Oxford University Press.

Tedesco, P. and J. Banaji. (2017). Giuseppe Salvioli's Capitalism in the Ancient World. *Journal of European Economic History* 46 (3): 145–56.

Temin, P. (2014). Price Behaviour in the Roman Empire. In F. de Callataÿ (Ed.), *Quantifying the Greco-Roman Economy and Beyond*, pp. 189–207. Bari: Edipuglia.

(2013). *The Roman Market Economy*. Princeton: Princeton University Press.

(2012a). The Contribution of Economics. In W. Scheidel (Ed.), *The Cambridge Companion to the Roman Economy*, pp. 45–70. Cambridge: Cambridge University Press.

(2012b). The Contribution of Economics. In W. Scheidel (Ed.), *The Cambridge Companion to the Roman Economy (Supplementary Material)*, pp. 1–8. Cambridge: Cambridge University Press.

(2006). The Economy of the Early Roman Empire. *Journal of Economic Perspectives* 20 (1): 133–51.

(2004). The Labor Market of the Early Roman Empire. *Journal of Interdisciplinary History* 34 (4): 513–38.

(2001). A Market Economy in the Early Roman Empire. *Journal of Roman Studies* 91: 169–81.

(1976). *Did Monetary Forces Cause the Great Depression?* New York: W. W. Norton & Company.

(1969). *The Jacksonian Economy*. New York: W. W. Norton & Company.

Temin, P. and D. Kessler. (2008). Money and Prices in the Early Roman Empire. In W. V. Harris (Ed.), *The Monetary Systems of the Greeks and Romans*, pp. 137–59. Oxford: Oxford University Press.

Thatcher, M. (1987). Interview for *Woman's Own* by Douglas Keay.

The Telegraph. (2004). Professor Keith Hopkins.

Thornton, M. E. K. (1971). Nero's New Deal. *Transactions and Proceedings of the American Philological Association* 102: 621–9.

Thornton, M. E. K. and R. L. Thornton. (1990). The Financial Crisis of AD 33: A Keynesian Depression? *Journal of Economic History* 50 (3): 655–62.

(1989). *Julio-Claudian Building Programs: A Quantitative Study in Political Management*. Mundelein: Bolchazy-Carducci Publishers.

(1983). Manpower Needs for the Public Works Programs of the Julio-Claudian Emperors. *Journal of Economic History* 43 (2): 373–8.

Tomber, R. (2018). Egypt and Eastern Commerce during the Second Century AD and Later. In A. K. Bowman and A. Wilson (Eds.), *Trade, Commerce, and the State in the Roman World*, pp. 531–55. Oxford: Oxford University Press.

Tompkins, D. P. (2013). Moses Finkelstein and the American Scene: The Political Formation of Moses Finley, 1932–1955. In W. V. Harris (Ed.), *Moses Finley and Politics*, pp. 5–30. Leiden: Brill.

Turner, P. J. (2016). *Roman Coins from India*. London: Routledge.

Van Alfen, P. G. (2012). The Coinage of Athens, Sixth to First Century BC. In W. E. Metcalf (Ed.), *The Oxford Handbook of Greek and Roman Coinage*, pp. 88–104. Oxford: Oxford University Press.

Van Minnen, P. (2001). P. Oxy. LXVI 4527 and the Antonine Plague in the Fayyum. *Zeitschrift für Papyrologie und Epigraphik* 135: 175–7.

Vasudevan, R. (2017). The Significance of Marx's Theory of Money. *Economic and Political Weekly* 52 (37): 70–82.

Verboven, K. and J. Poblome, Eds. (forthcoming). *Structure and Performance in the Roman Economy: Complexity Economics. Finding a New Approach to Ancient Proxy Data*. Brussels: Latomus.

Verboven, K. (2012). City and Reciprocity: The Role of Cultural Beliefs in the Roman Economy. *Annales: Histoire, Sciences Sociales* 67 (4): 597–627.

(2009). Currency, Bullion and Accounts: Monetary Modes in the Roman World. *Revue belge de numismatique* 115: 91–121.

(2007). Demise and Fall of the Augustan Monetary System. In O. Hekster, G. de Kleijn and D. Slootjes (Eds.), *Crises and the Roman Empire*, pp. 245–60. Leiden: Brill.

(2002). *The Economy of Friends. Economic Aspects of Amicitia and Patronage in the Late Republic, Brussels, Latomus, 2002 (Collection Latomus 269).* Brussels: Latomus.

Viglietti, C. (2018). Economy. In M. Bettini and W. M. Short (Eds.), *The World through Roman Eyes: Anthropological Approaches to Ancient Culture*, pp. 216–48. Cambridge: Cambridge University Press.

(2014). Prix de la terre, census, virtualité de la monnaie à Rome pendant la haute République: une hypothèse de travail. In C. Apicella, M.-L. Haack and Fr. Lerouxel (Eds.), *Les Affaires de Monsieur Andreau. Économie et société du monde romain*, pp. 141–55. Bordeaux: Ausonius.

Visonà, P. and S. Frey-Kupper. (1998). The Romanization of the Ager Bruttius and the Evidence of Coin Finds, Part II. *Revue suisse de numismatique* 77: 81–98.

Von Reden, S. (2012). Money and Finance. In W. Scheidel (Ed.), *The Cambridge Companion to the Roman Economy*, pp. 266–86. Cambridge: Cambridge University Press.

(2010). *Money in Classical Antiquity*. Cambridge: Cambridge University Press.

(2002). Money in the Ancient Economy: A Survey of Recent Research. *Klio* 84 (1): 141–74.

(1997). Money, Law and Exchange: Coinage in the Greek Polis. *The Journal of Hellenic Studies* 117 (1997): 154–76.

(1995). *Exchange in Ancient Greece*. London: Duckworth.

Von Reden, S. and W. Scheidel. (2002). Introduction. In S. von Reden and W. Scheidel (Eds.), *The Ancient Economy*, pp. 1–8. London: Routledge.

Walker, D. R. (1978). *The Metrology of the Roman Silver Coinage: From Pertinax to Uranius Antoninus*. Vol. 3. Oxford: British Archaeological Reports.

Wallace-Hadrill, A. (1986). Image and Authority in the Coinage of Augustus. *Journal of Roman Studies* 76: 66–87.

Walton, P.,and S. Moorhead. (2016). Coinage and the Economy. In M. Millett, L. Revell and A. Moore (Eds.), *The Oxford Handbook of Roman Britain*, pp. 834–49. Oxford: Oxford University Press.

Wardle, D. (2014). *Suetonius: Life of Augustus*. Oxford: Oxford University Press.

Wassink, A. (1991). Inflation and Financial Policy under the Roman Empire to the Price Edict of 301 AD. *Historia: Zeitschrift für Alte Geschichte* 40 (4): 465–93.

Weber, M. (1968). *Economy and Society: An Outline of Interpretive Sociology*. 1978 Edn. Berkeley: University of California Press.

(1949). 'Objectivity' in Social Science and Social Policy. In *The Methodology of the Social Sciences*. Trans. Edward Shils and Henry Finch, pp. 49–112. New York: Free Press.

(1947). The Fundamental Concepts of Sociology. In *The Theory of Social and Economic Organization*. Trans. A. M. Henderson and T. Parsons, pp. 87–157. Glencoe: Free Press.

(1946). *From Max Weber: Essays in Sociology*. Trans. H. H. Gerth and C. W. Mills. New York: Oxford University Press.

(1922). *Gesammelte Aufsätze zur Wissenschaftslehre*. Tübingen: J. C. B. Mohr.

West, L. C. and A. C. Johnson. (1944). *Currency in Roman and Byzantine Egypt*. Princeton: Princeton University Press.

Whimster, S. (2007). *Understanding Weber*. London: Routledge.

Whitby, M. (2004). Emperors and Armies, AD 235–395. In S. Swain and M. Edwards (Eds.), *Approaching Late Antiquity: The Transformation from Early to Late Empire*, pp. 156–86. Oxford: Oxford University Press.

White, H. (2014). *The Practical Past*. Evanston: Northwestern University Press.

(2000). An Old Question Raised Again: Is Historiography Art or Science? (Response to Iggers). *Rethinking History* 4 (3): 391–406.

Whittaker, C. R. (1994). *Frontiers of the Roman Empire: A Social and Economic Study*. Baltimore: Johns Hopkins University Press.

Wickham, C. (2005). *Framing the Early Middle Ages: Europe and the Mediterranean, 400–800*. Oxford: Oxford University Press.

Widell, M. (2005). Some Reflections on Babylonian Exchange during the End of the Third Millennium BC. *Journal of the Economic and Social History of the Orient* 48 (3): 388–400.

Wiemer, H.-U. (1995). *Libanios und Julian. Studien zum Verhältnis von Rhetorik und Politik im vierten Jahrhundert n. Chr.* Munich: Beck.

Williamson, O. E. (1985). *The Economic Institutions of Capitalism*. New York: Free Press.

(1981). The Economics of Organization: The Transaction Cost Approach. *American Journal of Sociology* 87 (3): 548–77.

(1975). *Markets and Hierarchies: Analysis and Antitrust Implications: A Study in the Economics of Internal Organization*. New York: Free Press.

Wilson, A. (2007). The Metal Supply of the Roman Empire. In E. Papi and M. Bonifay (Eds.), *Supplying Rome and the Empire: The Proceedings of an International Seminar Held at Siena-Certosa Di Pontignano on May 2-4, 2004, on Rome, the Provinces, Production and Distribution*, pp. 109–25. Portsmouth: Journal of Roman Archaeology.

(2002). Machines, Power and the Ancient Economy. *Journal of Roman Studies* 92: 1–32.

Wolters, R. (1999). *Nummi Signati: Untersuchungen zur römischen Münzprägung und Geldwirtschaft*. Munich: Beck.

Woodman, A. J. (2016). *The Annals of Tacitus: Books 5–6*. Cambridge: Cambridge University Press.

Woods, D. (2013). Aurelian and the Mark VSV: Some Neglected Possibilities. *Numismatic Chronicle* 173: 137–49.

Woytek, B. E. (2012). The Denarius Coinage of the Roman Republic. In W. E. Metcalf (Ed.), *The Oxford Handbook of Greek and Roman Coinage*, pp. 315–34. Oxford: Oxford University Press.

(2008). The Aureus Under Trajan: The Metrological Evidence. *American Journal of Numismatics* 20: 435–57.

Woytek, B. E., K. Uhlir, M. Alram, M. Schreiner and M. Griesser. (2007). The Denarius under Trajan: New Metallurgical Analyses. *Numismatic Chronicle* 167: 147–63.

Yarrow, L. M. (2012). Antonine Coinage. In W. E. Metcalf (Ed.), *The Oxford Handbook of Greek and Roman Coinage*, pp. 423–52. Oxford: Oxford University Press.

Young, G. K. (2001). *Rome's Eastern Trade: International Commerce and Imperial Policy 31 BC–ad 305*. London: Routledge.

Zanker, P. (1990). *The Power of Images in the Age of Augustus*. Ann Arbor: University of Michigan Press.

Zouboulakis, M. S. (2002). John Stuart Mill's Institutional Individualism. *History of Economic Ideas* 10 (3): 29–45.

Zuiderhoek, A. (2009). Government Centralization in Late Second and Third Century Asia Minor: A Working Hypothesis. *Classical World* 103 (1): 39–51.

Index

Printed in the United Kingdom by TJ Clays Ltd.